In these circumstances is dedicated to the radical presence of the body, to circumstantial thinking and to the joy of emancipatory, conflictual and loving practices that refuse to stop questioning infrastructures and their political implications.

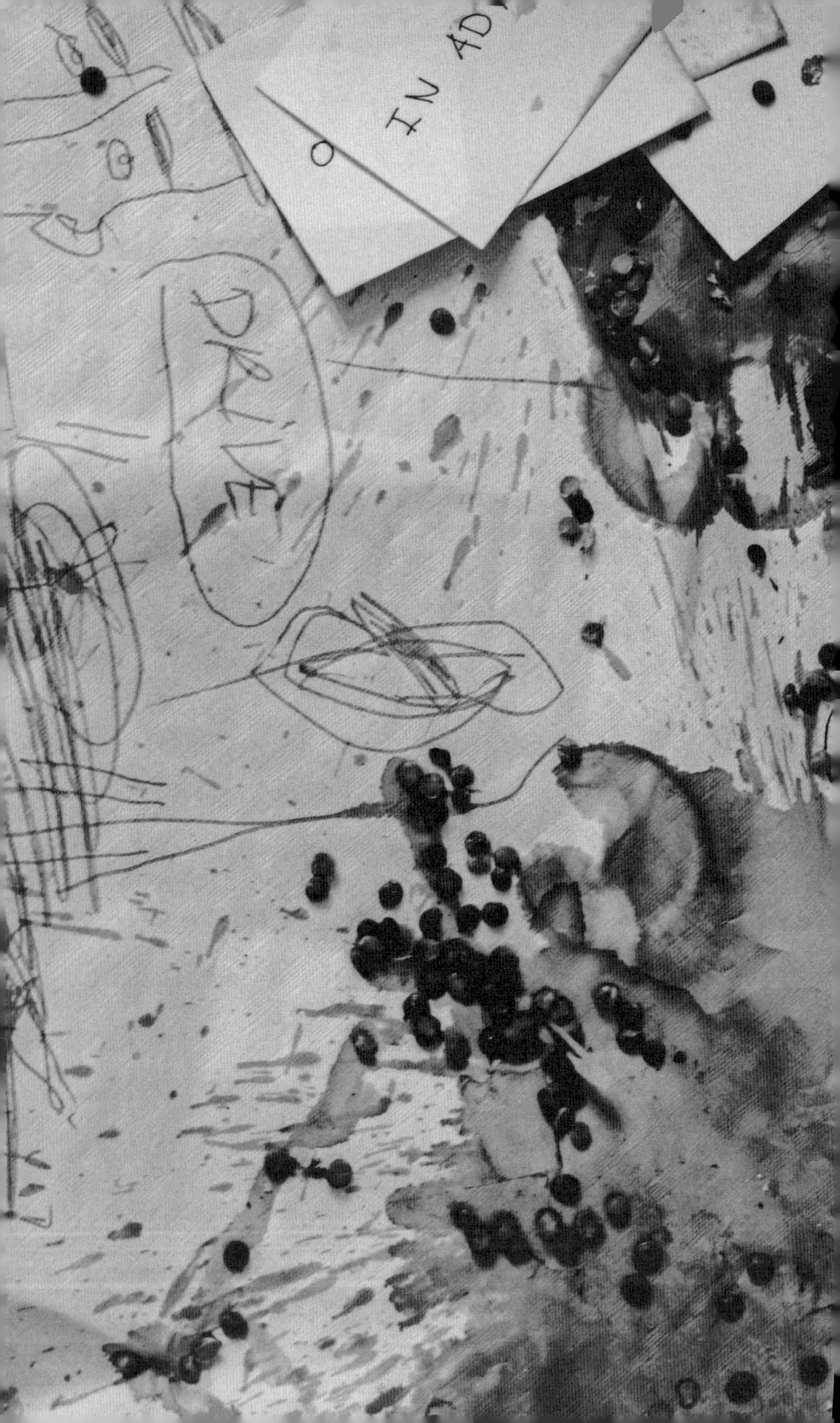

LONG WAY FROM HOME

THE

MARSEILLE IN '85

FIDDELING AROUND WITH OBJECT BETWEEN HER FINGERS

TRAVELLING AROUND WITH THE FELLOW TRAVELLER

AND THE SECRETARY DOES THE WORK OF THE

E IS

OUNGER

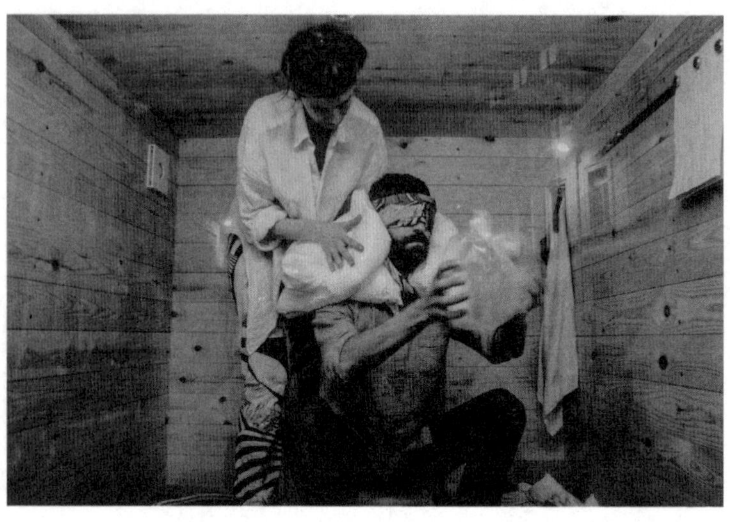

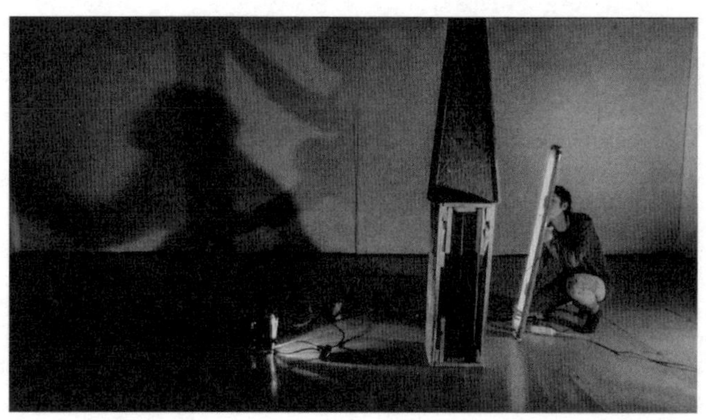

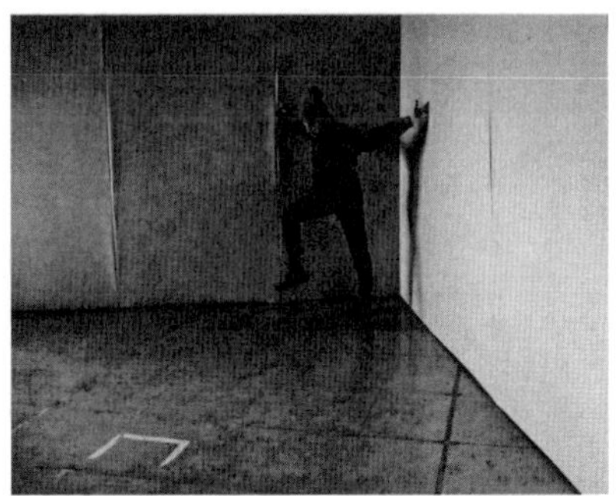

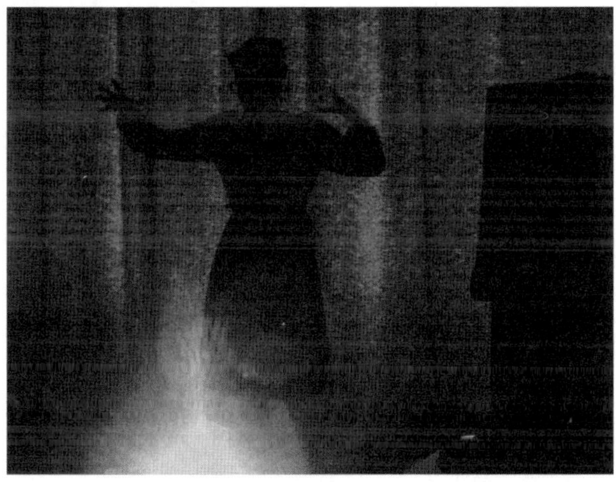

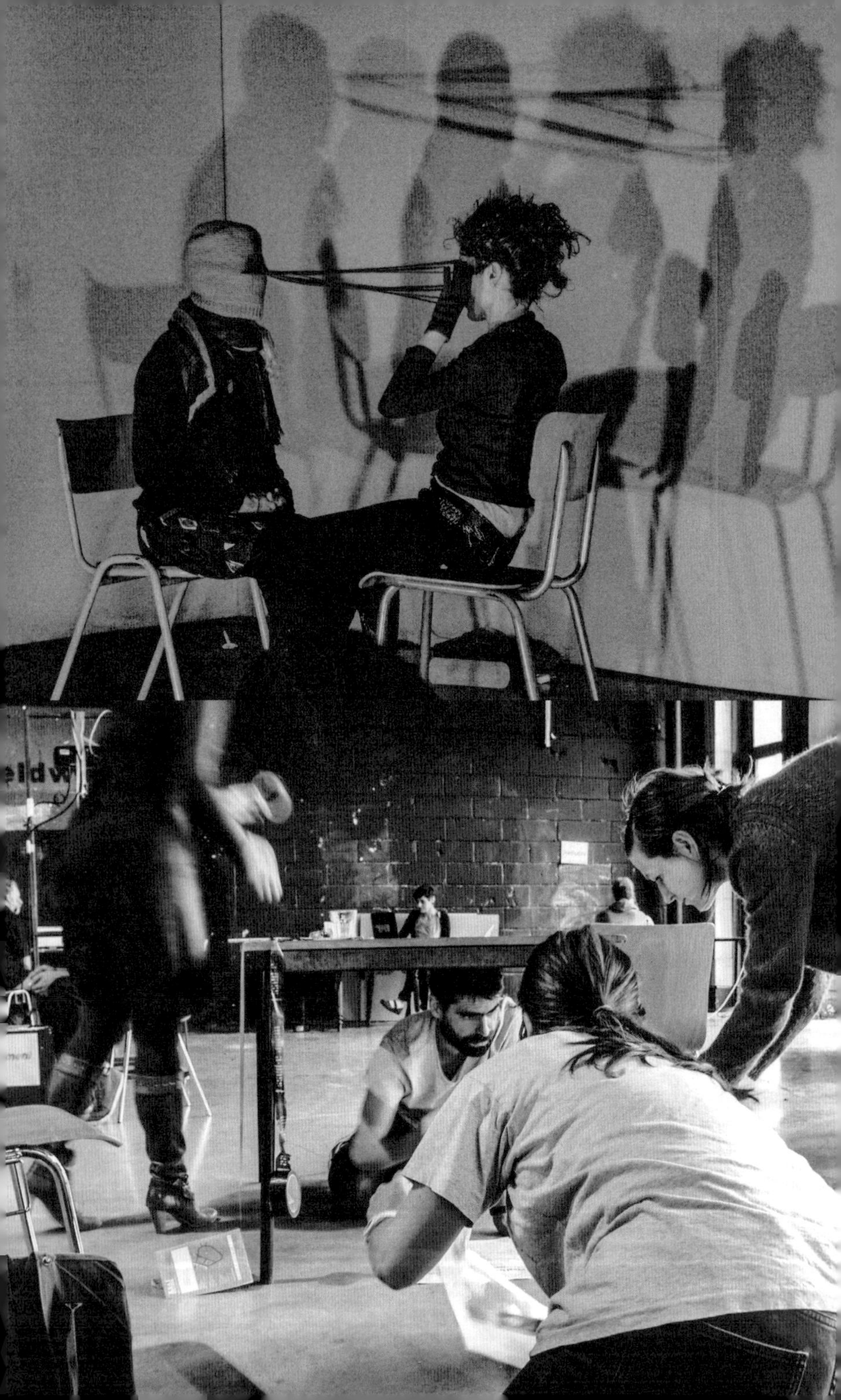

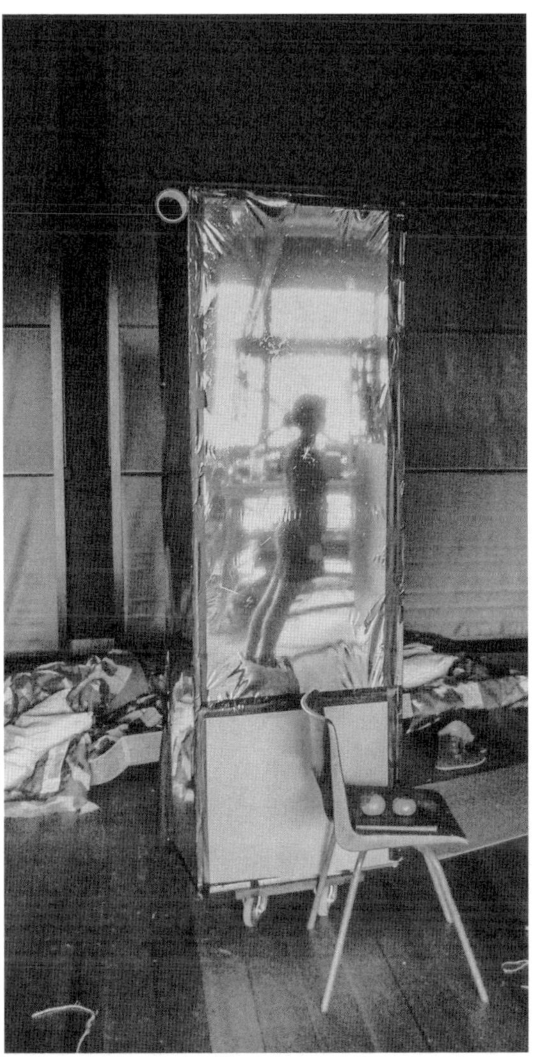

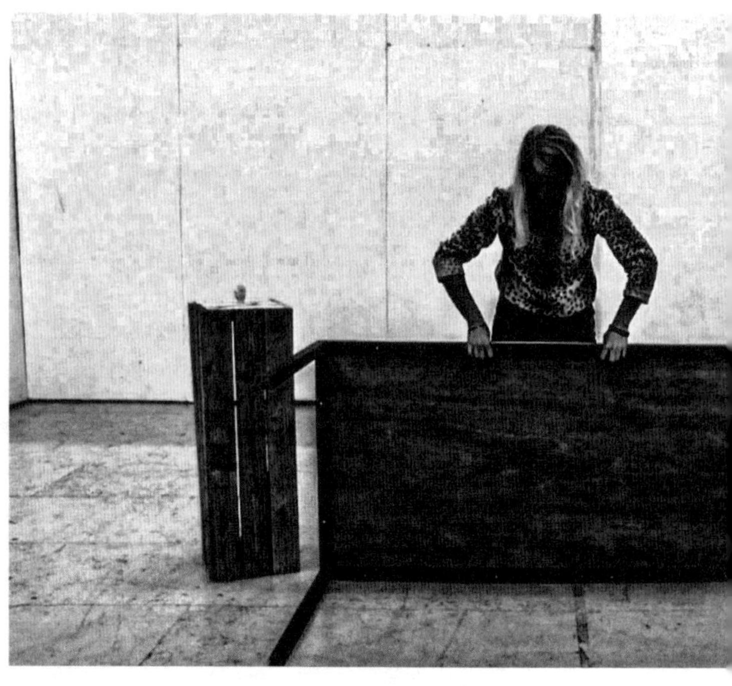

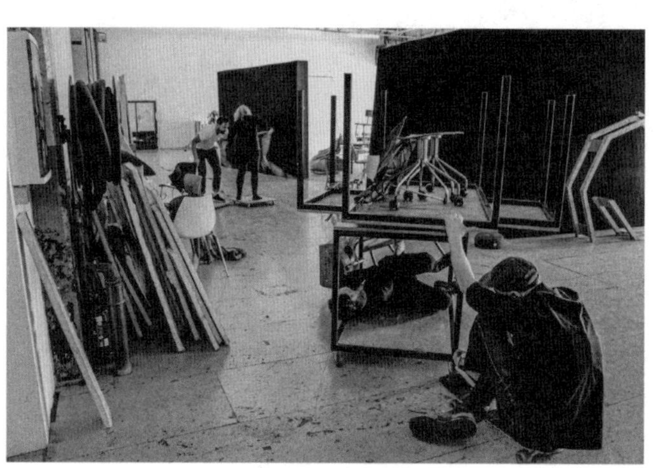

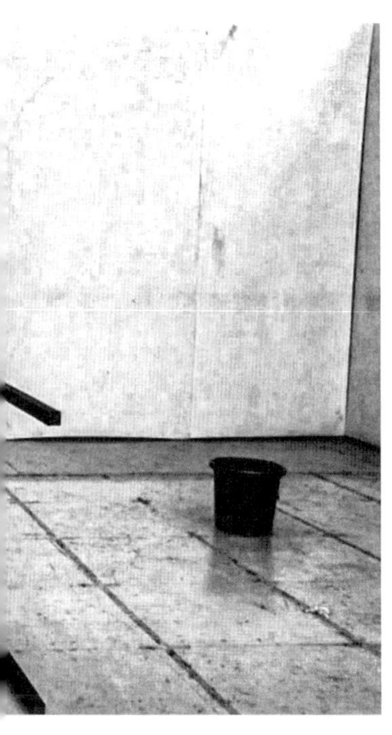

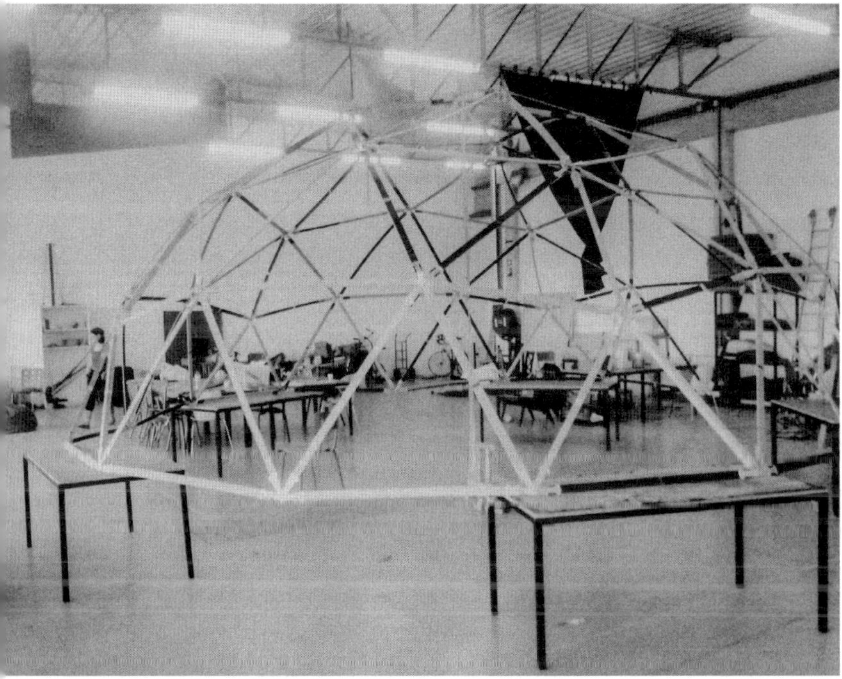

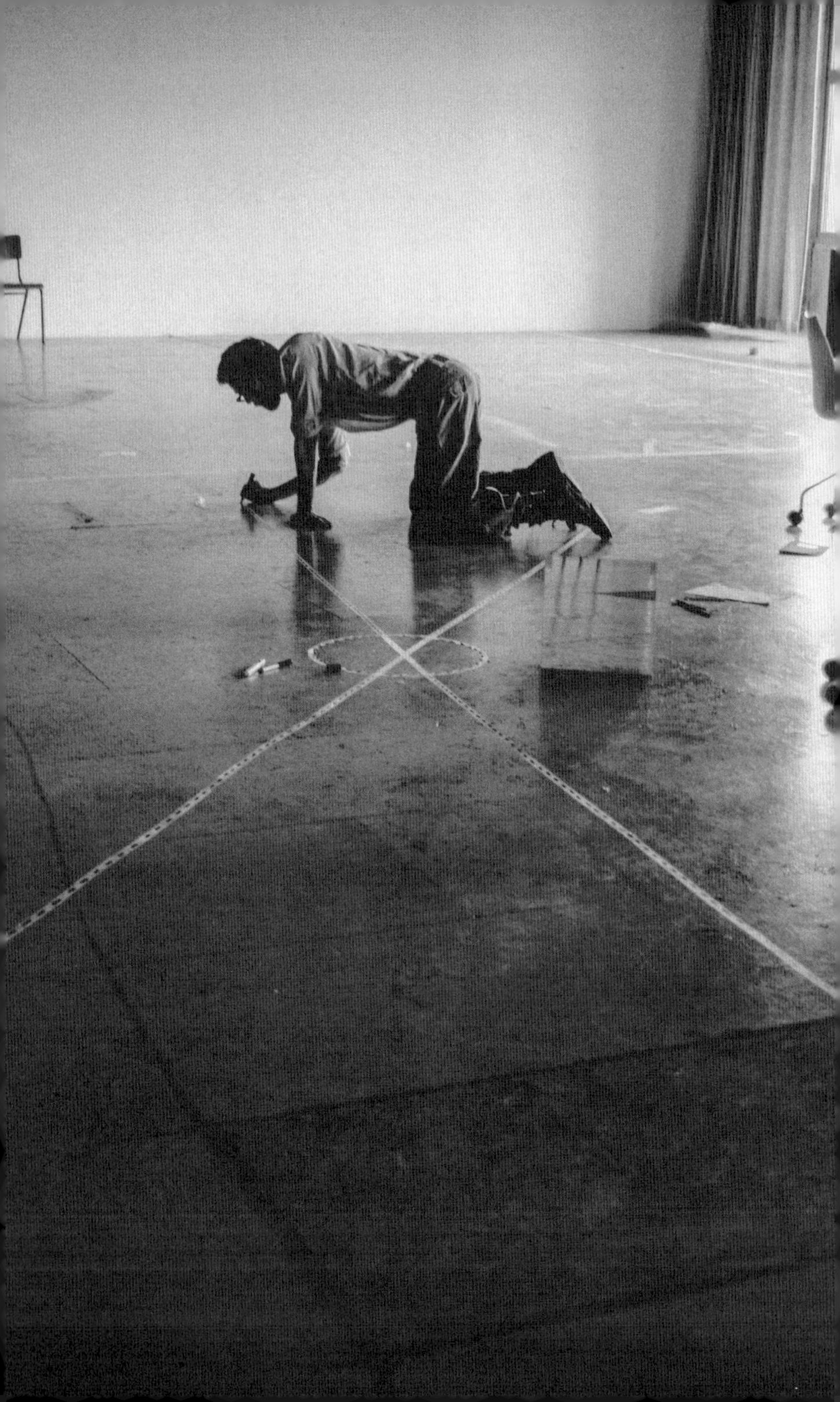

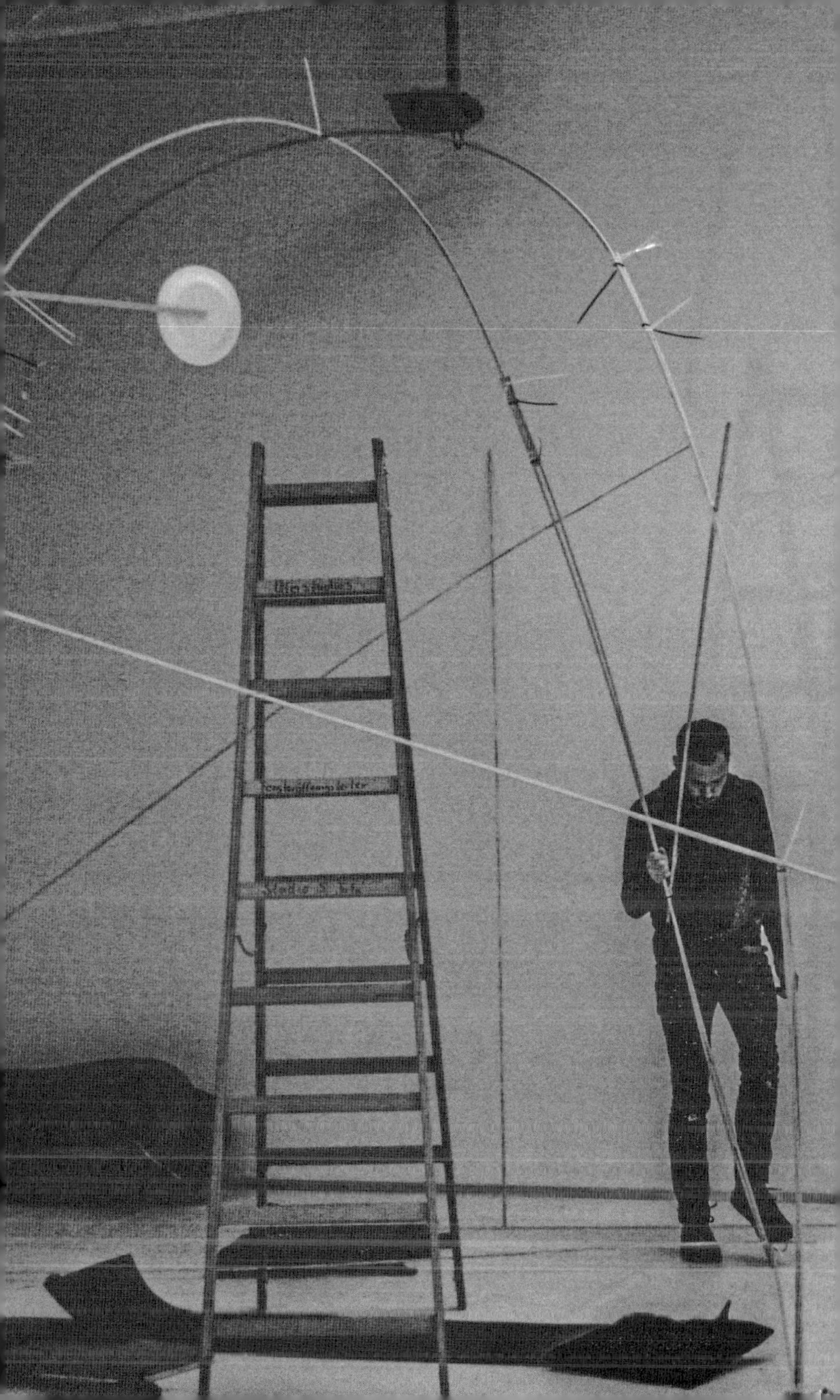

Contents

Part II INNER:
What's going on in there?

Part III PLAY:
It's all about practice!

Part IV INSIDEOUT:
Looking outside-in and inside-out

Foreword

In these circumstances is a publication about artistic research as it is practiced within the co-learning environment of a.pass. This book brings together an assemblage of curatorial, artistic and pedagogical approaches emblematic of an institution that fosters collaboration, self-organisation and transdisciplinarity in research-based practices.

In these circumstances presents itself as a printed version of the educational model of a.pass. It enacts its characteristics in a conversational and experimental mode, exposing questions and doubts as much as insights and convictions. It conveys a history of the stakes, qualities and methods of artistic research in the context of both an ongoing academisation of art education, as well as an abrasion of the once unbridled scene of artist-run organisations in Northern Europe. Documented here is how a.pass has carved a space for artistic research to deploy its tentacles with joy, risk and excitement, to imbricate in fields of both art and education, and to stir the sediments of disciplinary enclosures.

...

a.pass is an acronym for 'advanced performance and scenography studies': 'performance' refers to how practices act in their surroundings, 'scenography' is the production of space and context, 'studies' stands for a co-learning pedagogical approach, and the prefix 'advanced' is a dedication to challenge the frames of existing disciplinary determinations.

a.pass emerged in 2008 as a reconfiguration of an already existing school for scenography. It reconceptualised and radically transformed a disciplinary training into a collaborative structure that would effectuate the conditions for artistic research. Over the course of 14 years, a.pass evolved into two complementary modules: a postgraduate programme and a Research Center. As a collective environment, a.pass is perpetually under construction by the researchers enrolled in both its programmes, by the curators, the staff and the mentors and by the various bodies that emanate from or coalesce around them (such as the Participants' Assembly and the Support Group). Together, they 'institute'. They constitute active partners in thought and enact what an educational environment striving for an emancipatory approach to knowledge production can be. The institution and its members function as each other's support structure. They mutually and continuously invite one another to initiate critical practices that rehearse horizontal models of learning.

As its modus operandi, a.pass has an unorthodox stance in resisting definition of what artistic research is, sustaining the doubts, uncertainties and vulnerabilities of experimentation, process and speculative sense-making. Pairing artistic practice with research is a means to create open spaces for questioning how and why we make art. A transdisciplinary approach forces each specific (or disciplinary) methodology to deconstruct itself, and instigate singular ways of doing and thinking. It orients artistic research away from a categorical understanding of knowledge production in the arts, and opens up distinctive forms of addressing relationality, which we might call 'undisciplined'. As an emergent practice, artistic research enables the study of art in relation to its socio-political contexts. It creates critical space to counterbalance prevailing models of the 'solo artist' and the art market fostered by a neoliberal position on artistic practice, inviting collaboration and physical presence.

a.pass is embedded in the Brussels art scene, which since the 90s, is a zone of and for radical practices sustained by independent artists, artist-run organisations and politically engaged affiliations. In the last decade, however, these entities have become precarious due to a shift in subvention policies. In the case of a.pass, as a subsidised organisation for education, the commitment to practices of self-organisation aligns with a permanent awareness that autonomy is manifold and never absolute. Self-organisation is inextricably bound to existing institutions, and in turn, creates new regimes of governance that an institution heralding horizontality cannot be blind to. Since its outset, a.pass has committed itself to be a meta-institute, i.e. to research instituting practices by setting itself up as an experimental structure, baring its own premises for critical inquiry and speculative re-workings. This kind of institutional dedication depends upon tools that support processes of decentralisation, responsiveness, experimental ethos and sustainable self-reflexive practice. It also requires the continuous development of experiential methods, including bodily and subjective ones, to extend, question and transform collaborative infrastructures. Ultimately, these tools and methods reach beyond education, making it a breeding ground for collective concerns, for adhering to mutuality, and as such, for exercising modes of proximity that make society at large.

...

In these circumstances presents the experimental attitude of a.pass by staging a plurality of voices that hold the double impetus of self-organisation and instituting in a productive tension. Initially a working title, the phrase gained relevance during the process of creating the book, as working and living circumstances were in flux, as the institution laboured, as people continued to pass through it with practices and researches ever-evolving, and time galloped on.

With this publication, a.pass brings attention to how researchers – out of their different situated backgrounds, positions and practices – articulate critical perspectives on knowledge production in and with the arts, and to the development of tools to share this knowledge with a public. a.pass encourages publications which don't treat knowledge, art making, aesthetics, body practices and politics as separate channels of communication. Instead, it works on research publications under the hybrid term 'performative publishing': a concept coined to contain the multiplicity of transdisciplinary publishing practices. In line with this notion, this book exercises a mode of making public that forbears a conclusive or product-oriented gesture. It rather inclines to expose the process of research and instituting in a non-passive form, i.e. in order to facilitate a modality of witnessing a.pass in its unfinished and searching vulnerability.

This book consists of 27 contributions, many of them collaborative, from former and current participants, mentors, team members, guests and visitors of a.pass. The contributions range from concrete projects to interrogative speculations about artistic research, and how it operates institutionally through a complex intertwinement of practices.

They offer shared reflections concerning ways of working, diverse understandings of artistic research, a showcase of transdisciplinary practices, try-outs of methodologies and strategies for criticality, as a case study for contemporary education. Every contribution is a chapter in itself, and they have been – somewhat intuitively – sorted into four parts: 'Enter', 'Inner', 'Play' and 'Insideout'.

It is important to note that this book can't, and doesn't try to be, complete or exhaustive. There are many voices missing, it is not historical or linear and it bears repeating that there is no unambiguous positioning of a.pass as an institute. Instead, *In these circumstances* is another version of a.pass, an exercise in performative publishing, and in collaboration and contradiction without cancellation, a work necessarily always in process. As an image of a.pass' own practice, the book wishes to reveal the institutional will to enable a constant negotiation between the self and what might be a community interested in processes of equity, equality and democracy in artistic practice and learning environments. How do we cohabitate with differences? How do we enter into dialogue with what we don't know? How do we care for conflict? How do we practice inclusion without uniformising?

Part I: 'ENTER' compiles contributions that offer entries into a.pass. Aubrey Birch sets the tone with a personal, literary account that follows a snake towards a gathering in a.pass. Femke Snelting addresses 'entry' literally by discussing the politics of the keycard used to enter the a.pass building. Leo Kay and caterina daniela mora jara talk about how they entered a.pass as participants: Kay describes how he saw a.pass from the outside and mora jara talks about language, the forbidding English she grappled with to make her way in. Elke Van Campenhout leads us through her long history with a.pass through the lens of her own practice and Pierre Rubio shares fragments of initial conversations that led to his collaborative contributions in this book.

Part II: 'INNER', gives insight into different considerations and approaches that are at play in the institution. Lilia Mestre and Kristien Van den Brande exchange letters on artistic, curatorial and pedagogical considerations through the lens of artificial friendship. While Veridiana Zurita makes a case for a political take on artistic research, Adrijana Gvozdenović and Pia Louwerens self-fictionalise their art educational trajectories. Vanja Smiljanić introduces us to her idiosyncratic universe and is quizzed by Pierre Rubio in a conversation which co-produces them as interlocutors. Lilia Mestre and Philippine Hoegen talk with Peggy Pierrot about the urgencies and pitfalls of experimental educational bodies. The group of Associated Researchers who were part of the first Research Center cycle in 2019, and who then proposed to curate a block for the postgraduate programme, divulge their collaborative strategies and processes. Kate Rich concludes Part 2 with insights into the artistic potential of a.pass' administration.

Part III: 'PLAY' is all about practice. Rui Calvo, Tamar Levit & Yaen Levi (Muslin Brothers), Anouk Llaurens and Samah Hijawi share the work they did in a.pass, how they were affected by the a.pass environment and how their artistic practices changed as a result. Pierre Rubio and Laura Pante share a working session where they discuss and articulate preoccupations about experimental pedagogy, while Participants' Assembly members Amy Pickles, Chloë Janssens and Túlio Rosa reflect on the process of preparing the event On Coloniality which they recently organised with a.pass. Vladimir Miller converses with Krõõt Juurak on how to conceptualise and conduct a workshop from an anti-scholastic point of view. This is followed by Miller's introduction to his curatorial practice on re-negotiating institutional modes of spatial production in collaborative research settings. He shares the analysis of his practice's origins, its iterations at a.pass and the reconsiderations that lead to its reformulation.

Part IV: 'INSIDEOUT' zooms out to look at the larger context in which a.pass operates. Vladimir Miller and Ana Hoffner discuss artistic research within capitalism and the knowledge economy. With Mathilde Villeneuve and Guy Gypens, Lilia Mestre and Philippine Hoegen discuss a.pass' position in the Belgian field of (performing) arts. Sina Seifee and Pierre Rubio address the context of publishing and performativity in the digital realm. Digital conversations between members of the Support Group are edited by Lilia Mestre and Loes Jacobs into a polyphonic discussion on knowledge production and epistemology in artistic research, the responsibility of the institution and the 'ideal' artistic learning environment. Finally, a.pass is taken as a context in and of itself by Nicolas Y. Galeazzi, in a documentary theatre play in three acts where the roles of the artist, the curator and the researcher entertain a dialogue about the paradoxes of their positions.

At the beginning and end of the book are image compositions by Steven Jouwersma, that use pictures he archived throughout his years at a.pass. This contribution reflects his spatial aesthetics and his input in the development of pedagogical scenographies.

...

In these circumstances is edited by multi-disciplinary artist, teacher, activist and conference moderator Philippine Hoegen, an alumna of a.pass who is involved as mentor, and as a member of the Support Group and the General Assembly.

Hoegen accompanied the making of this book on its two-year long journey. The process involved a constant attention to ever-evolving institutional realities, requests, divides and hesitations, and an excavation of an abundance of practices (pedagogical, artistic, institutional, curatorial and more) documented in incomplete archives, carried by dispersed researchers. She activated different facets of methodologies from her own practice to assist people in translating and contextualising the multi-dimensional and sometimes evanescent daily practices of a.pass into printed matter with a public address.

As an initial gesture to unearth the expectations of *In these circumstances*, Hoegen conversed with all people engaged in the institution in 2020 to gain a better grip on the convergences and diffractions she was challenged to bring together. In line with the research she developed while at a.pass, she approached the project as a coming into being of a version of a.pass, a version that will perform and return the gaze. It will go off into the world and lead a life of its own, in dialogue with that world.

One of the questions asked in the initial conversations was, who would a.pass be if they were a person? Enmeshing the answers together gave 'a queer trickster as a mad scientist who is dipping their fingers into a big pot of glitter hair gel while stitching together the parts of several different bodies'. The paradoxes and the energy of this figure informed the editorial model, which embraces inner conflicts. It also fueled the aspiration of creating the conditions for this version to perform publicly, to converse and show its colours in a broader context.

Another question that was asked to the initial interlocutors was: Who should we be talking to if we want to talk about a.pass? The recommendations led to a variety of new exchanges and invitations to contribute, and to an open call to all alumni from the outset of a.pass until now.

The ways of writing translate the practices of the authors and the relation that these practices forge with language. The panoply of formats, varying between interviews, essays, correspondences, collage and poetic forms, exemplify how a.pass probes a dynamic space between practice, theory, community and their respective languages. Punctuation, grammar and vocabulary have not been entirely standardised throughout the book to accommodate the particularity of different voices.

...

In the final stages of compiling this book, the Ministry of Education put forth it may no longer subsidise the institution. This political decision reasserts the precarity of autonomous, experimental and alternative projects in favour of centralised and highly administrative structures of education and art production. After the Bologna agreement, we saw the demise of art academies which operated as single bodies, as they were merged into the academic field, regulating the regimes of artistic practice to that of scientific knowledge production constrained by conclusions, competition and marketable products. This political decision, aimed at uniformisation, will ultimately leave us with a lack of complexity and diversity in art education, disempowering and debilitating artistic practices, discourses and their contribution to society.

Once again, the intended indeterminacy of an in-between space like a.pass – which relies on the rehearsal of community formed by friendships, kinships, proximities, desires, elected alliances, disagreements, responsibilities, accountabilities and all their limits and interwoven complexities – proves difficult to sustain on a subsidised level.

At this point, the title of this book, *In these circumstances*, bends its meaning and reaffirms the importance of listening and giving voice to modes of transmission and governance that emerge from persistent practices of sharing, critical reading and imaginative rethinking, across art and education.

...

We dedicate this book to the radical presence of the body, to circumstantial thinking and to the joy of emancipatory, conflictual and loving practices that refuse to stop questioning infrastructures and their political implications. We hope that *In these circumstances* will be provocative in a useful way for you. We believe that in its variety you will find at least one voice that speaks to you, maybe even about you.

Lilia Mestre & Philippine Hoegen
Brussels, February 10, 2022

Part I

Six different ways to arrive

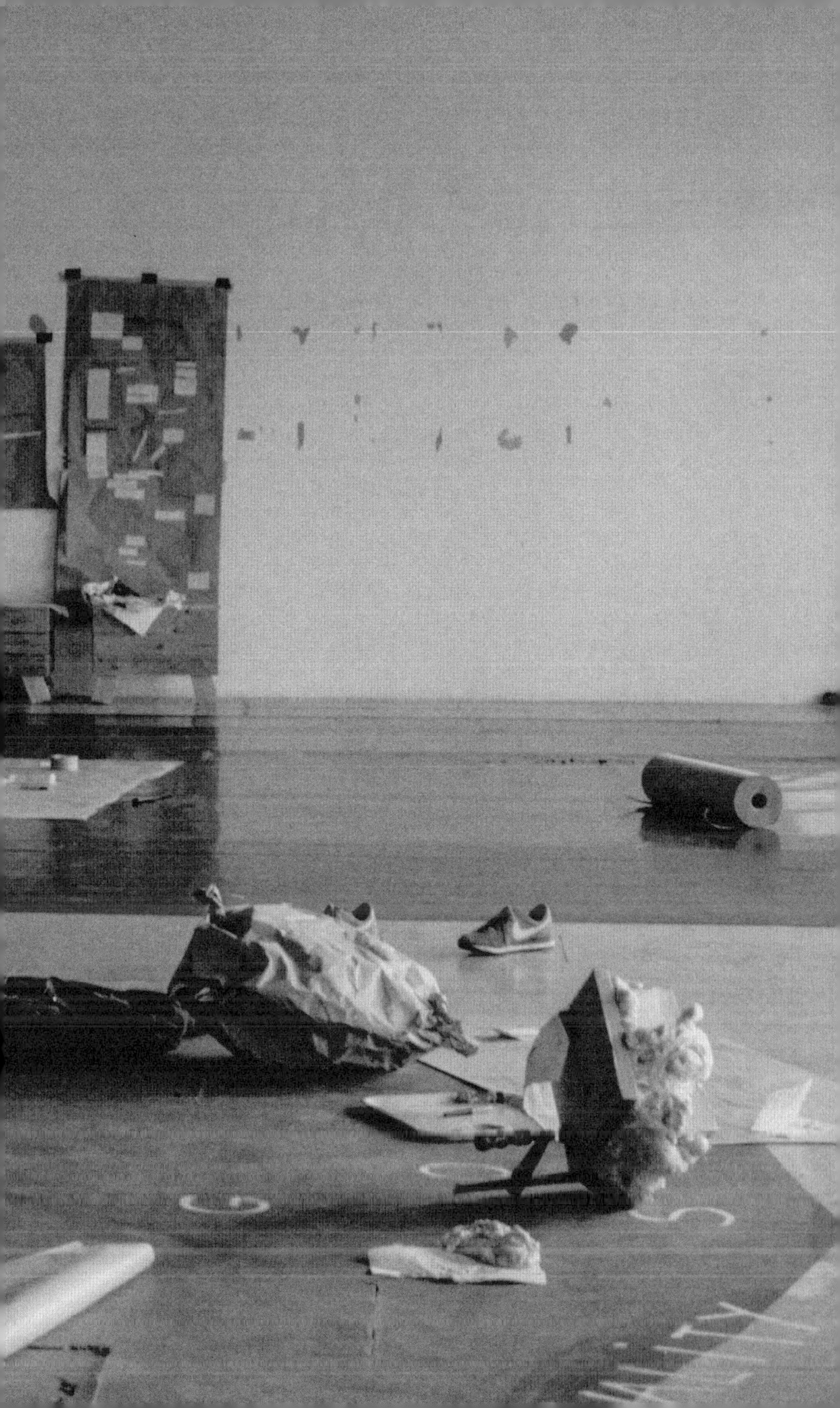

Aubrey Birch

Clumsy Fingers

(Serpents in the Off-Hours)

A female red-bellied black snake is ovoviviparous, meaning that her young are hatched from eggs, and those eggs are hatched inside her body.

Did you know that a snake can die from sun exposure? I did not, at one stage. I have felt the small egg sac of a baby red-belly, *Pseudechis porphyriacus*, through the thickness of its mother's flesh. I have felt the supple form of its hatched siblings, their length and breadth. I have accepted heat from their mother, a standard caloric transfer from the hotter body to the cooler; even though snakes are cold-blooded, even though she was dead. The knowledge changed my life, as a knowledge sometimes does; because I did not learn it from a book, because I learned it from a snake.

Can I change the light? I am standing at night under a bare sky, windstill. The waxing gibbous moon raises itself over the mountain that rises above the eastern paddock, which bleeds back into the mountain, which has worn away the fences, which lie rusting as a testament to an entropy that marks the hazy boundaries between two worlds.

What I didn't know that I knew was that the moon would rise further to the south this time. I knew it because I had been watching it rising, waxing, sinking, waning, for months. Accidentally, for the first time in my life I had watched it cycle. What I did not know had been registering in my body over time.

What kind of knowledge happens by accident? I could taste it. I could recognise a flavour and then I could recognise the recognition and still not pinpoint the learning. It's not exactly tactile, not exactly. It might be kinetic. I have read about the moon and the moon tastes different in a book.

Can I change continents? I'm sitting on the floor in a circle with others. It's very urban. There are ten of us maybe, on cushions in a large room with a high ceiling. I feel resistance. The walls get smaller, the space gets tighter and my body builds a space to push against it. We are doing nothing and it's somehow related to love. We are letting it emerge. What is coming out of me is more like rage. Perhaps heat is the first boundary line when the body's shell is breached. One of my colleagues says that it helps when a plastic bag is placed in the centre. The members of the group try to feel love for this sad, overlooked object and seem to succeed. I was not there, but the story increases my tenderness. It's very urban, and I'm nearly an urban creature. I have my weapons.

Will we survive the present if we are soft? And what kind of 'we' survives if we are hard? There are so many ways to use knowledge as a weapon, and there are many kinds of knowledges that can be used as shields. Sometimes we need the weapons, and other times we need the shields. Why all this war talk? When it's hard to lie down in the crossfire and look at the soil, seek the small grass flowers and the trafficking worms, you know there are grounds for this artillery.

Can I change the frame of time? I sharpen my tongue, as a child, in order to defend myself and my friend against the unnervingly unsurprising bigotry of a geographically-isolated town. I learn to laugh while sharpening my wit. My brain and my tongue play a game. I respond like a knife.

My parents began to say that I'd make a good lawyer, so I did a student internship at the local court, but the use of the law made me anxious. The law is about protecting the rule of law. It seems a labyrinth, but it's not. Within certain sorts of knowledge, there's always a compass. Within others, we lose our bearings; Foucault's Chinese dictionary, Sei Shōnagon's lists.

Knowledge-of-the-taste-of-things-that-touch-the-tongue and those-the-tongue-cannot-touch. Those-who-can-be-known-under-the-sign-of-the-hourglass and those-under-the-reign-of-the-clock. And-this-that-I-would-not-give-up-the-smell-of-iron-in-the-heat-after-the-rain.

Can we cultivate what in knowledge is accidental? To be an acolyte is to be porous, to not yet have learned the fullness of an armour. When we don't have it quite on, we always have it a bit off. Learning to tie knots, our fingers are clumsy. Learning to chop onions, the knife slips, our eyes water. On the fourth floor there is a balcony where people smoke, a kitchen without a sink. The frame of attention allows but is not confused by rage. Actually, there is no fence. I am here by choice, I can leave by choice. I stay.

Can you rehearse a spell? There is something happening that makes me understand my armour, but I only understand it in the off-hours. I only understand that I was touched when I feel the difference in my touch. In the circling, cycling empty hours, I hear the spell before I know it. What I learned I did not know that I was learning: it wasn't what I had come here to learn. At some scale nothing is accidental, at another nothing is not. An incantation is a figure that loops across this breach. I smelled the wet summer basalt for years before I understood that it might smell me back.

I'm in a room being asked to explain myself. There's the now-familiar leitmotif of 'what's your research question?' and the circling, cycling empty hours. What is my research question? When I blow an eyelash from my fingertip and make a wish, I always say: life. Someone told me never to reveal the wish or it won't come true. I told her anyway. It's always about how the abiotic and the biotic meet. The way we thread and knot the different scales. And how all attention is an incantation. She is my future wife.

Hildegard von Bingen depicted fertility as a gemstone. She was a neo-Platonic thinker, and I'm supposed to have a research question. It was Leibniz who said, 'there is nothing uncultivated, nothing sterile, nothing dead in the universe'. And it's not a question, but maybe I wouldn't mind fraying the edges of what is called Life.

What happens in the off-hours? We learn to sharpen our tongues. We learn lessons in defence, protection. And the on-hours? The arrows, the swords, the guns. And in the off-hours? We learn that we had learned to mistrust serpents. Under the hielaman and the aegis, we learn to fork our tongues. What might Lady Macbeth have otherwise said about *Pseudechis porphyriacus*? 'There is a flower, and there is a serpent underneath it. Let it be, and leave us in peace'.

I would like to acknowledge the Gamilaraay people, traditional custodians of the land that I call home, and pay my respects to Elders past, present, and future. *Pseudechis porphyriacus* is *Galibaay* in the Gamilaraay language.

Elke Van Campenhout

Love Revisited

I

a.pass started up in 2007, not yet by that name, but already with the intention to become what it later turned out to be: a hybrid learning platform for international and diverse, transdisciplinary artists with an attitude. Its beginnings were tentative, but radically influenced by the tone of the conversation then: the discussions around radical pedagogy, the politics of self-education and the problematics of knowledge (re)production.

Its ambition was to be an institute that was no institute, an endeavour that took on different guises throughout the years in initiatives and texts like the Don't Know![1] conference, the Tender Institute[2] gatherings, the Institute of Love plays,[3] and the constant rephrasing and experimenting with horizontality, chance decisions, flexible curricula, and open spaces to meet, share and (re)construct. The themes of these first initiatives kept transforming and reappearing in different guises throughout the years: the preoccupation with the status of 'knowledge' as it is processed in an artistic practice environment, for example, was first touched upon in the Don't Know! conference. This event was conceived as a gathering of research practices that diverged from the constraints of academic knowledge production procedures. The research practices presented allowed for a more intuitive, or practice-led form of research that would find its logics in the unfolding of the initial spark through the practice, rather than through a preconceived order of procedures. The hypothesis being that artistic research finds its methodology in the doing rather than the other way around.

---

1 Don't Know!, 1st a.pass Conference on the Art of Research, 15-17.09.2011 in Brussels, De Bottelarij.

2 The international conference, The Tender Institute took place on the 7th and 8th of September, 2012. It was an active meeting around the notion of the 'institute' in artistic practices today. In these two days, a.pass invited speakers, artists, and administrators to construct new imaginations of what the institute today might look like: how to think of an institute with flexible walls, how to administer an organic institute that grows out of the interests of the people working in it? What is the place of this kind of institute in today's society? In other words: how can an institute still stay an institute when it is embracing its 'tenderness': when it recognises its dependency on the interest of its users? The risk of becoming obsolete in the whirlwind of heterotopic interests? The challenge to reinvent its administration to shift from a politics of categorisation to one of attention and engagement? https://apass.be/tender-institute/

3 The Institute of Love was addressed in the article, 'Strange Love: How I Learned to Stop Worrying and Loving the Institute' by Elke Van Campenhout in *Turn, Turtle! Reenacting the Institute*, Edited by Elke Van Campenhout and Lilia Mestre, Performing Urgency #2, A House On Fire Publication, 2016 https://. alexander-verlag.com/programm/in-vorbereitung/titel/380-TURN_TURTLE.html?order_by=c.erschienen&start=

The questions posed in the Tender Institute were similarly recurrent: what is an institute that doesn't thrust forward on the wings of its profile, that is not building authority through a canon and stones, but swarms around the interests of the people involved in that particular moment and time? A Tender Institute, bound to blur and become visible, more like a Rorschach test of its time than a beacon of visibility and certainty.

And 'Love', weaving in and out of the discussions, as an antidote for neoliberal institutionalisation of sameness and repetition, of strait-jacketing practices into tick boxes and normative frameworks.

I cannot remember a time during the 10 years I was working at a.pass (2007-2016) as the initiator, the coordinator, the head of research, a mentor... that the institute was in total balance. Its form was constantly shifting; the architecture always slightly leaning this way and that, having to readjust at every new period to the strong choices made in the previous one. Some of these periods of strong choice were hard-core critical, others soft-core ritual, poetic or spiritual. In these ten years, I cannot say that any week was exactly the same as another. a.pass produced problems, creatively and exhaustingly, for anyone that was part of the institute.

These problems crossed the borders of work into the personal, into life views and decisions, into friendships and personal bonds and disagreements. a.pass was very much like any other ideologically driven experimental young institute in that period: a project of desire and love, of contradiction and libido which engaged whomever was around. In its quest for diversity and instability it carried the sign of the times on its shoulders, and moved it around this way and that, stumbling under the weight sometimes, making light of what is a heavy task: to combine the dependability of an institute with the unpredictability that is the dictate of horizontal organisational structures, and the ideology of critical theory ideologies. Trying to avoid a clear denomination, or a stultifying profile, a.pass played hide-and-seek in its communications, a strategy that was very much part of the subversive strategies of alternative work spaces in the 90s and later. To avoid profiling and identitarian narrowness, a lot of small and experimental initiatives avoided an all too clear line of communication, in order not to produce consumers, but actively engaged participatory networks. Unavoidably, most of these spaces therefore created insider circles of initiates that would function as their own critical audience and players. As did a.pass.

Over the years, the pressure to fit more snugly into the institutional profiling mould became more poignant. The fun of playing hide-and-seek for so long became tiresome. The desire to be understood, to gain a place in the international scene, to become heard and seen as a player in the research field, grew. Creating the problem once more of the 'how to'. How to combine clear profiling with the promise of flexibility and diversity? How to publish and become seen without adapting to the strong pull of academia to translate artistic research in terms of academic jargon and closed-circle access? How to translate the true value of the place which was not so much in the quality of the outcomes as in the vibrancy of the collaborations, encounters, individual process and creativity, that fuelled the life in situ towards an outside, in a way that is experientiable?

Looking back I see this tension flaring up again and again. The struggle between the horizontal (self-organisation, fluidity, diversity) and the vertical (institutionalisation, profiling, subsidy), between critical ideology and openness towards difference, between the institute of love and the squeeze of the wedding band of the institute, married to its 'end qualifications'. In the end, it made me flee the institute and construct the work in another context.

II

In the text 'Strange Love' that I wrote for the publication *Turn, Turtle! Reenacting the Institute*, I wrote:

> An institute that is fuelled by love has a complicated relation towards the individuals that inhabit it. On the one hand it is driven by desire: by the attraction that is produced by the actions of the other, which engages each and everyone in an ecstatic move. Out of their comfort zone, their self-recognition, and their identitary vanity. Not in order 'not to', but rather in a tentative dance of instituting a sense of social cohesion that is not based on agreement or negotiation, but rather on a forced cohabitation within a same space of interest. Desire is the force that pulls us out of ourselves, into the world. It is an external attraction towards a love object that frees us of our own confinement, and opens up new paths of flight, previously unknown and unpredictable. Every researcher knows this feeling of verging towards an 'expérience' (experience/experimentation) that oversteps the boundaries of the hypothetical set up, and shamelessly reveals its ecstatic pulsation in the naive practice of stepping on hot coals, or getting lost, following a 'holzweg' into the woods.

> What keeps this desirous centrifugal force field together, is the magnetic power of love, which not only keeps the ecstatic subjects connected to each other and the institute, but which also renders them porous to their environment and the world around them. Recognising the vulnerability of the other, makes you simultaneously aware of your own and the world constructed around you. The fragile is the instrument that breaks open the smooth surface of representation and branding, both on the level of the individual and on the level of the institute. An institute that has become porous to the world, both on the inside and towards the outside is a 'tender' institute. An institute with a small 'I' that distinguishes itself from the capital 'I' Institute that is profiling itself as a centre of investment and attention. The Institute that jealously guards its canonised knowledge, packaged and processed into ready-made parcels for consumption and recognition.[4]

Re-reading these notes that I made on what I then considered the core of an experimental arts education institute, I have to admit that this ecstatic spiral dance vision is highly coloured by my own desire for space, movement, change and breath within the walls of the institute. And that it all too easily glosses over the pedestrian stride of researchers entering and exiting the building, leaving huge portions of their lives and drives stored at home or at their outside jobs. Or the staff meetings and board assemblies that did not necessarily breathe in ecstatic union with the dream of the love institute. In other words, I talked about the ecstatic pull, the moment of expansion, but neglected its necessary counterpart, which is as much a part of the love dance as the falling apart movement, the move of contraction, turning inwards and processing the experiences, turning them into text, and document; traces of the desirous spiral. Talking about an institute of love today, I would put more emphasis on the mundane acceptance of the everyday, on the workers silently holding the institute together, the scenographers of the space that keep the work flowing, the technicians, administrators, producers...

Also, I see now, with some years of distance, that the porosity of any institute is only, and can only be, relative. The magnetic force holding an institute together is probably not so much love, or a lofty vision, but language: a language that all too often hides its ideological markings, or considers them to be self-evident. A language that creates clear demarcations of

4 Campenhout, 'Strange Love: How I Learned to Stop Worrying and Loving the Institute', pp. 143-144.

a history of experimental arts, leftist political discourse turned normative neoliberal marker, aesthetic references, and styles of engagement that unavoidably (?) mark the space of (non-) invitation. A language spoken by dossiers, essays, mentors, coordinators, and participants, that asks for adaptation and the construction of a shared world view. Which is not necessarily questionable. Or rather, that is silently accepted as a marker of the playground we move on. Every institute has these language markers, signalling their position in the field. Today a lot of these markers are shared over the borders of transnational collaboration, networking and peer-to-peer publications. It is this language that marks the territory of the love to share. The marriage contract that marks the ins and outs of the institute.

In my own journey, I can see that it was my desire that spiralled me into, but also out of, the institute: following the thread of my love for criticality, I tried to create a space for everyone to speak their own language. The Tower of Babel, precariously leaning Pisa-style to the Operaismo left, Rancière and Latour. In so doing, I co-created rather than a Tower of Babel, a language school that echoed the concerns of its time. A language that, incidentally, at a certain point no longer answered the call of my desire, which spiralled me out of the institute again. The critical was too narrow a harness to mirror the experiences I was working on. The hope born in the body, in my then research '*Bureau d'Espoir*'.

Which tells me that it is not the institute that is the love object, but the desire for a place where we speak, at least temporarily, the same language. A place in which my desire of the moment is mirrored, reflected back, welcomed and 'read'. Rather than the institute as a 'place to become undone', as I presumed in the text cited above, the institute is a place where I petition to be seen and heard, within the confines of an agreed upon language game. A marriage of convenience in the best possible way.

III

Today I am back at the institute, for the first time, after brief stints of curating and mentoring after leaving, as a participant of the Research Center. A researcher in the midst of researchers, searching for references, phrases, and ways to communicate what it is that I'm trying to get a grip on, what is pulling me out of my comfort zone into the complications, contradictions and inner inconsequences of my research subject 'The Sex Asylum'. I feel the call to make myself understood, to remember the language, to struggle with the resistance to use it. For the first time, I experience being 'in' from the inside out. Not taking care of the mould, but being moulded in the most pleasurable, inviting and inspiring way. I no longer expect the institute to be fuelled by love. Maybe rather by sym-pathy: the willingness to suffer with the other through their obstacles and blind spots. To open up new holzweg in the process. To be moved by the other, without necessarily losing my ground. I have become less of a radical, and more of an experimental pragmatist. With the Sex Asylum, I try to invent new practices to experience intimacy, fear and closeness between people, objects and scenographies. Desire machines that enter the houses of people, and seduce them into the twilight zones of libidinal confusion. The a.pass environment makes me question the self-evident monastic practice I have adopted, and forces me to find a language in-between The Monastery,[5] which I run as a fluid community in the countryside, a place to creatively work through alienation, desire and trauma, mostly through meditation and body work. On the other hand, the community of seeking artists, with their critical instrumentarium, and desire for the subversive turn of any unfolding narrative.

What it does to my work is to make me exceedingly aware of the idiosyncratic nature of the way I do what I do. The beauty of meandering between worlds, one that is organised mostly hierarchically, canon-based, and esoteric (the spiritual lineages), and one that is weaving in and out of certainties, taking every new wave as seriously as the previous one, and sometimes little aware of the relativity of the current paradigm. Challenged by both options, I have come to trust even more than before the practice itself. The doing of connection, the restructuring of the ground I stand on. A spiritual pragmatist, running a non-denominational Monastery. Inviting trauma and exhilaration as much as contemporary philosophy and community work. Monks ebbing and flooding the place, each one coming with their own practices, languages and convictions. A Tower of Babel for the spiritually challenged. Some habits are hard to shed...

---

5 The Monastery Live is a live-in fluid community of spiritual-(artistic) practitioners, buzzing in and out of the house. The Monastery is currently situated in Solwaster in Wallonie, and organises retreats, workshops and residency periods to people in need of recalibrating their life/work/body-mind equilibrium. https://themonastery.live

Leo Kay

Space. Negotiated.

Space, pace, breath slowed...
resisting conditioned urge to present,
settle in, listen in.
Prioritising public, private negotiation
Knee twist, leg flick,
breath,
jump back from limbic overload,
from burnout. System shutdown.

When I was a kid I believed, truly believed, that there was a culture that had it right. A place where everyone was happy, where humans knew how to act responsibly towards each other and towards the planet we share. A culture that was able to balance community, rest, care, collectivity, privacy, support, autonomy... I opened a magazine once and saw a large sunny square in Mexico City, all cobblestones and grandeur, accordions and leather shoes. There were couples of every age, dressed in their humble best, dancing Argentine Tango and for some reason, for a large part of my childhood, I thought that, in their warm Sunday calm, they had found it.

I've been reading up on polyvagal theory,[1] about the way our nervous system creates maladaptive stress responses. About how, when we experience a perceived threat, we can be projected back in time to a traumatising experience (or many[2]) and one's body can react disproportionately to the current danger. We move into sympathetic nervous system functionality, releasing increased amounts of cortisol and adrenaline causing a heightened state of anxiety: we function from our lizard brain and ready ourselves to take flight, or fight for our lives. I've been thinking about how this can be useful for fast response, hyperproductivity and aggression but within this mode we literally can't digest food and our ability to respond with nuance and consideration is impacted. I've been thinking about the need to digest on every level, not just in terms of gaining nutrients from our food but also from our experience. I've been thinking about the value of boredom, of doing nothing, to take time for processing, and time to understand past experiences and how they inform present action. This area of consideration includes the earth's need to digest, to process toxins and regenerate itself. Our current system doesn't prioritise this need, neither for ourselves or our biosphere, and so we remain in a closed repetitive linear trajectory between production and consumption without hitting the third point on this triangle:

1 Polyvagal theory was developed by Steve Porges in 1996.

2 Cultural somatics is a new area of research and activism surrounding the recognition of the impact of ongoing systematic racialised trauma. 'Cultural somatics' is a term coined by two American activists, therapists and authors: Tada Hosumi, and Resmaa Menakem in his recent book *My Grandmother's Hands: Racialised Trauma and the Pathway to Mending our Hearts and Bodies*, 2017.

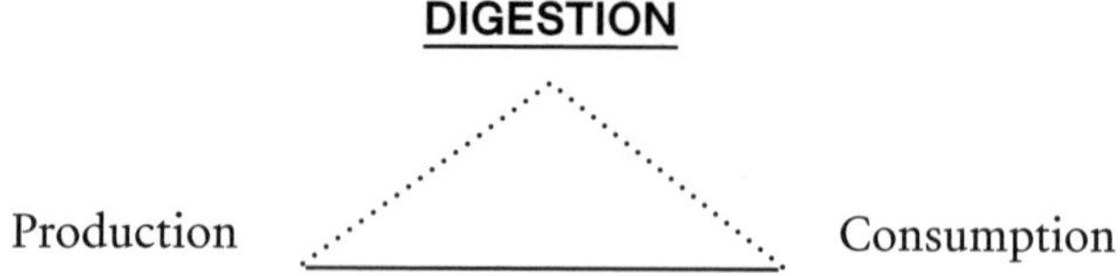

SPACE FOR CONSIDERATION

My current work takes a lot of inspiration from Donna Haraway's writing. One influential concept is situated knowledge:[3] the idea that we must recognise and consider the situated experience and identities of those who are voicing, when evaluating what is being said. There is no neutral scientific perspective from which to evaluate and analyse the world. The practice of situating knowledge asks for a level of personal understanding and transparency with regards to one's own history, difference and privilege. Another one of her concepts is 'tentacular responsibility'[4] which, simply put, suggests that we can generate energy to fight for change through understanding what we are deeply and fundamentally connected to in the world around us.

I moved towards a.pass in a state of exhaustion verging on burnout. I came with two questions: Can ritual and inactivity breed resilience and act as resistance against our broken system (the White Supremacist Capitalist Patriarchy)? And, how can I be in service of the changes that I feel must occur within our culture whilst attempting transparency and acknowledgment of my unearned privileges?

These two questions required me to reflect – to really reflect – which provoked a realisation that there was a lack of space for reflecting on the impact of our actions and for digesting previous experiences, and that lack has created much of the damage surrounding us on all scales. To me, a.pass and the context for artistic research that it carves out represents time and space. A commodity that it buys from its funders through ingenious justification and dogged bureaucratic tenacity. I don't see a.pass as a static utopia, I see it as a fiercely held space. An ever-evolving negotiation.

---

3 Donna Haraway, 'Situated Knowledges: The Science Question in Feminism and the Privilege of Partial Perspective', *Feminist Studies*, Vol. 14, No. 3 (Autumn, 1988), pp. 575-599.

4 Tentacular responsibility is a concept taken from Donna Haraway's book: *Staying with The trouble: Making Kin In the Chthulucene*, Duke University Press, 2016.

A negotiation between

State bureaucracy	*that demands justification, for its support, from*
The institution	*that demands justification, for its support, from*
The artist pedagogues	*that hold space for*
The artist researchers	*to create within.*

When I first heard about a.pass from an alumni, I was excited by the combination of elements and the child inside once again remembered the Mexican cobblestone square with its easy community and cohesive aesthetic. This was tempered by my developed understanding of the complicated and imperfect nature of life. But the mix of what this alum described: '*a performative, artistic research space that embraced the esoteric, the academic, the scientific, the political, the mystical, the philosophical, and the practical. A context that didn't delineate clear boundaries between forms of expression and invited all modes of artistic representation and exploration. A space where those present could co-design the content and contribute to the structuring of experience*'. Their description of this space opened my heart. It aligned with my own journey from stage to site responsivity, from product to process, from presentation to participation. During the four month study block that this alum enthused about, the curators had invited a Peruvian shaman to reside in the space and influence the practices of the artistic researchers. A shaman... This gave rise to thoughts concerning cultural appropriation and modes of knowledge production, it felt uncomfortable, challenging and exciting. They proposed, and problematised their own proposals.

Within my time at a.pass, it was clear that the institution didn't have one coherent ideology or belief in what art is or how art/life should be lived and experienced. It proposed a dialogue between the different curators, pedagogues and researchers. In this proposed continuous enquiry a.pass was far from the utopic cohesive context the child inside me had once dreamed of, but in the practical, administrative, social and ethical wrangles of humans making things up I found what I was looking for: space and time to chew over and reflect on entanglement, tentacularity and responsibility.

Haraway describes our entanglement with and responsibility towards the critical issues of our time as tentacular, as relating to the tentacles of an octopus: sentient, sensual, sensitive feelers into the world. She states that we are connected to many issues both near and far, but we are not connected to all issues. She suggests that we try to understand in what way our identity, history and experiences are entangled with current issues; identifying what issues our tentacles touch, stroke, suck on, and entwine with.

By doing this we can then generate a sense of connectivity and responsibility for certain critical political stances. This in turn generates the energy needed to engage in activism, to act in support of these issues.

I was born in London to descendants of Russian peasants and Hungarian German/Czech communists. Jews. First and second generation immigrants. I grew up there and experienced comparative privilege. At age 14, I started a 30-year relationship with a chronic health condition which affected my interactions with work, art and the social. A side effect of which meant that my gut biome was compromised and among other things, I couldn't digest industrialised wheat.

In 2014, a friend, Victoria Cristina Lelis Aranha, who has now passed away, taught me and my flatmate Alex how to bake sourdough rye bread. I was, at last, after years of buying everything but industrialised wheat loaves, taking back my bread sovereignty. I like to see my intolerance to durum and mass-farmed wheat as a slightly comic, subconscious political action: my body, resisting the onset and brutality of advanced industrialised capitalism.

I approached a.pass questioning my role as an artist and created a practice that decentralises my voice and aims at holding space for generative and negotiated creative engagement. It aims at being a platform for exchange, dialogue and ritual, in which and through which collective action, concepts and emergent ideas can be held, passed through and transformed.

Sometimes, for reflection and new thinking to emerge, people need a radicalised space, claimed for celebration, for consideration, for rigour, rest and encounter.

Maybe my utopia continues to hold elements of the Mexican village square: bodies in sensorial dialogue, moving in a gentle dance between and amongst one and other but now it is more like a 'Temporary Autonomous Zone', (examples of which are most recently seen in various cities across the US following the race protests of summer 2020).[5] A context which resists state imposition, where hierarchy is flattened and action is negotiated. Maybe the ramshackled bunch of pedagogues, administrators, technicians and artist researchers that make up a.pass, with all their contradicting positionalities and ideas, aspire to hold and secure some sort

5 Autonomous police-free zones popped up all over the country after the Black Lives Matter protests post the killing of George Floyd. [The idea] was created in 1990, derived from anarchist philosopher Hakim Bey when Temporary Autonomous Zones were proposed as areas outside of formal state control. In autonomous zones, there are no hierarchies or leaders – local governance is decentralised, and the main goal is creating a neighbourhood without police'. https://refinery29.com/en-us/2020/06/9879362/seattle-black-house-autonomous-zone-protest-meaning

of low-key autonomous zone; a moment of utopia, nested within circles of resistance. Still a village square but where individuals, couples and groups hold space for each other to make up the steps and dance together. A place where the rules of the dance are a little less predetermined. But, as with all current autonomous zones, they are by nature temporary, living in defiance of a societal inclination towards structure, order and safety.

In times of increased state and corporate coercion, the presence of these fiercely held spaces for reflection, digestion, conflict and emergent meaning become more and more urgent and worth fighting for.

Space and time...

...at a.pass facilitated the construction of my current practice that holds at its core a necessity of space and time; an appreciation of the enriching nature of shared contexts of negotiated action and meaning. This practice is called The Bakery Of Slow Ideas and is a social art practice based on the actions and metaphors present within the acts of sourdough bread making and other processes of food fermentation.

Femke Snelting

Contactlessness

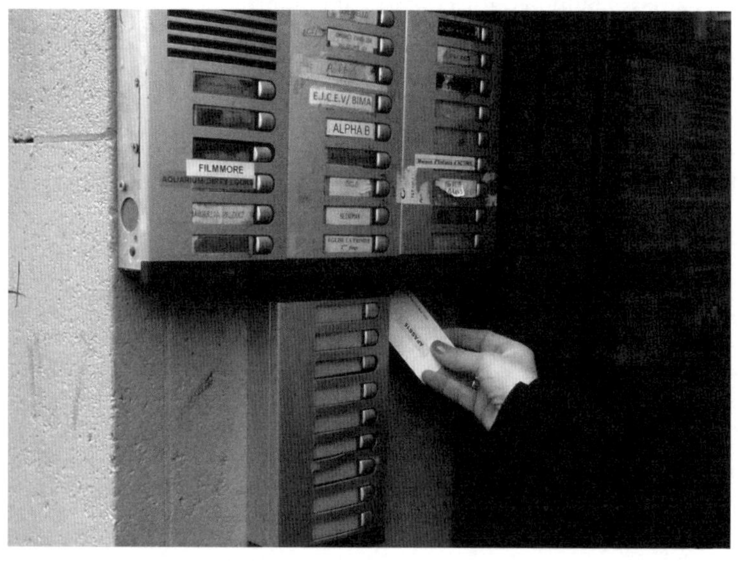

A white piece of plastic, exactly the size of a credit card. On one side, two numbers. A sticker reads 'R 820'. Another number is printed on the plastic itself: 001429256021,53000. The reverse side of the card is blank. I haven't used this keycard for over a year now, but for some reason it stayed in my wallet all this time.

Like in many other institutions, staff and participants at a.pass use on- and offline digital tools for daily communication, archiving, administration and production. They rely on a collage of self-hosted software and proprietary services, of borrowed tools and hardwired networks that are put to use without much space for reflection on what they do and how they actually work. Monday Readings were an attempt to bring these computational infrastructures within reach of the a.pass community and to open them up for interrogation and critique. Together with co-researchers Seda, Sina and Martino, we hosted five day-long sessions in which we read mundane technologies such as 'databases', 'streaming', 'networks', 'text processing' and 'keycards' alongside theoretical texts. By bringing the habitual tool-situations of a.pass in conversation with theoretical and political thinking, we wanted to excite the expertise of a.pass participants and staff, and to collectively pay attention to those powerful tools and devices that so easily blend into the background.

One Monday we started from the innocuous piece of plastic that opens the outer door to De Bottelarij, a former industrial site which houses among others a daycare facility, a theatre company, a traditional dance and music group, a campus of RITCs school of arts, and a.pass. We followed the path of the administrative-infrastructure in place and asked ourselves: What does it mean when opening a door becomes part of a data-flow? Writing this three years later, at a moment of intensified biopolitical optimisation and digital substitution, I would like to rephrase this question. What does it actually mean to carry keys in our wallets?

The a.pass keycard opens two automated doors, one for cars and one for pedestrians. These doors close off an area which Marc, responsible for technique and infrastructure at RITCs, calls the 'walled public space' of De Bottelarij. From here, one has access to outdoor stairs and an elevator leading to among others, the third and fourth floor of the building where a.pass' office, meeting room and studio are located. As one of the main tenants of De Bottelarij, RITCs manages access control for some of its users. The outer door is operated by an electromagnetic circuit hooked up to a computer, a system inherited from the previous owner of the building which apparently runs on a single, standalone machine located somewhere on the first floor. Joke, production coordinator at a.pass, orders read-only RFID cards from an American company, which have a unique 10 digit ID number installed on them. When new cards need to be initialised, she asks Bruno, who manages the system for RITCs, to add their ID to the database. Joke also numbers them according to a system internal to a.pass and keeps a record of who has been given which card. But currently, Bruno does not register the internal numbers in the database; sometimes cards are swapped between users, or stickers peel off. This porous registration means that there is no way to reliably trace the identity of who enters De Bottelarij. This is particular to the way that a.pass practices access control – students of RITCs for example, who carry personalised cards, might be subject to another level of surveillance. As Joke explains: 'because the cards are not personally assigned, there is a collective responsibility. We use the card as a key, and that's about it!'

For the Monday Reading on keycards, Seda invited her colleague Danny, a researcher in applied cryptography. He explained how the cards in our wallet fall under different categories of data management, and how each of them unlocks various technical gestures. And of course, when we each laid out our library cards, credit cards, public transport cards, student cards, ID cards and discount cards in front of us, it was obvious that they represent various challenges for privacy and security. We asked Danny to talk to us about the dataflows surrounding the a.pass keycard but once he had explained how simple identification requires 'only passive interaction', there was not much left for him to be interested in.

Lowest in the picking order of so-called 'contactless smart cards', the generic keycard in use at a.pass contains nothing more than a copper coil and a simple microchip which stores its ten digit ID number. When a card is held in the vicinity of a terminal, a radio signal is emitted to temporarily power the conductor sandwiched in between the plastic, just long enough for the access system to read the number off the card. The terminal checks this information with the database managed by Bruno, to know whether the card has been authorised to open the door. Only if the card is identified as such, the magnetic lock will be released. For more complex operations such as authentication, identity verification and electronic payments, a constellation of read-write interactions is required between machinic and human verifiers, carrier and chips embedded in the card. A keycard such as the one in use at a.pass is read-only, which means it does not contain personal data, nor can it be re-written. As a passive token, it resembles a physical key, in the sense that the system is not interested in who holds the token, but only cares for the relation between the key which authorises the unlocking and the database.

Most of the cards in our wallet fall under the ID-1 category, which regulates their exact physical dimensions (85.6 x 53.98 x .76 mm), their material qualities such as resistance to bending, chemicals, humidity and temperature. For some of them, brief instances of contact might be required. But all of them adhere to the ideology of contactlessness: optimising flows through the reduction of touch. As a convenient argument for the increased use of smart cards, issuers often cite the speed-at-scale of contactless processing. This feature is linked to the fact that the Near Field Communication (NFC) by which the terminal powers the card, can be read from within a short distance of the reader module. NFC allows for hands-free, touch free, tap-and-go processing, which reduces the time per transaction because cards can be used without being taken out of a wallet. It made contactless payments soar under pandemic conditions, since banks and shops convinced payers that it was safer not to touch dirty cash, and that speedy transactions would prevent busy queues. Another pragmatic argument is the possibility of 'revocation', the annulling of access that was granted earlier without the need to be in contact with the card and cardholders physically. Contactless revocation is efficient if you imagine that in the case of a mechanical lock with physical keys, you would need to replace the lock but also all keys in circulation when someone would lose or steal a single key. This is not trivial especially when access is shared with a large group of people. In the case of keycards, it suffices to change the authorisation for the card ID in the database and because plastic cards are cheap to replace, there is less pressure on issuers to demand their return.

Contactless smart cards have become increasingly hard to avoid when moving through daily life. They are issued by institutions and organisations for many different tasks that involve some kind of administrative authorisation. They cut out the need to employ humans to be present on site and continuously oversee who can withdraw money, lend a book, eat a sandwich, take the bus or enter the premises. The thing about keycards that should concern the a.pass community, is not their problematic relation to personal privacy, or at least, not in the first place. What should worry us is the way they contribute to the efficient translation of life into a series of contactless transactions that are authorised at a distance, and how they facilitate technologically managed membranes of inclusion and exclusion. The banality and uninterestingness of the technologies, processes and repeated movements that culminate in pointing a piece of plastic to a terminal, make it easy to forget what logic is being domesticated in the background. It is not without problem that the ubiquitous objects which regulate our relations to spaces for critique and creation, for physical and intellectual nourishment, for public transport and education are each modeled after credit cards and it is also not without consequence that the gesture of opening a door now resembles a financial transaction.

As Philip Agre explains in 'Surveillance and Capture: Two models of Privacy', such small gestures of continuous authentication are seemingly insignificant processes that we take for granted but which culminate into a paradigm shift which has real implications for the way we live.

The displacement of access control from a situated negotiation at the place of access, to technological infrastructures operating out of sight, slowly but surely folds life into a continuous repetition of separable transactions, gestures that are characteristic of bureaucratic capitalism. The same systems that so conveniently allow for revocation, are based on the dispossession of individual and collective agency and weakening of institutional strength. Our urgent concern should be with the way that the gestures of authorisation and transaction are being performed under the premise of contactlessness, a regime in which access can be revoked without being in touch. Contactlessness turns technical infrastructures into intangible environments, and trains its users to become the medium of what Agre calls 'partial perceptions'.

The minimal viable mode of access control practiced at a.pass ('We use the card as a key, and that's about it') could point at a collective hesitation about the hands-off paradigm, but the point is of course how to resonate differently with keycards, how to shift the way that the objects in our wallets make us perform our relationship to the world. Monday Readings proposed a radical staying-in-the-presence-of techniques and technologies that regulate daily life. We assumed that to study the intricate interplay between tools, institutions, ideologies and social practices that keycards tap into, requires the kind of rigorous undisciplinarity that artistic research can offer. It staged the a.pass Research Center as the appropriate setting for attending to the implications of separability, for inventing 'grammars of action' that instead of capturing life into reduced transactions and contactless authorisation, would allow for complex interactions and proximate modes of negotiating shared access.

In 2018, Seda Guerses, Martino Morandi, Sina Seifee and Femke Snelting organised five Monday Readings at the a.pass Research Center. https://apass.be/monday-readings

Philip Agre, 'Surveillance and Capture: Two models of privacy', *The Information Society,* 10:2, 1994, 101-127.

Orit Halpern, Robert Mitchell, Bernard Dionysius Geoghegan, 'The Smartness Mandate: Notes toward a Critique', *Grey Room*, no. 68 (Summer 2017), 106-129.

Lucas Silva Figueiredo et al., 'Prepose: Privacy, Security and Reliability for Gesture-Based Programming' IEEE Symposium on Security and Privacy (SP), 2016, 122-137.

Interlocutors: Danny De Cock, Joke Liberge, Marc Vandermeulen, Bruno Tuyteleir.

caterina daniela mora jara

The untrans-latable a.pass: The politics of remaining

BEFORE THE BEGINNING

I moved to Brussels without speaking French, nor English. I prepared my a.pass Skype interview in Buenos Aires, October 2017 with my friend and English professor, Mariana. With her, I prepared all the possible questions we could ever imagine for the interview. During the interview I had with me, next to my computer, several annotations and phrases prepared for potential questions. That morning, my hands were sweating more than normal in my apartment.

The first day of a.pass on Monday, April 30th, 2018 was the first official day in my life where I encountered English for six or seven hours nonstop. I could feel the pain of developed, stocked and disoriented cells in my brain. I had a headache during the first five months after I started. The headache was right after each a.pass session. The cells in my brain were dislocated by the amount of English going on. I used to ask a lot for second or third explanations and I took the habit of asking people where they were coming from, because I was very worried about native English accents.

THE HEADACHE AND THE BLOCKAGE OF THE FIRST BLOCK

During my first block in a.pass, I was busy trying to open up questions in relation to the reggaeton phenomenon. I started looking at the stereotype construction of Latin-imaginary through two concepts: *semio-capitalism* (Franco Berardi, known as Bifo) and *imaginary communities* (Benedict Anderson). I was obsessed with how reggaeton videos and especially the famous song 'Despacito' were/are framing stereotyped ways of 'Latin-ness'. Due to the absence of a more appropriate terminology to translate 'lo latino', I choose the phrase 'the Latin imaginary' owing its relevance in relation to the imaginaries. My questions were: Which signs are reproduced by this construction? How are Latin bodies perceived in the Brussels context? And how is it possible to make artistic operation on this imaginary? So, I tried several things, among others: mapping the places related to 'Latin-ness' in Brussels, interviewing 'lo latino' experiences, YouTube videos with the voice of Google Translate, creating reggaeton songs through the comments of others, re-appropriating choreographies made by others that illustrated 'lo latino', offering a brunch in my garden during summer.

I was completely trapped by the stereotype and those exercises showed that I was reinforcing the stereotype itself, instead of questioning it or opening it up. During the End Week in PAF[1] I found out the limits of these ways of addressing stereotypes.

SECOND ROUND, INSPIRED BY APHRA BEHN

This is why it was clear to me that for my second block I needed to try another strategy. At the same time, I was very frustrated with my hyperdependence on Google Translate. After my first block of a.pass, even though I became better in my English, it was very rudimentary. So, one of my mentors told me to bring that conflict from my daily life into my artistic research. And I started to translate like crazy. From dance to text, and vice versa. From text to maps, and vice versa. From photos to videos, and vice versa. From economic inflation in Argentinian pesos to economic inflation in euros and vice versa. From emotions to choreographies and vice versa. From movements to draws and vice versa. From dance to dance and vice versa. I found out something interesting in this one: from dance to dance. This is how I started to translate from ballet to reggaeton.

At the same time, I read theory of translations with gender perspective, so I discovered the name of Aphra Behn, who has inspired and guided this research since then. Behn lived between 1640 and 1689. She named herself 'translatress', and she was the first woman to earn her living by her writing. She worked as a spy for King Charles II and her life is for me and so far, a story of admiration. This is why I took her input and I called myself like her, a translatress, busy with poetry and pleasure as sources for creation.

At the end of this block, I was very touched by the possibilities of my research. Coming from Argentina, for me a.pass was a luxury environment for research. I had a key to the building, the alarms of the building, the possibility to pay someone who listened to my questions, the possibility to re-try, rehearse, re-question the same questions as well as re-expose, re-exchange, and re-feedback through and with the same, different and diverse people.

1 **PAF** is the acronym for Performing Arts Forum, in France. It is a place where the entire team of a.pass moves (participants, curators, mentors, administration, sometimes family) for one week and where the End Week presentations of each project take place.

Although a.pass doesn't consider itself as a 'rich' institution, for me it was indeed a rich environment due to the privileges related to conditions of production. And this richness for me was untranslatable.

In the middle of this block, I arrived to formulate the question: What resists translation? What reclaims the agency of being untranslatable? Until now, I am still more interested in what remains untranslatable, rather than what is translatable. This is because usually, for me, what remains untranslatable is related to privileges, pleasure and violence. Privileges of context, interiorisation of violence, and in this particular research focus, on the interiorisation of violence through the techniques, methods and styles of dance.

'THE TRANSLATRESS IN HER OWN PERSON SPEAKS', APHRA BEHN

After, I skipped a block and I went a lot to *a.pass* for one particular task: using the space in the morning for my training and for the translation. This also ended up in my presentation at Performatik 19, the Brussels biennale of performance art. a.pass presented a group proposal and I created for this occasion the first bastard-cheap lecture performance called '18 minutes of a Poor Cheap Bastard Lecture Performance'. In the description it says:

> For this project a.pass provides bright paper, a platform, a microphone like Madonna, cables, speakers, lights and they/we transport the handmade ballet barre. I provide 18 minutes of my embodied research, a plastic crown of 10 cents of euros and music from my cell phone that I bought for 67 euros. This is an attempt to bring high and low culture closer but maybe it's too pretentious. I am trying to dance critically: from *l'exagération de a sociological situation* to the pleasure of *mostrar los dientes*.
> All of you are welcome.

I didn't know at that moment, but after the creation of the first I have been busy with the following ones, which don't have a sequential timeline because they are not in chronological order.

TRT

For the fourth and last block I was afraid about how to continue my research after a.pass. Also, I had the necessity of framing all this year in some way. So, my mentor told me: ‘Do it into method!’. I remember this phrase, but it doesn’t make too much grammar sense in English, so my corrector has suggested: ‘Make this into a method!’

After this intervention, Transversal Research Training (from now on TRT) emerged in May 2019. TRT is a constellation of methodologies (in plural) for artistic research, and of course they are not mine, they are there, existing outside of me. Conceptualised not long ago, what I wrote in May 2019 remains, guides and challenges my practices. Below a fragment of the TRT explanation, that you can find more or less in my a.pass web portfolio: Focusing on the development of strategies to articulate training, research, feedback and communication, TRT is a device for artistic practice being created in recognition of the historical contribution made by the figure of the translatress Aphra Behn.

- TRT develops critical and optimised coordination by exercising an ecosystem of practices based on the respect for the territorialisation of practice, interdependence by engaging a diversity of dance practices while aiming for a non-hierarchy by inviting others’ bodies.
- TRT encourages strategies for sharing/shaking through taking care of the production context in art practice.
- TRT is situated research that questions, through translation, the legitimisation of authorship.
- TRT does not claim uniqueness or originality.

It is transversal because it tries to encourage transversal relations among power structures in dance.s, conditions of production in artistic research, problematising entertainment, shifting north-south, east-west and questioning authorship. Those concepts embrace themselves in the training.

It is a training because it looks at processes that endure in time and processes of endurance engaging art/life. Like any training, it is linked to a way of facing knowledge in process-education. Like any training, it is looking for preparing and contextualising practice focused on elasticity, concentration, balance and coordination of different tasks.

It is research by acknowledging the colonial growth of this word. It seems like the word 'research' gives the frame of 'artistic research' another status. More powerful, more legitimate, as the word 'art' wasn't enough or wasn't already legitimated. So, that's why TRT is also busy with the critique of the device called artistic research. I am here in front of a paradox: I am engaging with TRT as a device to do artistic research that is also criticising the device of artistic research. This brings me to another problem...

I continue with the previous quote: this brings me to another problem, but this problem is addressed in another text about the Eroticism of Practices.[2] Actually, TRT is the consequence of remaining and the trace of several enunciation try-outs. When I was writing the previous quote in May 2019, I realised that TRT is nothing 'new' because it is the outcome of several re-enacting, re-try-outs and re-petitions. This is why this text is focused on what I called the 'politics of remaining', and it is configured by wondering: What remains there, in my/our/your/their practice to be conceptualised, to be enunciated? What does this remaining do? And what is the politics of that?

My aim was to do an erotic article about how my methodology in artistic research was produced by multiple essays. I don't know if I succeeded through this text which elaborates a little bit how the things were appearing. This particular research is not mine, it is there at some point in Brussels or Stockholm territory, it is here in this English grammar without proofreading, it is there in some Bastard-Cheap lecture performance, it is here currently doing a PhD in Stockholm, it is there trying to go to Argentina, it is here reminding and addressing what remains invisible.

Circular time is for this research a possibility to deal with pleasure as a source with potential disruption, to interconnect pleasure with seduction and magnetism with the desire in our dances-practices. Because some practices and thinking can re-appear and re-inform others' practices and thinking.

In the middle of this research and in the middle of this text resonates specific a.pass vocabulary such as methodologies, HWD (Halfway Days), blocks, skip block, internal mentors, external

2 The other text about Eroticism of Practices had as a starting point the following question formulated in March 2021: 'How and when will we dance together again? How to invite a grammar that magnetises again this 'we'? How to deal with the flat, cold and square screen today and the physical separation that has been imposed as a protective rule?

mentors, End Presentations, publication, room 117 in PAF, break, headache, break, breath, break. In the middle of a.pass, the act of gathering together, discussing a lot, sharing food and spaces and the most important thing: not-being friends.

The politics of remaining that a.pass proposes is busy with discursive problems, dreams, nightmares, necessities and fantasies of artistic practices. The politics of remaining are entangled with a lot of 're': re-mind, re-act, re-explain, re-expose, re-try, re-peat, re-sense, re-cook, re-taste, re-configure, re-enchantment, re-fall-in-love, and so on.

Remaining is also resting and resisting.

A little part of my affective references, in a non-alphabetic order:

My sister Marilina - Sherry Simon - Bifo - Benedict Anderson - My partner Lucas - Aníbal Quijano, Enrique Dussel - Silvia Rivera Cusicanqui - My cousin Belén - Marie Bardet - Aphra Behn, the translatress - Gloria Ansaldúa - Katie Briggs - Ramsay Burt - Susana Tambutti - Susan Leigh Foster - Audre Lorde - Eduardo Grüner - Maradona - My mum Nancy, my dad Daniel - Luis Biasotto - Luciana Acuña - Femke Snelting - Luis Martinez Andrade.

Another little part of my references, in form of alphabetical order:

ANSALDÚA, Gloria, 1987. *Borderlands-La Frontera: The New mestiza.* Aunt Lute Books, San Francisco.

ANDERSON, Benedict, 2006. *Imagined Communities: Reflections on the Origin and Spread of Nationalism.* Verso, London.

BERARDI, Franco, 2009. *Precarious Rhapsody: Semiocapitalism and the Pathologies of the Post-Alpha Generation.* Minor Compositions. London.

BRIGGS, Kate, 2018. *This Little Art.* Fitzcarraldo Editions.

BURT, Ramsay, 1995. *The Male Dancer: Bodies, Spectacle, Sexualities.* Routledge, London and New York.

FEDERICCI, Silvia, 2004. *Caliban and the Witch: Women, the Body and Primitive Accumulation.* Autonomedia, NY, USA.

GRÜNER, Eduardo, 2000. *De culturas e identidades nacionales, o que la verdad tiene estructura de ficción* en Boletín N° 120 de la Biblioteca del Congreso de la Nación. Buenos Aires.

LORDE, Audre, 1978. *The Uses of the Erotic: The Erotic as Power.* Kore Press (reprint 2000).

NOVERRE, Jean Georges, 1760. *Lettres sur la danse, et sur les ballets.* Retrieved from https://libraryofdance.org/manuals/1760-Noverre-Lettres_BNF.pdf

QUIJANO, Aníbal, 2000. *Colonialidad del Poder y Clasificación Social* en Festchrift for Immanuel Wallerstein – Part I. Journal of world-systems research, Vol.XI, Number 2.

RIVERA CUSICANQUI, Silvia, 2010. *Ch'ixinakax utxiwa: una reflexión sobre prácticas y discursos Descolonizadores.* Buenos Aires: Tinta Limón.

SIMON, Sherry, 1996. *Gender in Translation.* Routledge, London and New York

TAMBUTTI, Susana, 2012. *Reflexiones sobre la danza escénica en Argentina Globalización. La misma danza bajo todos los climas* en las Actas de las IV Jornadas de investigación y crítica teatral.

Pierre Rubio

Fragments of a Recorded Message on Cybernetics and Collective Artistic Research

to Laura Pante, Sina Seifee and Vanja Smiljanić

‘Hi Laura, Sina, Vanja. This is Pierre speaking…’

(…)
‘As entry points, when I considered the possibility of creating a space for us to write interesting texts and/or dialogues under the circumstances of this publication, I shared with you some text fragments and questions that I wrote in relation to some of the problems that I can pinpoint from where I stand and that, I think, an artistic research curator, pedagogue, or mentor faces. I was “interested in your interest” in some of these ideas and questions, but in tension with your own questioning about the curatorial propositions you formulated and activated at a.pass and the problems shaped by your work in general. This dialogical process created a transitional space as individual positions and common issues often diverge, but when they are articulated in a grey area of risk-taking, then perhaps, new perspectives can be glimpsed and unexpected challenges might be raised. On this ridgeline, our work has generated different and specific forms of textual connective fabrics stitched by problems that we decode through our practices, questions that we decide to pose to ourselves and concerns we want/need to talk about and share in this context’.

(…)
‘We are all connected to a.pass – this always-already ungraspable but very much actual object that brought us together – and we are developing or have developed within this institution complex processes that intertwine forms of knowledge production, political positionings and more or less assertive ideas about what art and artistic research are or should be in contexts of collective experimentation. This institutional connection – or connection through an institution – has become for us one of the themes of our discussions more or less directly, and we have tried to decipher our complex relational systems around ideas of participation, technology, publicness, design, identity, control, power, knowledge and more’.

(…)
‘At first, I shared with you a constructive critique of systems of curation and of artistic research projects occurring at a.pass in relation to ideas of cybernetic systems of control and to theories conceptualising the multiple metamorphoses of information generated by and generating performative processes of individuation and transindividuation. But why launch our writing process from there?’

(...)
'Systems of control'.

(...)
'Cybernetics is the science of self-regulating systems that gauge, anticipate and respond in order to intervene and change conditions. This idea of self-regulating systems has historically oscillated – and still oscillates – between two utopias. That of achieving total control through unlimited surveillance and that of abolishing hierarchies within horizontal, participatory and inclusive social forms. My working hypothesis is that, in artistic and research environments such as a.pass, the historical succession of cybernetic theories, as different waves, is played out and replayed in a cyclical movement through a logic of accidents which determines individuation(s) and transindividuation(s) – I am not an academic like some of you are, my hypothesis is formulated by me-as-an-artist, so not very scientifically. I mobilise this hypothesis in order to read situations, rather than attempting to prove it. So, through the filter of cybernetics, one can perceive artistic research projects or methods or environments as different ecologies of ideas and practices powered by performative relationalities. The individual research projects, the institution, the curatorial frames, and everything that takes place between these poles, become assemblages of multidisciplinary systems-thinking exerting forces on each other and within each other. One can call these forces systems of control as they are aimed at generating determinations in many different directions and in many different ways. I believe that our different relations with control – that I compare with the divergent relations of cybernetics theories to controlling – play a central role in the possibility for a research project, for an artist-researcher or for a curator, pedagogue or mentor to individuate, i.e. to activate their potential to become. And methodologically speaking, from my point of view, one of the multiple conditions of possibility for observing and deciphering these control forces-operating-through-relations is to consider the systems which generate them as structures in becoming or in a process of individuation and to seriously consider the metastable nature of these systems – the state in which they are full of potential to evolve – generating these forces and at the same time being generated by them. In other words: being individuated and individuating'.

(...)
'How do protagonists in artistic research environments individuate themselves and their projects on the basis of determining information systems that they follow, resist, construct, or criticise?'

(...)
'Individuation'.

(...)
'In a.pass, an artistic and research project, or an artistic research methodology, or a curated pedagogical apparatus, aimed at generating knowledge collectively, can be thought of as trajectories of individuation. A trajectory of individuation is made of successive "individuating encounters" inducing the formation of ways of thinking, practicing, acting, organising, understanding, and perceiving. A project, or proposition, or institution is never completely individuated, it maintains a part of metastability in itself, an unresolved part of itself one could say, that I identify as a condition for its future encounters with "beings" (other projects, other institutions, people, ideas, struggles, non-humans...) and as a condition for its potential resourcing and transformation i.e., its individuation. A metastable-project-as-individual is not essentially defined by its individuated parts, but through what is not individuated within it! A metastable-project-as-individual is therefore a being partly composed of acquired "behavioural" structures, and partly of its plasticity, its capacity to transform when in contact with an experience. Simondon calls this an archipelago structure – a composition of the individuated and the not-yet-individuated or open to transformation – and in his theory, metastability is the condition for an individuating encounter. An entirely structured individual cannot experience any individuating encounter. The entities, who are "meeting", are already partly individuated, but in truth, it is only between what is NOT individuated within them, between what is metastable or unresolved, that a transformative encounter can happen'.

(...)
'How do artist-researchers and artistic research curators/pedagogues individuate their projects in contexts structured by accidents generated by a constant interdependence between interiority – them – and exteriority – the others, the institution?'

(...)
'Information as singularity'.

(...)
'Coming back to the idea of control, one can look at artistic research projects and curatorial/pedagogical structures as systems of control that deal with and transform the metastable milieus they exercise forces upon but are in-formed by these very milieus as well. Here, the notion of information plays an important role because it has to be defined as an in-between-matter,

as a medium for the performative inter – or intra – relations between the different systems of control and their possible individuation horizons. The definition of information I play with was conceived during the second wave of cybernetics theory and challenged previous definitions that focussed exclusively on the sender and its message abstracted from any other types of relations. The notion of information was redefined, more politically, by some "new" cyberneticians, including Simondon, who drastically changed the perspective by considering the position of the receiver as a constitutive part of information itself. That is to say that information is considered through its potential effects and equivalent to a singularity. The information-singularity, or active information, does not exist as such in a consistent duration and identity, it is not a thing nor a substance. There is no such thing as an essence of information-singularity, it is in a particular metastable milieu that any given thing will be in-formed and undertake an informing function, which it may not undertake in another milieu. The information-singularity is not something, it is an agent of change, it is an operation that generates individuation; a change in the state of the individual. By evolving, the metastable milieus, here the systems constituted by research projects or curatorial/pedagogical apparatuses, can provide themselves with new singularities, such as new thresholds, new configurations of matter and structures which can bring into play other effects of production of form. But, there are singularities that are "not expected" by the systems. In fact, there is a random factor in the conditions of possibility for a change to happen (an individuation as Simondon would say) in artistic research processes and environments. But why and how can randomness be a decisive operator in this traffic of individuations?'

(...)
'Randomness'.

(...)
'The Western conception of the individual achieves a problematic unity in the refusal to allow space for real historicity, which is that of transformation, without necessity and without finality. In the classical definition, whether as an a-temporal essence opposed to the temporality of accidents, as a substance, a person or a self, the individual is what escapes time. As its theoretical foundation, the concept of the individual has identity, be it logical, ontological or psychological, and identity in general is reluctant to change. The "classical" individual evades the effectiveness of historicity. Posing the question of the temporality of the individual is already displacing the problem of the solidified individual, which is only an abstract cut in time, to the process of

individuation, which is the real genesis of individuated entities. The idea of individuation reforms the traditional concept of the individual from two perspectives. First, from a temporal perspective which posits that the "real" individual is not the constituted and frozen individual, but the very process of individuation. Second, from a relational perspective, which revokes the idea of the substantial individual based on an essence or a nature, and replaces it with a notion of a relational system whose identity is constituted in its relationship to exteriority. From this point on, the second myth about the individual self-unravels. The idea of an individual closed in on itself, possessing all of its being within itself is obsolete in light of the idea of process, because the function of process is to constantly bring exteriority and interiority into contact. However, as soon as the idea of finality – for us, here, finality means the intention to fabricate within an artistic research project for example – does not govern the totality of the transformation, this confrontation with exteriority can be legitimately questioned in terms of randomness'.

(...)
'Can artistic research projects and artistic research contexts create some conditions of possibility for the generation of other compatibilities leading potentially to the individuation of new forms?'

(...)
'Compatibility'.

(...)
'Not any random information-singularity will prompt new individuations or new becomings because everything cannot be compatible with everything and not everybody can be compatible with everybody's art or research. Singularities randomly trigger changes only when there is compatibility between the information and the receiver-metastable milieu. Any information can operate extensive or minor modulations but not all of them will do so. Randomness is a significant player in this theatre of operations, but it is a "constrained randomness" conditioned by compatibility factors and restrained by the amount of compatibility of one actor/object with the other. Therefore, acting on the compatibility ratio seems to be a working horizon to be privileged for those who want to play with the randomness of individuating encounters to possibly generate new forms. As I pronounce these last words I hear your voices objecting loudly: "but Pierre, this is a precise description of the ultimate goals of deep marketing and one of the most potent resources of capitalism's liquid superpower!"

And, unfortunately you are right, as always. It is also an accurate description of the heavens and hells of cybernetics torn between a world imbued and nurtured by generative relationalities, and another one, drained by a morbid utopia thirsting limitlessly for the total control of human engineering. Sad smiley'.

(...)
'Which kind of effect does a.pass generate by assembling transversally a multitude of systems-thinking projects and apparatuses exercising determining forces on each other?'

(...)
'Et voilà! I wanted to share this (long) recap with you today. I thank you all for your participation in this transindividual process of textual generation. See you soon in other dimensions. Be well. Bye...'

Laura Pante
At a.pass, Laura questioned the degree to which bodies are subjected to propaganda through the exposure of corporeal images on digital 2D screen devices to analyse the seductive power of the body and its use and abuse by former totalitarian regimes and contemporary globalised technologies. She also collaborated with artists and researchers to create zones of expanded thinking where visions of the future and past are generated collectively in order to destabilise and rewrite conditioning narratives. Within the framework of this publication, she engaged in a series of conversations and shared urgent concerns, rephrasing and randomising notions of pedagogy publicness and collaboration.

Sina Seifee
Sina's work is committed to social dimensions of imagination in the intersection of techno-media and globalism, with an emphasis on the heritage of zoology in West Asia. At a.pass, Sina researched and curated, and as an art form, constructed and programmed digital interfaces for artistic research projects. In the frame of this publication, Sina engaged in a series of dialogues and operated a reversal of some initial points of discussion through his systematic suspicious attitude to, and allergy of transparency.

Vanja Smiljanić
In her practice, Vanja bridges fictitious and experiential universes, comprising technical apparatus, diagrams, and sci-fi povera sculptures. For the circumstances of this publication, she participated in a series of interviews where she navigated the questions with hybrid methods that eventually liquefied and transformed the dialogical space when she proposed to process the interview through a fictional dysfunctional machine.

Pierre Rubio
As co-curator and mentor at a.pass, Pierre's work questioned modes of individuation and transindividuation in/through artistic research collective practices. For this publication, Pierre positioned himself as a non-neutral interlocutor and proposed a collaborative process generating forms of written dialogues: an attempt to transcribe the phenomena of writing together and the process of individuation at work when talking about (trans)individuation.

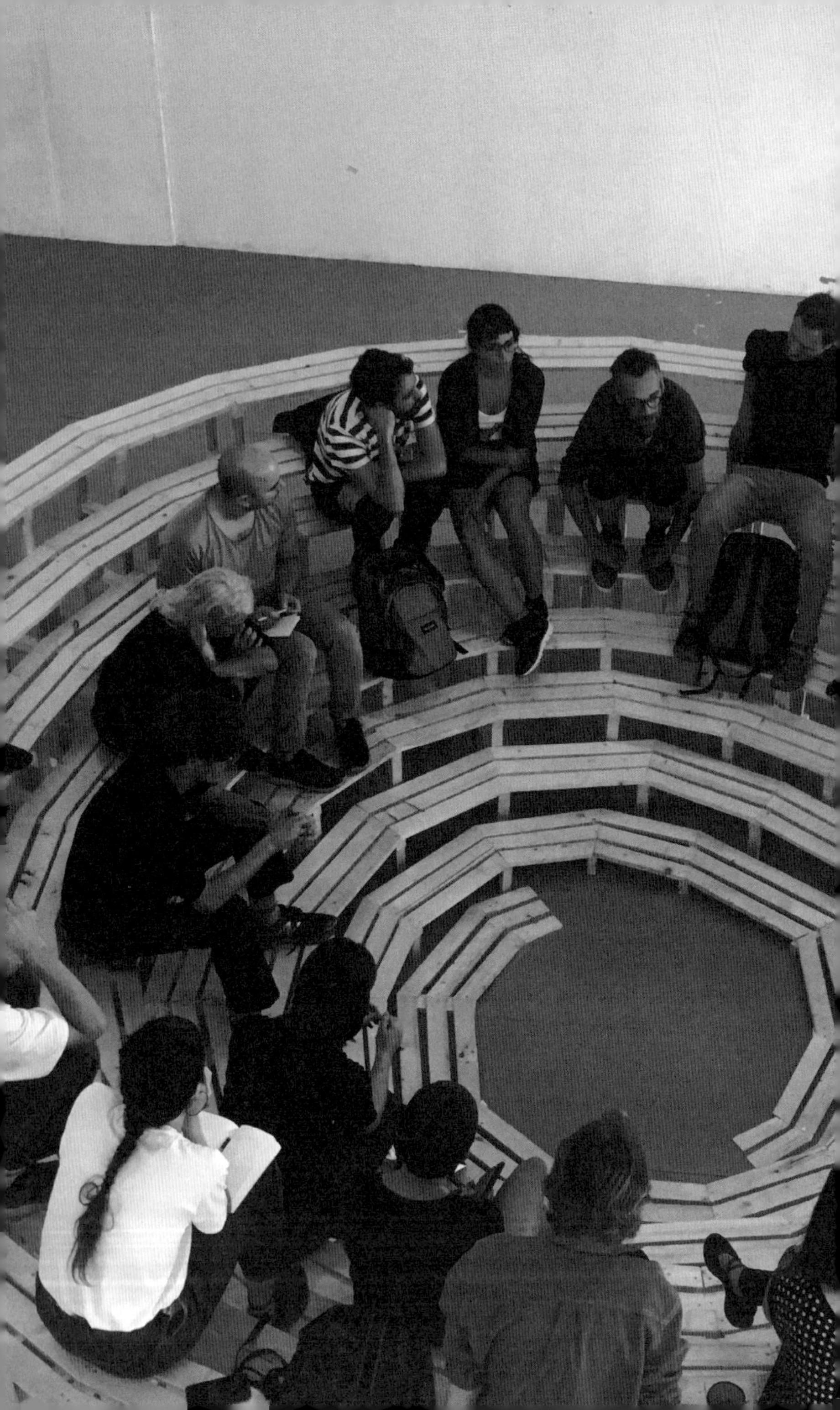

Part II

INNER

What's going on in there?

Lilia Mestre
Kristien Van den Brande

Letter to You: A Correspondence on Artificial Friendship, Curatorial Practices and the Precarious World We are Living In

Brussels, October 8, 2020

Dear you,

We most probably have not met before and we might not meet again. That doesn't matter so much now. Meanwhile, between the past and the future, we are here together, reading or listening to the same words, each of us in a different space and time. Me and you giving attention and attending to the words and presence of each other. In different temporalities, political constellations, economies, concerns and forms of awareness.

I hope you are well, I really do, and I also hope that you are able to deal with all the questions that come through this terrifying moment that we are living, and that you can, in one way or another, embrace them.

While writing these words, I remember the first verses of the book *Parable of the Sower,* by Octavia Butler, which I read throughout the first COVID 19 lockdown. The story tells about a dystopian world where survival becomes the only concern of all living creatures, humans and non-humans. Despite the dystopian reality, a sense of hope is carried by the main character, the 18-year-old Lauren Olmina. She believes in community building and in the possibility of re-seeding a new world. A world she doesn't know yet. To support her belief, she collects all of the knowledges at her disposal: books, tools, guns, seeds, landscapes and behaviours. She writes verses in her diary as a way to communicate her thoughts to others. The first verse is:

All that you touch
You change
All that you Change
Changes you.
The only lasting truth
Is Change
God Is Change.

Regarding the question about 'curating and performing in times of halting and transformation'[1] launched by Roselle Pineda, to which I decided to write this letter, I ask myself how to curate change? and I tiptoe towards the question. I don't see any other way than to attempt to get closer to the will to accept change as a

1 Performance Curators Initiatives (PCI) Symposium 2020 – Conversations on Curation and Performance in the Time of Halting and Transformation.

determinant intention. And, I don't want to thwart that possibility in any way. So I decided to write a letter because its address forms a 'you'. A 'you' I want to entangle with.

I will most probably deviate from the task of telling you about my approach to the curatorial in the time of the pandemic but I hope you don't mind, because in that deviation I hope to touch the very heart of it. This approach takes time. The time to suspend fast conclusions. The time for observation. The time for caring and holding, the time we share. Maybe the time to not address everything at once but to focus and be closer to what we are doing. The time when we reach out. When we make ourselves visible to others. When we are seeking connection.

I like the way letters bring thought, feelings and words together. The writing of letters proposes a certain attention for the thoughts that appear, the involvement of the self, the looking out of the window, the starting again from the beginning to make sure the thought follows. To be thinking about you in every step. Maybe this is not just happening when writing letters but that's my feeling now.

I have to think about the project, 'Time has fallen asleep in the afternoon sunshine' initiated by Mette Edvardsen, which I'm part of. In this project, a collection of 'living books' reads individually to one audience member at the time, a book they've learned by heart. This project takes place in libraries and raises many questions around the artwork in terms of authorship and spectatorship, but actually the most important is what happens in the encounter. Two people, a specific situation, a certain time, many questions. The text – learned by heart – passes through the performer in several ways, multiple times, and it is always new every time the performer retells it to an audience member. There is no way around it. Whatever happens here is in the in-between of the encounter. In the time we spend together.

And when COVID-19 made encounters impossible for a while, Mette asked us (the books) to write to our readers in case of not being able to meet in person. What a beautiful thought to write the text again, this time not as one of the strategies to learn by heart but to actually send it to someone. Someone like you, someone that we have never seen before and probably will not see again. The intention of such a process engages in taking the audience as a friend. The epistolary calls for intimacy at distance. I will never forget you.

The last time I received a letter was the 4th of September, 2020, not so long ago. Tom Engels, a writer and dramaturge, and at this point also mentor at a.pass, an educational artistic research platform where I've been working for about 12 years now, presented himself by writing a letter to a.pass. It was great to be addressed personally, with precision and in such an attentive manner. In my experience, that letter made connections across the personal, the people in the room and the world outside. We were woven at that moment between the personal, the collective and the world. The letter was a way to create relations through what really mattered to Tom at that moment, his vicinity and the actual political context of homophobia. We were caught in between story and history, both making each other simultaneously.

The world is on fire. Don't you think?

In my work as a curator at a.pass, I continuously developed a research on scores that I later titled Scorescapes. When I was asked by former director Elke Van Campenhout to curate at a.pass, I got obsessed with the idea of creating a modality of work with the postgraduate researchers that could encompass several types of research in the arts with multiple modes of expression. A kind of infrastructure that could support difference, even conflict or at least dissensus. A support structure for critical dialogue through making and articulating artistic practice. Not a place of unity, conclusion and certainty but a place of vulnerable co-existence where the capacity of learning and transformation is most important.

The practice of Scorescapes consists of creating a correspondence between several artistic researchers through a combination of presentations and writing practice. We don't address each other directly, as in a normal feedback activity, we address each other with the delay of the letter, the delay of reflecting about what a critical response could be and how we want to formulate it with which language. The delay of the letter produces critique as a modality of care. I'm holding on to you, while responding to your work. I carry you with me every day. I think through you. You change me. I'm totally in love with the idea that a critical world can be a world of change. An inclusive environment of transformation.

I want to mention that I see critique as a responsibility towards the constitution of the 'we'. A 'we' that is constituted by taking the difference between me and you very seriously. A 'we' that questions, speculates, embraces and takes responsibility for the 'we'. I think this is a place of utopia. A place to hope for. All together and all apart at the same time. No restriction of thought. No fear. What could be the politics of such a place?

Maybe the community that Lauren Olmina, in the book *Parable of the Sower,* is aspiring for, is a community without identity. Meaning a community not based on recognition, similarity, identification, solidity and niceness but a community where difference can be shared. Always vulnerable but not weak. Always reflecting but not unifying. Where collected knowledges are the starting point to take action. Where change is the only truth.

COVID-19 made visible some curatorial approaches that have made sense to me for a long time. Many of these forms are not new but maybe they attach to the precarious and vulnerable environment of the arts in a different manner. For example, to bring people together in smaller groups, one on one performances, to use private spaces to perform and to work with what is there at hand as the conditions for the work. Many of these strategies have been practiced by artists even before the pandemic.

It may be because I'm getting older or maybe because I care for alternative and experimental settings – where the art situation is not about consumption but about processes and experiencing exchange through aesthetic practices – that I'm attached to this kind of work. Attached to the experience of attending to a poetic construction of the world. To attend to a specific sensibility and logic that makes the world a richer place for each of us. This is probably what art can do and this is not a minor gesture.
I strongly hope that we all continue to practice it.

During the lockdown, from March until July, the a.pass researchers and myself used one iteration of Scorescapes to keep in touch with each other, but also to keep in touch with ourselves and our individual practices. We called it 'Scorona'. That ironic touch made life lighter while the world was collapsing. It made us laugh. The practice of the score became a way to try to make sense of our lives without panicking about what was going on in the world. Somehow it poeticised and articulated the moment of confusion, despair, isolation, precarity and sorrow that the lockdown ensued. Through the score, we shared and discussed our impressions, conditions and fears. We diligently worked on hopes, desires and aspirations for the world. What else other than collective imagination can empower social change?

Scorona, like the other Scorescapes iterations, was a weekly practice. During the course of three months, on the same date and at the same hour, each of us sent a five minute video, text or sound file to someone in the group. In response, two days later, we would get a personal email with a reflection upon the material received. These responses led to other videos, sound files or texts, and so forth. Every week we let chance decide to whom each of us would send the material and to whom we would respond. Because we couldn't meet in person, we were somehow obliged to stay with the mediated supports at our disposal through our computers. Those mediating tools suddenly seemed so uncanny. Too familiar and too mediated… or had we never thought of them as existential devices? Somehow, they have been naturalised or socialised or humanised or colonised through COVID-19. We had to look them in the eye.

The only resistance against acting as if the world was normal, was to stick to the delay of the responses we sent to each other. Wait a second! A delay that makes you stay in touch. Is this a paradox or the possibility to extend the connection? The delay in the score enables performing the gap between distance and intimacy and doesn't let the mediating devices somehow smooth over the space between the me and the you. A delay that hopes and transforms the experience of the other not as an image but as a person, somewhere there. Somewhere with a body. Somewhere with feelings and thoughts besides the computer. The correspondence acted like a side effect, a metabolic experience of life. A form of resilience that could be sustained softly. Just keep writing in whatever way. Just keep an addressee on the horizon. You are not alone.

Can we see the curatorial approach in pandemic times as the production of delays? No fast solutions, no pre-digested arguments, no statements, no filling the void, no certainties, no looking for good strategies, no guilt, no accusations, no sellable goods and goals. But maybe correspondence with a delay in the response, intimacy in the distance, while you go. The time of digestion, the care for the other, the other we don't know at all. The time to hangout with the doubt of not knowing but trying. To let the time of the delay affect our logics of production and attachment. Corresponding.

We know at this very moment that the world is collapsing. That the neoliberal forces that are, at this moment, directing movements are the ones that are most surely leading to collapse. We know that we need new forms of governance that propose resilience on a global level. We know that we don't know what is going to happen. We know that we need each other. We know that art can't solve this in a global manner at all.
I think it's important to take curation literally as an act of care. To take care. But to take care of what? Maybe to take care of what we ask for. To take care of the singularity of each artist. To take care of the conditions in which the work is done. To take

care of art as a form of openness and questioning. To take care of each individual work as singular and attached. To take care of poetics. To take care of the paradoxes, conflicts, the estrangement that art can offer. To take care of the environment of exchange. To take care of the audience. To let in that difference that calls for solidarity.

What do we want to experience when we engage with the world through art? I'm aware that this is a very big question and I think we want to experience many different things since we are many different people. Nevertheless – and in my opinion this is an important question to keep in our minds in all situations – what do we expect from artistic practice?

COVID-19 raised the question of sickness and general burnout as a symptom of the general distress the world is carrying. Time appeared amidst the pandemic as a fundamental lack to care for each other. Suddenly there was no feeling guilty about not being able to attend or assess a certain task in an immediate manner but to engage in thinking about systemic economic and social equity. Suddenly there was an understanding of tiredness, emotional distress, understanding of the time one needs to make sense. The time one needs to make sense of the world. A confrontational reality check that could put in perspective the urgency of collaboration. How many solidarity moments appeared in the past months? Many.

Here I wonder: what is the responsibility of the institution with such a gesture? I want to mention a long term collaborator and a.pass co-curator Vladimir Miller, who has been working for many years on a spatial practice titled Settlement. Vladimir invites the participants and collaborators of the Settlement to share their processes instead of their products in a self-organised, DIY, co-working space to research, amongst other things, a different mode of attention and participation. In this last version happening at the moment at a.pass, Vladimir introduced the question of 'The Unconditional Institution' as his contribution to the three week co-working environment of the Settlement. He asks the following questions: Can we imagine institutions with unconditional access? How would that work within a society where conditional access is the very foundation of social and economic life? Can we create a utopian imperative for institutions to give unconditional access to their resources like space, time, materials as part of their structural organisation?

These questions make me think about a non-curatorial collaboration between the Beursschouwburg, a theatre in the centre of

Brussels, and Globe Aroma, a platform that hosts refugees and asylum seekers through artistic practice. Together, these institutions opened up the entrance of the theatre, a large area often unused, to support homeless people and people in great distress throughout the confinement. This kind of collaboration made a difference. Or, an initiative taken by State of the Arts (SOTA), an open platform to reimagine the conditions that shape the art world today. This artist-run organisation connected people with financial stability to people facing precarity as a result of the COVID-19 crisis in Belgium through a direct donation tool.

I call for Artificial Friendship.

I call for – Artificial Friendship – and here you are. I open up the potential of friendship with you, in order to make myself available to write to you. I call for – Artificial Friendship – as a form of dedication to the unknown. A form of care for the ones we don't know. A form of practice to engage with the precarious, the vulnerable, the alien... Dear stranger, how are you? How do you feel? What do you do? I've been thinking about Artificial Friendship as a concept for a long time. By creating scores as an infrastructure of encounter I can observe and experiment with a relational shift in my approach to others. A mode of relation that is based on taking seriously what doesn't correspond directly to my understanding of the world as a valuable companion in life. To take into consideration, not the symbiotic but the intra-dependant relationships, the close and the far at the same time. The known and the unknown and the inbetween.

I've been asking myself, how can friendship and artificiality be partners towards an infrastructure of care for the other. Paradoxical at first instance, both these concepts, if allied, can create the conditions for a sociability of commitment, dedication, attention, patience and inclusion. I have been working with scores, in their artificiality, to set a series of scheduled moments in time and space with clear constraints, where one can perform what friendship does, and even become art friends, without having to have a friendship in the first place.

This is an invitation to spend time together. To meet in a place of availability that can engage with the moment of being present to each other. The sort of agreement one can commit to when visiting a friend. I would like to propose we think seriously about this when we think about curatorial and performing approaches in times of halting and transformation. About the spaces and the conditions that want to propose forms of attendance that are not consumeristic but that involve the vulnerability of coming together as a form of co-constituting care for the other. A form of care to the complex societal ecosystem that can embrace change.

In the current conditions of work that has become more and more precarious, I also have to think about several projects that use the epistolary. The use of this practice became dear to me because it claims a space for attention in simple ways. I see it being of help to other forms of curating or performing.

Letter to an unknown person by Kaya Freeman, my daughter, is a project she did with her friend Victor Guezennec not so long ago. Kaya is now 21 years old and I'm quite impressed by the will of these young people to create spaces for hosting the audience in an intimate manner. They turned a gallery into a crossing place between private and public and the letter functioned as an invitation to enter the space of their project '*La maison des poems*' which in English is 'The house of poems'. This letter described the situation the performers were inhabiting inside the gallery, and the reader could witness it through the window. At a certain point, the letter invited the audience to take the place of the writer inside and to be part of their temporary form of life.

Another project that comes to mind is *Letter addressed to the audience as an attempt to construct spectatorship otherwise.* This letter was written by choreographer Adriano W. Jensen and sent by post to many people. In this letter, Adriano addresses practice-based spectatorship as a form to stay entangled with what we see. This entanglement being a constitutive part of the performance. This letter invites the reader for further correspondence and co-thinking of spectatorship.

And to finish this letter, I would like to make reference to a beautiful letter that Bojana Kunst wrote in the beginning of the confinement, *Lockdown Theatre (2): Beyond the time of the right care: A letter to the performance artist.* She writes: 'The attendance is also care, but, as the notion of care itself, has many articulations. Marder writes about the difference between the forms of attending, like attending as mere presence (visiting an event, observing, standing by, etc.) and as attending to other, presence to other. This presence, attending to other, you know well, is crucial to theatre in whatever way it happens. It should be put in the focus, but maybe in a different way as it was done until now. How would a performance change for all, if we attended it as a rich web of practices? The performance as a mesh of environments and processes, ecological correspondences, a mesh of articulations and imaginations, which would enable life to all its players, a field of caring with. No particular projects and interests, but the knitting of the environments and correspondences, a web of co-survival and support, a continuation through the time as the balls of wool'.

And with this, I stay with the delay of possible responses. I stay with the desire to be part of a community of strangers that through the arts stay within the complexity of life to imagine forms of co-existence as a contribution to the world.

Warm greetings,
Lilia

Brussels, February 1, 2021

Hi Lilia,

When you were young, did you also exchange 'friend books'? At my school, they existed in two forms. Square books, with all the pages blank, which you'd pass to your friends, one by one, to make a drawing dedicated to you. This was early childhood, before we could properly write. The convention was to take a double spread and make the drawing on the right side. You could write your name or maybe something a bit more elaborate on the left, in big shaky cap letters. As we got older these square books got replaced by portrait-shaped books with two pages of set questions: What's your horoscope? What's your favourite colour? What's your motto? – these sorts of things. The principle was that the book would return to the owner who then chose the next friend in line. Often there were several of these books circulating at the same time. It was always an honour to write. A space for (re)formulating who you were, for inclining towards each other, and also for peeking into what others had written. I don't remember schoolyard dramas about not being chosen or not being chosen first. Not even the question, 'who's your best friend' was reason for upset. Maybe as children we understood the importance of continuing to circulate these books; their social value was more important than one's personal status in the fabric it was reflecting and creating. I do remember distinctly the aspect of delay. There usually was an agreed expiration date, like you could keep the book for a week maximum, a time during which anticipation and care would converge into a specific emotional charge on both ends. Mauss' analysis of how gift cultures rely on endurance over time instead of immediate and monetised compensation captures how these books featured in sustaining an intricate set of relations. The built-in delay, the wait for return, the extended search for the right words, the interplay between intimacy and publicness, these books were quite an astounding practicing ground for upholding relations of trust later in life. Sometimes a week would turn into two weeks, a month, or even more, with or without former agreement of the bookowner, which created a difficult tension between dissipation and expectation. Was your friend overcaring or did they stop caring? You might already feel where this is going. I'm so sorry to keep you waiting. In my own defense – not that it is a good one – this is the third document I've started in response to your letter. The first started like this: I've listened to your letter a second time around and have now taken some notes. A curious thing to do, because nowadays we read letters – if not from an occasional page, then mostly from a screen – in any case, interfaces upon which the flow of words takes a fixed form. It is easy to read and reread, get hooked on a specific fragment or even phrasing, and respond in the firm belief that *I* read what *you* wrote. Now I have my memory to return to, impressions and mood, and a page or two of transcriptions, your words mixed with my thoughts, in a handwriting that even I can not always make sense of. Already I am multi-modifying what I heard into something I can grasp or work with. Correspondence is metabolic, I believe you said, but I am tempted to listen again. I want to know precisely what *you* meant, how you said it, what it referred to. Instead, I'm accepting your troubling tenet by Octavia E. Butler: 'the only lasting truth is change'. It's all the more true for spoken words and the attunement they require. The fading traces of your tiptoeing altered by me hunting after them with slightly bigger feet. That's how we tread paths, writes Tim Ingold in *The Life of Lines,* a book that accompanied me as an antidote during the first confinement. Paths are social, he says, but unlike the structure of a palimpsest – a surface *upon* which layers have been *added* – they result from *impressing* movements *into* the earth. Upon or into, it might be a minor difference, but it is crucial for his attempt to give primacy to lines over blob-like ontologies. Blobs have distinct boundaries, they can be isolated or conglomerated into new blobs (today's bubbles), whereas lines tend to entwine and form new strands that can't be pulled apart so easily. Magnetising response, your footprints are losing their distinction, but only if they were conceived as isolated marks in the first place. Not only do they carry the weight of shared experiences, sense-making and backtracking, they also cast the addressee into the semblance of an intimate and reciprocal relation. *Dear you*, sent out into the ether, it is a missive that speaks to an anonymous and faceless mass, yet as a performative gesture, it invokes familiarity and repositions its multitude of auditors – including myself – into an ambiguous space where simply listening is already to engage *as if* one were a correspondent.

I got stuck in this ambiguous zone, somewhere between 'real friend' and 'artificial friend', 'witness' and 'interlocutor'. I think I was too aware of the public aspect of our correspondence and it became more of a lofty essay than a reply to you. I was aiming to ask you about some of the stages in the curatorial and pedagogic approach of *Scorescapes*, its start as a writing score with a clear Q&A structure, and its development into a multimedia set-up that relies more heavily on interpretation, you-me entanglement and triangulation. Taking your oral letter and my own listening-experience as a starting point, I was wondering if the Bubble Score calls for another type of subjectivity than the Writing Score, more mesh-like than blob-like. And If so, if you could say something about the challenges and limitations of a mesh-like pedagogy in relation to the subjectivities that contemporary art or life require. I wonder if I myself would've liked to receive such a question.

I decided on another approach and started writing you a story. It was inspired by an observation Svetlana Boym made in 'Scenography of Friendship', namely that the majority of philosophical reflections about friendship are made by men and describe male friendships entertained in relation to a public life. This bias created a conceptual map in which female friendships are much harder to understand, are devalued to the private sphere and gradually imbued with negative connotations – as Silvia Federici shows with the word 'gossip' and its initial meaning 'female friend'. In her essay, Boym calls for theoretical fables and rigorous storytelling that stage affinities that would otherwise slip through the cracks of patriarchy.

My attempt at storytelling was leading me too far, and to be honest, it wasn't very good. I'm not going to copy-paste it. However, I was hoping that it would raise a question about where the public is located in relation to the participants in the score. Clearly *Scorescapes* has a pedagogic function. It is a training of discursive, artistic and relational faculties within the closed environment of an educational programme. In his text 'Self Writing', Michel Foucault stresses the historical importance of regularly writing to oneself and to friends to exercise one's discourse and one's tenets prior to trial in real situations. In her text about *I Love Dick* (Chris Kraus), Karolin Meunier opens the possibility of another pedagogy of letter writing, based on Virginia Woolf's assertion that letters are 'the school of writing for women'. She writes: 'As if, in this particular space of correspondence any kind of writing and thinking is allowed and thus excessively exercised, like a kind of underground training for the invasion of the public'. With *invasion of the public* and *excessive exercise*, we are far from Foucault's ascetic inquiries of the self. How do you see the pedagogical project of Scorescapes within a tension between self-writing as a form of training oneself for a public life, the formation of underground communities and counter-voices, and the performative exploitation of correspondence and friendship? Something along these lines was going to be the question.

Early this evening, it finally dawned on me that I'm trying to answer my own questions instead of offering you something and letting the score do its work. Third attempt, in exactly 100 words.
In your letter, you described the characteristics of friendship and I remember they all had a positive value. In my notebook I have: 'sociability of attention, dedication, commitment, patience, inclusion'. Maybe there were more. I was wondering if the concept of 'artificial friendship' includes the possibility of betrayal within friendship, or a betrayal of what we usually understand as friendship. Something unfriendly covered by friendliness, along the lines of what Laura Riling wrote: 'you must agree with me that the relation between letter writers is unfriendly, though the magic essence of letters consists in a friendly concealment of the fact'.

x Kristien

Brussels, June 12, 2021

Dear Kristien,

How are you? It was very nice to get your response to my letter. Thank you so much! I have been waiting for it with much curiosity. The way you wrote and rewrote your thoughts made me think of the concept of *ritournelle* as G. Deleuze and F. Guattari talk about it in their book *Mille Plateaux*. A sort of tune or air that recalls something that needs attention and one cares for. Something one knows or is on standby, and that sticks to one's mind, calling for return; for being tackled or processed. They say that the *ritournelle* is linked to the problem of territory, and to the processes of entrance or exit of territories, meaning to the problem of deterritorialisation. They use this concept in relation to the physical territory surrounding one's own environment (home) but I like to expand the idea of home to bodies: thoughts and ideas that circulate around one's own body, constantly re-forming the self and the others.

I'm not super familiar with their concept but the correspondence practice proposed by the score, installs a kind of bug in one's own mind that reminds you that the other one is there, thinking about the same thing, eager to get some response about something that was launched while corresponding. One has to write to keep the connection up but also to keep the thinking active, as something that is alive. Something that is alive besides one's own ideas and desires but that is fed and grows in the correspondence. Maybe coming in and out of one's own territory, forming, informing and cultivating culture as a mass or sticky stuff. Like a double skin made of otherness. What do you think about this?

I like your question about which kind of subjectivities the different score practices propose. How do the different materialities entangle and what kind of subjectivities, but also collectivities, I would say, are generated by ways of relating to each other's work.

I copy here your question so that the reader can follow our thinking. (The reader here comes in as the audience of our friendship – don't really know how to deal with that. Some kind of exibitionism is at stake?) So your question: 'I was wondering if the Bubble Score calls for another type of subjectivity than the Writing Score, more mesh-like than blob-like. And if so, if you could say something about the challenges and limitations of a mesh-like pedagogy in relation to the subjectivities that contemporary art or life require'.

So, I think that with the Writing Score, the first one I proposed in a.pass in 2014, the researchers were invited to write a text about their research and to read it out loud in the weekly meetings. The collective reading practice entangled through oral transmissions the histories of that community. After the readings, which lasted for about four hours, the group used a chance procedure to assign who would address questions to whom. (These questions are very important because they are the trigger to develop the thinking about each other's practices but also about each one's writing about their practice and about the collective. Do you remember? We did this weekly for about three months!).

I would tend to say that the epistolary practice proposed by the Writing Score creates mesh-like subjectivities. Each participants' writing is like a baseline transforming through the listening and of the questions coming from the collective week by week. This mesh can be disentangled at any moment. The practice itself is a documentation of a process of entanglement and its deviant off-springs. It follows somehow a linear form of thinking and reacting, a sort of cause and effect relationship that can be depicted.

On the other hand, I would say that the Bubble Score is more a blob-like structure. The entanglements are far more complex and the continuous baseline proposed by the writing practice is gone. What happens here differs from the Writing Score in two major ways.

First, all of the responses to the questions coming from the collective are expressed not only in writing but also in the medium chosen by the participant (like stage performance or video material), opening up the spectrum of attendance (how do we attend to something?) and of discourses that are produced. Secondly, the participants respond to questions addressed to someone else's work or practice. There is an indirectness or deviation of response that engages in more than one view point. Each response doesn't only have to find a connection between one's work and a question but also between one's own work and the work of another.

It is like a threesome relational entanglement that opens up for complex subjectivities that are maybe more in accordance with contemporary work and life. Or at least to the one I perceive as being of positive change. A sort of neverending entanglement attachment. A sort of permaculture field? In both scores, the reading out loud or the presentation of the responses are like the air or the atmosphere around the collective. The place from which we all feed. This moment is the indirect rubbing against each other's differences which forms each of us and all of us from unexpected sparks, connections, proximities or paradoxes.

The publicness of the entanglements between works, view points and sensibilities and their reaching out to the world (collective) is what Scorecapes can do. I do believe that subjectivities emerge in these moments of sharing in collectivity. The audience, the more than one, is always present when we address the other. Maybe this answers your question about letter writing and the publicness of such pedagogical exercise, a kind of intertwinement of the self and the collective that don't exclude each other but encourages other kinds of communities and counter voices? I think I'm seeking a mix of blob and mesh and maybe other forms. This makes me smile as I always think about monstrous constructions that can encompass many different shapes. Difficult environments that bring together several species with different histories and appetites.

I enjoyed so much reading the text of Svetlana Boym, 'Scenography of Friendship' that you mention in your response. She speaks about the theatricality of distance and proximity and I can relate to this as a mise-en-scène of artistic research for the 'intertwinement of the plurality of voices that encompass our existence in a world or worlds'. Boym's approach to diasporic intimacy relates so much to what we practice in Scorescapes that it feels like I have a new friend. She says: '... in inadequacies of translation, diasporic intimacy is not opposed to uprootedness and defamiliarisation but is constituted by it. In contrast to the utopian image of intimacy as transparency, authenticity, and ultimate belonging, diasporic intimacy is dystopic by definition; it is rooted in the suspicion of a single home, in shared longing without belonging'. Further on: '... Diasporic intimacy is not possessive but tender. Tenderness is not about complete disclosure, saying what one really means, and getting closer and closer. It excludes absolute possession and fusion. Not goal-oriented, it defies symbols of fulfilment (...) In tenderness, need and desire are joined. Tenderness is always polygamous, non-exclusive. Where you are tender, you speak your plural'.[2]

I imagine again that the territory is not fixed and that singular materialised homes go far beyond buildings and bricks. And that the process of deterritorialisation is so important. We need to create environments that help us construct new subjectivities that don't fix us in identity paradigms where differences are stigmatised rather than permeable subjectivities that make us engage with alterity. Being these other humans, animals, plants, structures of all kinds, the universe...

Vladimir Miller, the other day, sent me a text by Tori Abernathy, 'We're Here to Make Friends', which reflects on the consequences of artistic practices if they would intake from the experience of prefigurative politics to 'rehearse' a possible new world. The question is: How can we create structures that support us to enact other kinds of social relations and decision making processes? Practices that self-organise forms of interaction that don't want to be perfect already but that are open to other relationalities that we don't know yet and can help us to resist hegemonic modes of interaction?

I think that friendship can help us with this. Friendship as a social phenomenon is the ground for exchange otherwise. It can be the setting for the myriad of attachments every existent substance has with the multiple worlds that exist. A 'place' where one can call these attachments, be it backgrounds, emotional states, family, war, love, or can be called by them. Maybe the positive conditions of friendship that you recall in my first letter: 'sociability of attention, dedication, commitment, patience, inclusion' are the basis for possible betrayal while being accountable for it. I called somewhere the score a perverse partner, pushing contradiction and directing friends (participants of the score) into not so easy conversations. There is a question of satisfaction that comes from the neoliberal paradigm of success that maybe pushes us to be in conclusion modes instead of assertive doubts, into deadly competition instead of positive contradiction. The transparency

---

2 Svetlana Boym, 'Scenography of Friendship', *Cabinet* 36, Winter 2009/10 https://cabinetmagazine.org/issues/36/boym.php

friendship entails, creates trouble, one needs to love trouble, to care for trouble, to agree to disagree. Maybe to think of no, not as a rejection but 'no' as caring for the love of difference and space.

Abernathy writes: 'It would be dangerous to assume that a "friend", however, is someone who simply seems to share your political values, your artistic sensibilities, reads the same magazines, or wears the same shoes. It is also harmful to assume that the "friend" is something you can determine based on your proximity to another's social or geographical locations; this love-of-the same is a corrupt form. Instead, the "friend" is a relationship based on a camaraderie that reveals itself through time and through activity in common (particularly in a struggle, maybe)'.[3] Abernathy became a new friend too. An intermittent companion that challenges my approach. The whole idea of Artificial Friendship is an attempt to practice otherwise, to try to go against our own prejudices and to not feel weak about them but to take them with the possibility to change.

oufffff Kristien! This was a big stretch! So, with a smile, I think art, by its capacity to imagine and speculate, can introduce formats that engage other paradigms than co-dependent approaches between things. Let's try!

The other day on the radio I heard Vinciane Despret speaking about her latest book *Autobiography of an Octopus* and she said that love is about keeping the necessary distance. I totally sympathise with this idea. I don't think that it is through osmosis that one loves but by trying to see the other in its singular blob and mesh and use the tentacles to spark unknowns.

I was thinking again about the *ritournelle* I mentioned in the beginning of this letter. I feel that I write that way, in, out and around my thoughts. The other day Antye Guenter, who is a curator at a.pass at the moment, spoke about cognitive processes and mentioned that rhymes help to stay with an idea in mind. So I would like to ask you to send me a song or a poem as something you'd like us to hum along to while apart together deterritorialising. What do you reckon?

I hope this letter finds you well. Looking forward to reading you.
With much love,
Lilia

---

3 Tori Abernathy, 'We're Here to Make Friends', *Temporary*, Jan. 24, 2017, https://temporaryartreview.com/were-here-to-make-friends/

Brussels, December 8, 2021

Dear Lilia,

If I imagine a future reader, say 20 years from now, coming across our correspondence, then I anticipate that they will amalgamate the dates with which our letters start – October 2020, February 2021, June 2021 and December 2021 – into one stretch of time, under the rubric of 'pandemic writing'. We do this with other historical pandemics. They begin and they end. But the idea of an end obfuscates the long period of sophisticated living with a virus, during which ethics and technologies of cohabitation evolve. Reading your first letter now, during the 4th wave of Covid in Europe, it strikes me that some of your pleas, for example about 'delay', and how you welcomed its potential, have been overtaken by new demands for immediacy and fast solutions. We are no longer house-ridden in a collective lockdown, atomised in front of computer screens. We are back in the thick of intimate, social and institutional lives, moving back and forth between risks and consequences, administered by tests, incubation days, illusive distinctions between high-risk and low-risk, vaccination certificates and their expiration dates... The little corona-crisis we had last week at a.pass while we were in residency at PAF makes me skeptical of all our investment in regaining control and certainty over the virus. Shouldn't we combine these approximations with more practice in how to live with an ongoing sense of indeterminacy, which includes 'difficult trade-offs, ethical dilemmas with imperfect and sometimes brutal outcomes', as Maggie Nelson has it in *On Freedom*?

As a *ritournelle*, I want to send you the insistent vocal raging on the album, *(In) The Abyssity Of The Grounds, by free jazz legend Linda Sharrock*. It is one of the last concerts I saw when I was living in London in 2016, and the album cover had a prominent place in the first home I was welcomed in during the pandemic. At the time, I didn't know about her earlier career. I only knew the mind-blowing concert I had experienced in Cafe Oto, from the back of the room, on my tiptoes, to catch a glimpse of the dynamic cues and prime attention between vocalist and ensemble, that made this guttural wordless explosion possible. Whaaa WHAAAA WHAAAAAA. On end. After a debilitating stroke, Linda Sharrock made an unparalleled comeback to the stage, turning speech impairment into post-linguistic expression, screaming, wailing, howling, moaning with and for heightened interdependence. Why don't we scream all the time, asks Harmony Holiday in a podcast about The Black Catatonic Scream?

Whaaa WHAAAA WHAAAAAA. On end.
Kristien

Veridiana Zurita

Artistic Research: A Mode of Práxis

We are in 2021. I am in Brazil. That's an orientation for you to know from where I am writing. The year. The location. The specific encounter with the collapse. And that's crucial because it's impossible for me to put any reflection in motion without considering the existential, civilizatory, planetary collapse we are in and the increasing intensity as it becomes accelerated by the political situation in Brazil. Yes, there is a double crisis here. The pandemic and its virus, Bolsonarism and its fascist desire. Both in convulsive circulation, and the more it convulses the better it circulates. Both retro-feeding each other while negationism nourishes Bolsonarism, and vice versa, as a tool for overcoming the pandemic with a project of genocide. Yes, it's a project. Let's stop considering that it's about an adrift ship. It's not.[1]

What we face in Brazil right now is an eruption of our most morbid symptoms as a society which has never restored its history in the present. So here we are with Bolsonaro as a president living a phantasmagorical moment where it's impossible to deny the ghosts that were historically set aside. The ghosts that dispute narratives about Brazilian history, ghosts that corrupt the narration of history in order to manage structures of power and oppression, ghosts that navigate between flat-earth-theory and vaccines that can turn you into a crocodile. Fake news' ghosts are directly implicating the production of knowledge and how it's set in motion. And who produces knowledge? Who puts it into circulation? Who can access it? Who sets up its legitimacy? Who funds it? Who narrates it? An obvious problematic – when considering that hegemonic production of knowledge is always implicated in structures of power – which takes a further leap in the years of Bolsonarism. In such a battle, because we are clearly in a battlefield, any counter-hegemonic production of knowledge is threatened (not to say erased) by the state of things. If even hegemonic science has been neglected as a knowledge to be heard, one can imagine what has happened with artistic research in the tropics.

WHAT IS ARTISTIC RESEARCH

I would never attempt here to define artistic research. That's a concept in dispute. What I exercise is reflection, through the project (Don't) Eat The Microphone which I worked on both in Belgium and Brazil. That transcontinental practice with the same object is crucial for my understanding of artistic research as a mode of Práxis. A revolutionary Práxis. For those postmodernists that have taken the contra-revolutionary bait thrown by social democracy, let's recall briefly what a revolutionary Práxis wants.

---

1 Jacobin Magazine, 'From Anti-Politics to Authoritarian Restoration in Brazil', jacobinmag.com/2020/12/anti-politics-authoritarian-restoration-brazil-jair bolsonaro

PRÁXIS

I am referring here to the notion of Práxis in Marx where theory and practice are in constant dialogue, without subordinating each-other. Práxis as a 'human sensuous activity' where critical-practice is a revolutionary activity. Revolutionary because it wants to push the interpretation, the critique of the world towards its transformation. The retro-feeding dynamic between theory and practice opens up such a revolutionary activity while it needs to mobilise, to experience the very materiality of social relations in order to formulate the theory to transform them. It can't be materialist or idealist, it needs to be a revolutionary Práxis. 'The philosophers have only interpreted the world in various ways; the point, however, is to change it'.

Artistic research is driven through such a demand. It needs to open up a process of horizontal dynamic between what's artistic and what's research. It can't be orientated by the subordination of one another where the research dictates the artistic practice or the other way around. It needs to be a dialectical walk. The research is an artistic practice, the practice is an artistic research. The research is guided by the questions arising in the artistic practice and, at the same time, the formulations of the research, its theories and methodologies, are feeding back into the practice which will return with new questions to the research. In that sense the relation between object and subject in artistic research also challenges the opaque hierarchical relation of an object of art subordinated to the subjectivity of the artist who produces it. When artistic research sets in motion situations which need to be heard in order to feed back the formulations of the research, the very object of creation needs to be considered as a subject that speaks, that it needs to be heard. In that sense artistic research needs to mobilise a quality of active listening. The artist leaves the inspirational channel and occupies the mediating channel between research and practice, between practice and research. It filters and translates from practice to research from research to practice, in a concomitant flux between one another.

(DON'T) EAT THE MICROPHONE

I arrived at Dr. Guislain Psychiatric Centre with an artistic research project. That was in 2014. My proposal was to act in the fissure of language between neurotics and psychotics. I enter their space. They are gathered for the morning meeting. I join THEM in a near circle. Now it's my turn to speak. I-SPEAK. At first, I stumble upon the hegemony that carries me. I present an articulated project, a priori, typical of those who project a situation detached from the emergencies of the territory (no Práxis). My speech is precise and articulated enough to handle the theoretical euphoria, but imprecise for those who listen to me. To speak, it is necessary to listen. The hegemonic language is interrupted. I feel out of language and alone in neurotic hegemony. Alone in efficiency. Alone in the logic of projections, of projects, projections of projects already projected, projections of desired desires, projects of neurotic acceleration, acceleration of achievements, achievements of success.

This first day at Dr. Guislain Psychiatric Centre (Belgium) was the crack awakening of my perception upon artistic practice as a mode of Práxis. But I guess the revolutionary fold of such a perception has appeared more clearly when the project happened in the Pólo Experimental of the Bispo do Rosário Museum (Rio de Janeiro - BR) in collaboration with 'mental health patients' (or as we prefer to say in Brazil: 'users of the public services of mental health'). But before bringing (Don't) Eat the Microphone to Brazil, the project had a long life experience in Belgium. That experience was crucial for me to understand in practice how methodologies in artistic research can translate what I mean by Práxis. Not necessarily the final format of the methodologies but how they come into being through the research. (Don't) Eat the Microphone started with nothing. Of course, that 'nothing' could only appear after the exposure of the neurotic projection
I experienced on the first day, and such a 'nothingness' was fundamental to the kind of listening the situation demanded.
So then, we started again. There was a garage in the back storage of one of the facilities of the psychiatric centre, a table with coffee and cookies, myself and Petra van Dyck (my partner in crime). There we waited and waited for visitors to come. And they came. And they came more regularly. And they became participants. And for that listening to happen we started brainstorming about elements that were needed for the voices to be heard and for the ears to listen carefully. After some years, the set-up started growing. The last edition of the project (2019) was set up in the garden of the psychiatric centre, we had microphones spread with eight metre long cables, costumes, materials like stones, records, instruments, Lygya Clark's[2] inspired relational objects, an external kitchen, guests, artists, musicians, insiders and outsiders. What (Don't) Eat the Microphone had become throughout the years was a set-up for a kind of socialisation that could resist the neoliberal rationality, which is everywhere, in every person, in every

2 Lygia Clark and Suely Rolnik, 'Politics of Flexible Subjectivity: The Event-Work of Lygia Clark', http://4.pucsp.br/nucleodesubjetividade/Textos/SUELY/Flexiblesubjectivity.pdf, Suely Rolnik, 'The Body's Contagious Memory: Lygia Clark's Return to the Museum' https://transversal.at/transversal/0507/rolnik/en, Suely Rolnik, 'Molding a Contemporary Soul: The Empty-Full of Lygia Clark' caosmose.net/suelyrolnik/pdf/molding%20_john_nadine.pdf

social organism, every interpersonal relation, every legitimisation of institutional functioning. Resistance to neoliberal rationality doesn't have a final stop. It's not about an act that manages to overcome, through resistance, the demands of neolibeal rationality. That would be too heroic, and for sure naive, considering an ideological apparatus molecularly set in motion from the dreams we dream to the words we speak.

Resisting neoliberal rationality is about creating conditions to expose such an apparatus, to take off its veil of 'freedom', undercovering precariousness while delivered (imposed) by entrepreneurial narrative. But a context that wants to create conditions for 'taking off the veil' needs to sustain 'nakedness' (no veil of promised entrepreneurial freedom). It needs to sustain 'nakedness' once we know how such a narrative (you're responsible for your success or failure) has become part of how we desire and understand our social roles. Such a resistance was present in the garden where (Don't) Eat The Microphone took place. It was present in contradiction. We were, on one hand, within a psychiatric centre – a lab for neoliberal framing of cure and efficiency – but on the other hand, being confronted with the impossibility to perform neoliberal productivity through the interpersonal relations we were agents of. That was because of the kind of context we had created. Setting up microphones everywhere confronted us with an object fully protocolised by the tight relation between success and speech. A mic. A voice. A message. What if we stutter?

What if the lack of prescribed message convulses the medium? Resisting neoliberal rationality was present through speech, through how one can 'stutter' its meaning, its functions, its order, its ordering, its place, its... It was present from the first day and it persisted echoing through each mic that was taken (or that took us) by the desire to formulate anything. As the hegemonic desire for formulation aims to successfully deliver, any formulation on that register was condemned to fail. Práxis was present in that very contradiction. We had to set up a situation where resistance would give place to formulation, to proposition, to a socialisation that would not only resist the hegemonic one but would provide a context for other ways of being together. We had to set up a situation where failure could happen successfully. And what was failing? It was not really about individual failure. It was about failing with the social contracts, the fictions of social interactions that pathologies operate. Operations where inclusion and exclusion play a fundamental role in defining normality and abnormality. Well, in our garden the neurotic as the universal subjectivity had to be pathologised too. The neurotic was constantly suspended, dislocated from its universal role and estranged. What we were failing in the garden was the normative interpersonal interaction which allows the fluid circulation of neoliberal rationality. That one where individual efforts guarantee success especially if the other (always as an adversary) is eliminated. Such a logic can take more literal formats but also more undercover ones. It's a micro and macro operation of an ideological narrative brought up to legitimise neoliberal economic agenda. That dynamic can be easily perceived while inside a psychiatric institution where external surveillance, which manages the demands of economic efficiency, is not solely external, but more and more internal to the subjects neoliberal rationality produces. Or more precisely, as Gino once said, 'We watch each other. Everyone denounces what's deviant to please the power. The chief watches the doctors, the doctors watch the therapists, the therapists watch the nurses, the nurses watch the patients, the patients watch each other. We all work here, we are all employees of the institution. We watch. Everybody's gossiping. I feel empty, I can't understand the other person and when I want a hug, I'm afraid of vulnerability'.

What we managed to shift in the garden was the stagnation of certain social relations. Their paralysis and apathetic functioning. Of course, that shift couldn't change the intensity of institutional operation, but it started mobilising an inside-outside space for suspending some of the fictions that have for so long been naturalised. That was possible because of the set-up we created and the methodologies that we rehearsed formulating in the garden. The fundamental methodology, that we understood as a possibility to unfold, was that twisting the function of social roles and creating conditions (the set-up) for that shift to happen could guarantee the presence of radical (in the root) questions: What's to be cured in a psychiatric institution? Who's the one that cures? What holds responsibility for that illness as much for its cure? Is the institution ill? We considered that as a methodology because that shift started orientating the sessions in the garden, an orientation of how to sustain that shift, what kind of spatial set-up we would need to host that kind of shift, but also a set-up that could help us to identify potential shifts, to have signs in the space that could indicate to us where that shift was happening and how we could sustain its happening. That could take different forms, from a patient taking over the kitchen and cooking lunch for the whole group, a guest coming to give a lecture and ending up receiving a sensorial treatment session from another patient or even a doctor who, while coming to rescue a patient who had run away from the crisis unit, was confronted with the same patient, seconds ago violent, in a garden calm and singing a song into the mics. The shift of understanding that the context was ill as much as its individuals, or perhaps more, or in fact in a dialectical way; the individuals are produced by a context while reproducing its coordinates. This became a bold frame for reading, interpreting and perhaps even planting seeds for shifting relations within the institutional psychiatric context. What we read was that the concomitant reproduction of a system – where individuals are produced to be cured, to fit, to perform life and reproduce the prescriptions of economic efficiency – was not a problem of the psychiatric institution alone, on the contrary, such a context was just a zoom-in, an intensified version of the life coordinations that are outside of the psychiatric institution as well. What's out of the psychiatric institution sustains what's inside. What's inside sustains what's outside. Changing the context had to do with a change in and with the subjects that are subordinated by it.

KNOWLEDGE IS SITUATED

What methodology in artistic research signals, is that the knowledge being produced is situated, it isn't generic or abstract knowledge but one that speaks about and with a concrete situation into which the researcher dives. That could not be more evident than when the project DETM happens both in Belgium and in Brazil. Geopolitically, we have two psychiatric institutional contexts on continents characterised by crucial differences. On the one hand, Belgium experiences neoliberal policies at the centre of capitalism and on the other, Brazil is experienced as a neoliberal laboratory on the periphery of capitalism. The consequences that any institution suffers because of neoliberal policies, be it in the global north or south, are remarkable. However, the impact that austerity policies have in the territories of the coloniser and the colonised are incomparable, and that is the same for what's resisting neoliberal rationality and how it's resisting. What DETM encountered in the Pólo Experimental – a facility for art creation in collaboration with Museum Bispo do Rosário and CAPS (Psycho-social centre assistance) – was a context where formulating resistance was already in motion. One can't detach that from the territory's history. While Dr. Guislain Psychiatric Centre is named after Joseph Guislain, a rich white doctor and psychiatrist, celebrated by his psychiatric-treatment inventions, the museum in Brazil and where most patients gathered throughout treatment is named after the artist Arthur Bispo do Rosario, black, poor, crazy, internalised in the Colony Juliano Moreira, where he produced all of his works during 49 years of hospitalisation. The former invented medical tools for treating the others' madness, the latter created art objects (to be worn) in order to sublimate the violence of an institution. This is not a fetishisation of colonised bodies and contexts, since we know that the precarisation of psychiatric institutions in Brazil beats the ones in Belgium, but instead it is an orientation for understanding how such historical differences will inevitably inform and change practices and the formulation of resistance in the present.

ARTISTIC RESEARCH AS A TRANSFORMATIVE WEAPON

After living in Europe for nine years, a period in which I developed my artistic practice as artistic research, I came back to Brazil just before Bolsonaro's election. What became clear from the beginning was that geopolitical dynamics coordinate (not to say dictate) the debates and urgencies to be addressed in different countries. What an artist is compelled to address in Brazil can be highly different from what would be in the centre of capitalism. Even if the topics can intertwine when referring to artists whose practices and researches are conducted for the transformation of reality, even if in both centre or periphery we are considering political art, the priority of topics and problems, conflicts, resistance to be addressed, voiced and heard are directly linked with the geopolitical positioning of each place. While in Europe there is space for a narrative of the pandemic's social limitations as an apparatus of biopolitical control, here in Brazil we struggle to have a minimum of pandemic coordination towards sanitary and security from government to the population. While in Europe, there is space and time to question the use of masks as a social contract, which guides bodies coercively, in Brazil we struggle to make our own president use a mask and to stop mobilising crowds without masks.

In such a scenario artistic research gains different potential. It can't only be a practice which resists and denounces, it needs to be a Práxis that formulates spaces for breathing, exits for confabulating new worlds which need to be practiced and tested, in order to gain and grasp people's desire towards a form of socialisation outside of capitalism and its neoliberal redimensioning. That also means that artistic research needs to, and can get out of the artistic/cultural bubble and put its methodologies into practice within other disciplines that are struggling to create exits from this mess. The call for considering artistic research as a direct instrument, as a weapon for political change, be it institutional or not, be it partisan or not, be it social movements or not, be it neighbourhood collectives or not, artistic research has a strong potential for strengthening any form of political organisation. It has a capacity to create a dynamic between theory and practice that political organisations need in order to mobilise the desire for change. Art for art becomes (more than ever) an obscene notion in the middle of the collapse. We are definitely not in times where artists can choose themes to work on as if from a menu. We are in a time of emergency where in order to do the impossible we will need to gather efforts for creating new worlds. Let's start rehearing the demands of such a collapse and instrumentalise our research to transform reality, from the most immediate problems until the active imagination of a revolutionary horizon.

Adrijana Gvozdenović
Pia Louwerens

This Artist

This is a story about you, becoming the artist that you are today. You became a full-time artist, and for you, being an artist means a constant establishing and dismantling of this role. Yes, that means that you think about yourself a lot. You often write in the first person. But not now. This story originated from at least two I's, who came together to be you. They are juxtaposed, placed side by side, not fully merging.

A few years ago, you discovered what it is to be an artist-researcher, which transformed many artistic anxieties that had built up over time. You understand that part of doing artistic research is producing the infrastructure for the research, an economy of knowledge that has an aim to go somewhere else, to be shared. For lack of a better word, you use the phrase 'ecosystem of artistic practice' to describe this fundamental aspect of artistic research. You tend to believe that artistic research, in this regard, could even be an alternative to the artistic practice that goes into the market. You went to a.pass, an artist-run programme for artistic research. Let's mark the words: transdisciplinarity, experimental, the blending of discourse and practice, and practicing together. And we go further back in time to provide a background for what made you become the artist that you are today.

This artist didn't start working as a child already, like some artists do. She did notice that she was able to draw what she sees more realistically than other kids, which is what grown-ups considered a talent for art. Her parents, of good standing, took her to museums, with work by dead artists. Another story says that she first learned about art from her uncles, who showed her books with black and white reproductions. The big museums were in the western countries that she would visit one day. When she went to museums she would have illogical subjective favourites. Usually paintings of women that seemed kind. She would fixate on these, as if they were made for her personally, and then she would buy the postcards of these paintings in the museum shop.

Her first conscious pedagogical encounter with art was in the 'craft' class at her high school, which together with 'drawing' formed the art curriculum. The craft teacher liked to use the powertools and would give students a high grade if they asked him to assist them. She graduated, but with a peculiar conceptual work: a half-folded cube of paper, which explored the border between the two classes: the fastest way to go from drawing to craft is to fold the paper, she reasoned. The teacher said that maybe she should look into the art academy, 'they like these sorts of things there'. She registered herself without telling her parents, who got angry with her. Or perhaps she thought about applying to an art academy, but she thought there were only 'special' people going there. Since she was quite sociable and even popular, she thought she was neither eccentric nor talented enough to be an artist.

During the first admission round at the art academy the coordinator asked her who her favourite artist was and she answered: 'Miró?' He told her to look at more art. For the second admission round she brought her sketchbook with some drawings in it – her best. Her aunt told her that she shouldn't show a half-full sketchbook because it would seem as if she didn't have enough passion to finish it. She quickly filled up the sketch book with random drawings and collages. This artist got accepted into an art academy.

On her first day of art academy, during the opening speech, the head of the department said to all the new students: 'No one is waiting for you'. When you think back to this, you want to sit down next to your former self, and clarify that it is possible to sustain a practice even if no one is waiting for you: 'Unhelpful conditions like these might even be subverted in order to become the foundation of your practice. You will meet someone who calls it radicalisation. When you align with your conditions you will see that they are not separate from the work, they are its material: this will be the way to break the spell'.

She liked it at the art academy, but she also cried a lot. Teachers were called 'masters', and one master didn't like her paintings, he thought she was not expressive enough. Once, he got so annoyed by her slow and intermittent movements with a brush that he took her hand roughly in order to make an expressive movement. The brush broke in their hands.

In the second year, all of the students had to choose a discipline. This artist chose printmaking, because it was the only thing she couldn't learn by herself at home, she reasoned. It was the only department where people would work together in groups, because of the printing press. Hanging out with people and talking about art and life is the thing she liked the most. You still do, and are now finally exploring how this could be an artistic practice. Also, the department was the only one led by a woman for a long time; actually she was the only female professor at the academy and the only known female artist. She was a master nevertheless. The master would come twice a week, to look at her students' drawings. They were only allowed to make self-portraits. She would take a look and select a couple of drawings which they were permitted to print.

It could also be that this artist chose sculpture, safely away from the bullies in the conceptual department. They didn't have group classes anymore, only individual studio visits by teachers. When they came she had to talk about something. She got very good at talking about things without making anything. She would have liked to have group classes but her teachers said: 'When you're an artist, you won't have classes either'.

She was alone a lot, she was supposed to work in her space, a studio. She would sit behind her desk, and then she would fall asleep. There was very little urgency to do anything at all, except for the four times per year when the students had to present something to be graded. She always pushed the deadline. She would always cry. She had to force herself to work, which made her think she wasn't really an artist. She fantasised about making immersive installations, but she didn't have the energy or the means. She got into Duchamp.

At a certain point she made her first video-performance. She had filmed herself reading a script in a forest. The head of the department asked her why she wasn't standing in the middle of the frame – she didn't know. He said that in art you should always know and choose these kinds of things with precision. After this, this artist started thinking more about what was expected of her, and what kind of art those expectations produce. Now you cannot see art without the frames that were already proposed.

In 2011, the year before her graduation, national politics had turned against art. Even the person in charge of the cultural department said that he wasn't interested in art. 'Cultural entrepreneurship' became the magic word. This artist had to take a class on how to write a business plan, the students were encouraged to print business cards. They were very focused on the graduation show, because curators and gallerists would come by and it would be the perfect moment to 'network'. The coordinator of her department had favourites, mostly boys who used drugs. Thus, he would direct the professionals to pass by their work spaces; they were presented in all the 'best of' graduation shows.

After exiting the hierarchical framework held by the masters of the academy, she was suddenly on her own. She wondered: When am I going to be an artist? When is it going to come? Is it just going to show itself to me?

She worked as a babysitter, cashier, dog walker, technician, security guard, tour guide, hostess and more. She broke up the long relationship she had with an older artist and went back to living with her parents. She made jewellery with her sister, who had just finished high school, and they made some money selling it on the internet. She wanted to leave her home country so she started applying for MA studies, but she couldn't afford the visa.

Life felt like a series of loose events that wouldn't turn into a narrative. She got really good at writing applications. She had an exhibition here and there, in kitchens and project spaces, over which she would expend many tears. Always during the openings she would feel detached and empty, like nobody cared about it really, not the curator, nor the exhibition space, nor the audience. She was on her own.

She came to Belgium and started her MA studies: a new life. Today, you would not accept to study in a place where there is a majority of male professors. Back then, she was surprised too, but she was just completely overwhelmed with all the changes. Besides the crazy bureaucratic procedures that this immigration required, she had to find a way to support this new life. For the studies, she started reading the kind of art theory in English that she wouldn't even have been able to understand in her own language. It was not just her, the whole group of students struggled to understand things. The teacher, a prolific writer himself, would contribute very little to help the discussion. You are still not sure whether it was a style of pedagogy, or a lack of it.

After this master's there was another master's. Or: she never pursued a master's. She couldn't imagine getting grades for her practice. She was alienated by the whole enterprise of art, it seemed to be something that she didn't want to do and maybe also couldn't. She was always told by her parents: 'If you're good at something, you will find a place in the world'. You are not so sure about that anymore nor about what it means to be good.

She wanted to study or work abroad, but every residency rejected her. Except for a.pass, in Brussels. By this time, she had already become hyphenated as a performance-artist, artist-writer, artist-cashier and artist-babysitter. When she arrived at a.pass, however, she understood: she was an artist-researcher. On her first day there was a girl with big eyelashes, wearing some kind of space suit or worker's jumpsuit. Another new artist-researcher said that he was into sourdough and a writer in the group was experimenting with subtext, interested in protocols and psychoanalysis. You remember this well – you were so happy to meet these people. They used words that you didn't understand, but then they also sometimes didn't seem to understand them themselves. You can still recall the first time she heard the word 'phenomenology'. It didn't sound like anything to her. They often gathered as a group to concern themselves with these un-understandable things, whether it was some speculative theoretical object, someone's proposal, or the institution itself. They would talk about them for a long time.

Sometimes, she was concerned about spending too much time there with other people which meant she was not making money for a living. Sometimes she would get confused about this privilege and accessibility of knowledge and worry what would happen once the programme was finished.

Sometimes, she would remember that she was supposed to be an artist with an individual practice. She would be mildly disconcerted, but then the concerns of the group would move her away from herself, like a big wave. Without realising it, her perspective was shifting. Art used to signify the work, an object or a piece. The presentation of them, and what they would mean for her, what they would do for her. But people kept mentioning 'practice'. All the separate events and choices she had made became connected like beads on a necklace. Then there was another word: 'research'. Instead of objects, she thought about questions and the people who shared them. This made them her colleagues.

You say that it reminds you of certain moments at the academy, when watching and analysing films with your peers, for example, or during reading groups. You would be working together, but not for the production of work or art. It would be a different kind of sociality. Now you call it transindividual knowledge production.

They would sit at the table or on a carpet, on chairs or pillows, and talk about the institution. The institution considered itself to be a practice, a dynamic, speculative structure. For the first time, this artist who was always becoming an artist was in an institution which was always becoming an institution. Through this process she learned how to play and perform the conditions for work, as if those are hers. Her anxieties transformed from being the symptoms of pressure for success to being the symptoms of something like hope.

During a.pass, as she extended and dissolved into all of the other practices and issues, she became the oceanographer-artist making an archive of encounters with the ocean, she also became a dancer translating and dancing ballet into reggaeton, and a charming storyteller connecting medieval bestiaries and animal videos circulating on the internet, and an architect-dancer who guides us to experience the same space differently. She could feel what it is to be obsessed with things you own and objects that surround your living interior, she could feel what happens with your body and the collective body if you walk at the slowest possible speed, if you become impersonal or if you close your eyes and you talk about your habits and your research horizontally whilst someone touches your hands.

You are a full-time artist-researcher now, which in your case means that you think about yourself a lot. The self seems porous and strange. You've met other people who feel the same, sometimes to such an extent that you don't know who is voicing when you talk. You still have a hard time writing about it, this becoming through each other. You try anyway.

Pierre Rubio
& Vanja Smiljanić

Ex Astris, Scientia

Ripening Minister

I AM a mid-career Minister of Cosmic People for the countries of Ex-Yugoslavia, Portugal, and former Portuguese colonies at the time that I ENTER a.pass.
I HAVE A DESIRE to expand and reassess the area of my activity.
In the course of the a.pass programme, my ministering vehicle starts transforming:
My pinky-finger nail, my antennae, my moustache, my fang teeth, and my pectoral muscles – they grow.
A tool box I USE to tackle hybrid identity issues within my research also begins to complexify:
A rearview mirror to diffract the ex/post-Yugoslavian disenchanting influence on the formation of my political body.
A laser comb to dissect the curating concept of a LOL archive, to pick out the historical, cultural, and temporal contingencies, and to tickle the position of an archivist.
A magnifying lens to oil the wheel of idiotic questioning, and to burn into my flesh the initials of my overseer: I.A.B.

3 IN 1? MULTI-PRAKTIK!

The change is gradual.
At first, while translating the documents from the Library of Light, I START to slightly modify the documents. That brings me to identify myself with the role of a Senior Architect of the Cosmic People's archive.
In this manner, I CEASE perceiving myself as a mere lubricator of their ideological apparatus but, by reshaping certain documents from the archive, I CREATE new extensions of their religious body.
My power grows.
Along with the power, the intolerance to the anti-epileptic medication I TAKE is also developing. It manifests itself in a form of narcolepsy, meaning – I AM constantly falling asleep during our daily a.pass meetings.
A fine period – I REMEMBER. A bit problematic at first (being seemingly disengaged). Occasionally slightly uncomfortable, but with time I EASE myself into this zapping mode. I LEARN how to navigate and operate joyously with them.
Logging in and out. Receiving fragmented messages. Noise.
A lot of it.

Embodying the double. Softening the borders. My power grows. It is when it came to me: DIGITAL SOCIAL REVOLUTION! A must in the ongoing cyberwar between Cosmic People and Saurians. A step up in my ministering career.
Approaching the last block, I BEGIN to work with Flag Nation Society – a global alliance of worshippers who are expressing their beliefs through a very particular body practice called 'flag worshiping'.
Their action of flagging in the 3D earthly plane seems to have a resonance in the immaterial plane.
How interesting...
I AM SHIFTING between a clairvoyant vision of a dystopian future, where Cosmic People are in a cyber war against their primordial enemies – Saurians, and present time where I AM a software developer, building a defence system against hacking attacks.
In order to propose a new collective dance practice which would fortify Cosmic People's community and lead it towards the Digital Social Revolution, I SUBVERT the orthodox flag worshipping vocabulary, and present the NEW ALPHABET FOR DIGITAL PROLETARIAT.
It becomes a manifesto.
It becomes a self-inflicted annihilation of my ministry within Cosmic People.
The complexity of the project, together with a growing over-identification with a submissive, yet ambitious minister, places me in a Schachmatt position where my only possible move is towards the leader of Cosmic People.
Through all of this time working with Cosmic People, I was firmly ideologically against this shift, soon after finishing a.pass, I DECIDE to place my ministering vocation on hold.
Writing about it now, calls her back. She starts possessing me. It feels good.
The Bluetooth remote control appears again in my left hand.
I USE it to control a Powerpoint presentation from the future.
I GET the boost of self-esteem. My posture is properly aligned.
I FEEL grounded.
My face muscles are relaxed, eyebrows slightly raised. I FOCUS on continuing where I left.
To fulfill the mission of crushing Saurian-driven hackers and igniting the DIGITAL SOCIAL REVOLUTION.
I CALL for YOU.

GLOSSARY OF TERMS (*)

Cosmic People An Internet-based UFO religion founded in the Czech Republic in the mid 90s, within the socio-political milieu of the post-fall of the Berlin Wall. The moment of rethinking and reinventing the new socio-political identity coincided with the process of commercialisation of the internet. Both of these affairs had a notorious impact on the Cosmic People's foundation. **Ideological Hierarchy** This society's belief system is based on the dichotomic relationship between the Cosmic People; an extraterrestrial civilisation of evolutionarily advanced beings led by an alien intelligence Ashtar Sheran, and their opponents; harmful inhabitants of the lower dimensional planes – Saurians. **Saurians** Evil, reptile-looking aliens that have deeply infiltrated our socio-political structure. They penetrate human psyches via computers, televisions, smartphones, and consumerism in general, in order to stop personal evolution and enslave humans to their will. The Cosmic People interact with humans in order to protect them from the Saurians. **'Library of Light' (LOL)** An immense online database, made out of a broad spectrum of digital documents: digital images, e-books, sound and video documents that contextualises Cosmic People. LOL is translated into 19 different languages and can be accessed for free on one of their 71 web domains (e.g. www.universe-people.com). As Cosmic People exist exclusively on the Internet, LOL can also be perceived as their cyber temple. **Light Workers and Time Crashers** The seemingly chaotic accumulation method applied in Library of Light, of various characters, objects, phenomena, from different intellectual traditions that, in a historical sense are at odds with each other, is ultimately challenging the notion of linear time. By directly referring to, for example: Michael Flatley, Jesus, Buddha, Barack Obama, and cat memes, as workers of 'Cosmic Light', Cosmic People become a reason for the existence of every entity 'tagged' in their archive. In this manner, they monopolise the notion of three-dimensional time, and position themselves as the protagonists in a reconfiguration of the world. Hence, the historical narrative changes its shape from a two-dimensional linear graph of consequent historical facts, to a Tesla-lamp-like object, where Cosmic People are in the orb, (a small sphere in the centre of the lamp), and the rest of the world – gases inside the lamp, are the byproduct of their existence. Seeing Cosmic People in the course of this pre-Copernican, geocentric model, they become the epicentre that maps and classifies the World. **ETH** Cosmic People welcome the hypothesis that has been bound to the idea that UFOs are material spacecrafts sent from another civilisation or planet. This theory is named 'extraterrestrial hypothesis' (ETH). As a unified concept, it merges all imagery of flying saucer sightings, abduction reports, and testimonies of contact with nonhuman aliens. **IDH** Cosmic People also welcome the 'interdimensional hypothesis' (IDH). Defined in such terms, is a theory by ufologist Jacques Vallée, who claims that alien entities are multidimensional beings that coexist with humans, but act beyond the spacetime paradigm. In that way, IDH justifies on a practical level all pieces of evidence that testify to the sudden appearance and disappearance of people and monumental vehicles. With equal effect, it is unnecessary to explain any propulsion method as it holds that UFOs are not spacecrafts, but rather devices that travel between different dimensions. **Ministering** Since 2012, Vanja Smiljanić is translating text-based documents from the English department of the Cosmic People's archive into Portuguese and Serbian, and is working on enlarging the following digital domains: www.andjeli-neba.com.hr www.anjos-ceu.pt

This involvement leads her to self-proclaim herself as a Minister of Cosmic People for the countries of Ex-Yugoslavia, Portugal, and former Portuguese colonies, and to transform the process of translation into their mutual currency of exchange. In the ministering parkour through the Library of Light, a particular focus is given to the analysis of digital documents which are problematising the full assumption of digital immateriality thus creating a permanent crisis within the research.

(*)Glossary of terms developed for The European Conference of Institutional Ideators (ECII) convened by The Office for Joint Administrative Intelligence (OJAI), first presented during the conference SELF-INSTITUTIONALISATION AS ARTISTIC STRATEGY, held in Wuppertal, Germany in October 2019.

Triple interview diffracted by an inception labyrinth with Pierre Rubio and Vanja Smiljanić

This is a labyrinth.
Its official name is 'Past Life Therapy Machine'.

It is a tool
that has been designed
to be manoeuvred.

Its function
is to breach
the linearity of time
through a spirographic modus operandi.

Both formally and physically, it is a three-dimensional inception labyrinth grounded on four golden paws and mounted on a gyroscopic body; it is equipped with two hands that polarise the surrounding space into east and west.
The way the labyrinth is constructed enables the labyrinth-rider to engage with it on three different levels: macro, meso, micro at the same time.

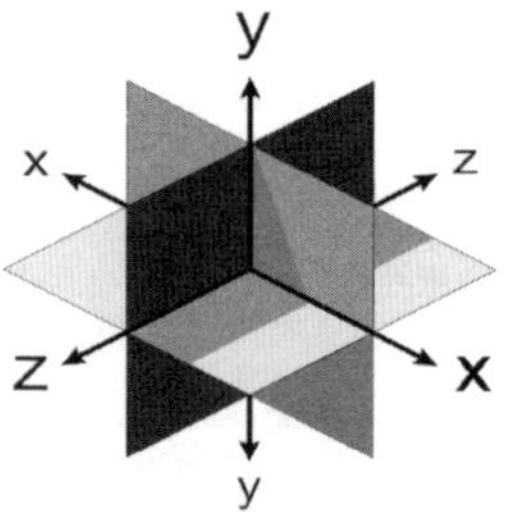

Level 1 – macro

Placing attention on the labyrinth's main construction blocks/planes/axis.
(three actants: x, y, z)

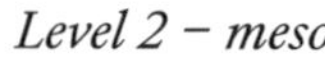

Level 2 – meso

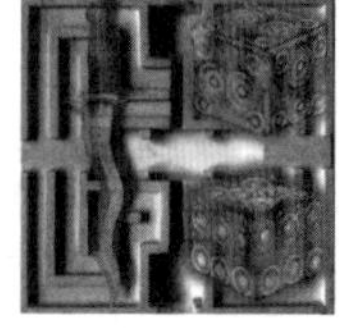

Zooming in and focusing on both sides of the labyrinth's construction blocks/planes/axis.
(six gateways: x-x', y-y', z-z')

Level 3 – micro

Further zooming in and concentrating on the interactions of actants and gateways. (eight dimensions: I, II, III, IV, V, VI, VII, VIII)

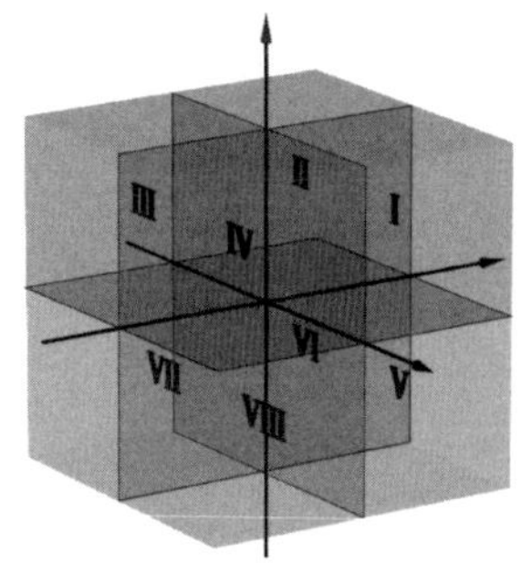

We load the labyrinth and qualify its main construction blocks with three interviews between Pierre and Vanja:

x becomes a written exchange gathering disembodied responses to a series of questions.

y becomes an expanding video interview transcribed in footnotes.

z becomes a performative and transversal mesh-out of images-as-words.

FIRST we enter the labyrinth.

THEN we reach the centre.

THEN in a mirrored movement we exit the labyrinth.

We enjoy the ride.

How is 'your' material generated?

once, she chose an archive
egalitarian structure
she asked to become a document
(one of 7952 documents)
rejected
asked again (92 times)
she became a stalker (of a stalker)
it conditioned the next 10 years of her work[1]

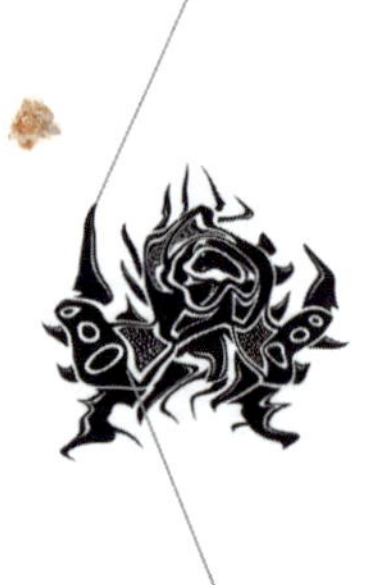

1. WORK

PIERRE: This dialogue will clarify some problems, questions or concerns. It might also open others. I will start by asking you two questions. First a very general one, and then another, more particular. The general one starts like: 'On a good day...' – I use the expression 'on a good day' because artists often experience 'bad days'. They try to cope with the changing structure of the world we are living in. They navigate hybrid methods and practices between theory, activism, creation, research... So, on 'bad days', they doubt the relevance of these hybridisations – What, on a 'good day', do you think is worth doing in your work? Why do you think what you're doing is relevant? That's the general question... Now the particular one: You are from Serbian and Portuguese origins, do you think that is a problem or a solution? Do you think it's a curse or a chance? These are my two questions for today after reading your haiku-like answers.

VANJA: I'll start with the particular question in order to reach the general one. I definitely feel a relief operating with both identities. I can juggle and actually dismiss both of them. Plus, through self-proclaiming myself as Minister of Light for the countries of Ex-Yugoslavia, Portugal, and former Portuguese colonies, and advocating photon rights, my desire was, and still is, to somehow dilute this concept of 'birth-blood rights'... to complexify this equation. Anyhow, I became Portuguese as one part of my family was fundamentally incompliant with Milošević's regime in what was then Yugoslavia. So Portugal became a very important milestone within the formation of my own identity. It was a safe haven where I exiled every time there was a political... hmm... problem in Serbia... by problem I mean the rise of turbo-nationalism, and the implications it had on the whole region.

What is the nature of 'your' material?

and a jellyfish dreams of becoming a redwood tree
she thinks about accessories needed to perform this transformation
at the same time (it is 2015) a drone called Lily is launched
it is one of the first (commercial) drones that has a follow-the-target option
a bracelet with an antenna allows this feature
she imagines having seven arms and on each 54 bracelets
she is running through a field with a swarm of drones following her
the drones are crashing into each other
mayhem[2]
the material is appropriated, it has been de/re-contextualised by the power of subtitles
she is enjoying following its metamorphoses
she contributes to its proliferation

What epistemology – and technique – does 'your' material require to be constructed like that, to be (mis)understood like that?

with each object, tool, performance, she generates a particular lens
each zoom-in is a singular journey
particular and concrete, rather than abstract
the materials she works with are mostly stigmatised and marginalised
('poor' materials in a physical sense, as well as systematically oppressed)
she navigates a spectrum of practices to empower them, to glorify them
this approach can be seen through a feminist epistemological lens, though she does not claim this position
the tools are multilayered and have multiple features

What I find interesting is that the percentages within my ID-cocktail are constantly fluctuating, and that keeps influencing and feeding my artistic practice. Questions like: What are the prerequisites for constructing identity? Which documents does one need to reinforce it? or to destroy it, deconstruct it, keep it in permanent flux – are always tangential to my research. A lot of my artistic work has this promise of reaching liquid identity, which means to abolish sedentary structures and allow perpetual renewal... 'becoming undone' is the term that I used in our correspondence... constantly trying to destabilise the ground, make it wobbly. And through that, creating different modes of existence. So that may be a bridge back to the first part of your question which I find very difficult because...

2. MAYHEM

PIERRE: You are never having a 'good day'... ?

PIERRE-VANJA: Hahahahaha... (laughing)

PIERRE: What I call a 'good day' is a day when you can work without being overwhelmed by doubts. When we are creating new forms grounded in what you just qualified as 'being undone' or 'inventing different modes of existence', you can have days when you struggle with problems of composition, with composing these different elements. It can be overwhelming. I invite you to elaborate on your assembling systems, or modes of composition, which make sense at some point for you as an artist and researcher.

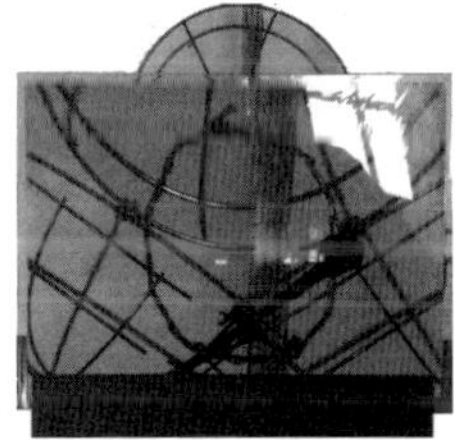

Is 'your' material somebody's?

she works with open source softwares, libraries, tools
their nature enables modifications and redistributions
she works with collective memory
she is interested in the possibilities of hacking it

Is it a crossroad? or an interface?

interfacing[3] allows her to create a short circuit between independent and unrelated systems from different dimensions

What does 'your' work bring together?
Does it articulate different types/textures/dimensions of reality?
How is it related to time? To history? To cultural tropes?

1. history of political disenchantment caused by the change of political regime (from socialism to turbo-capitalism) and the bloody domino effect that this triggered.
2. recipes for (re)construction of an identity (DIY political re-enchantment, self-optimising through DIY hardware)
disruption of linear time
vertical incisions
projections in the future
quantum leaps
a call to slow down
idiotic questioning
operating in spirographic motion

3. INTERFACING

VANJA: Okay, first of all, I'm a deadline junkie... So I often find myself immobilised, floating in this jelly bath of conglomerated research subjects that are a bit at odds with each other. So, a 'good day' comes when I feel the urgency to move. For example, I must share my research within four days. So I enter a Space Odyssey tunnel where things start... blending... and making sense with and to each other. Everything else ceases to exist, and I'm able to put aside all those vampire slugs that, as you've said, occupy, demotivate, and paralyse us. And it liberates me to create short circuits between concepts, methods, elements... to see the clarity between them, or within them. Like Neo deconstructing the Matrix at the end of part I.

PIERRE: I am sure we will go back to the idea of 'the urgency-junkie', but, can we first talk a bit more about identity? What forms of expression and outreach does this liquid identity, this identity in a constant state of construction or reinvention, provide you with? How can this type of identity make a possibility for you to reach out to others — to spectators, collaborators, to the communities of research that you have been part of within the long track-list of your successive immersions in collectivities-that-research-together - ? Which kind of empowerment does your specific experience and practice of identity give you in terms of relationality, in terms of connections?

But what does 'your' very work generate?
Is knowledge what you expect to generate?
If yes, then, which kind of knowledge?
If not, then...?

she generates sinkholes in the pastoral landscape of Critical Theory
the network of sinkholes creates a system of interstices[4] that is used to circumvent socio-political constraints
this requires a radical imagination that operates as a political tool
she is making a full circle by walking backward
from empowerment to camouflage
losing the central position comes as a victory over human exceptionalism
it announces full symbiosis with the surroundings and a step towards acknowledging other non-human agents (hyperobjects, pandas and rivers) in knowledge-making practices
being contingent, co-productive and co-constructive
enacting a world by being in the world and taking the responsibility for it
she also defines knowledge-makings as survival strategies
introducing different methodologies for nourishing radical imagination that leads toward In-Real-Life potential political actions

4. SYSTEM OF INTERSTICES

VANJA: Yes, I've been exploring this complex configuration of identity, nationalism, and body politics by engaging with different communities that operate on the fringes of normcore grids. By re-visiting particular practices from their repertoires, my intention is to (re)present them as empowering tools within the current socio-political context. This expansion of their field is the first step towards liquefying and transforming. Inviting 'and's and 'as well's instead of 'either/or's. On another level, situating these practices in a new context is something that particularly excites me. I'm interested in creating environments where we can collectively explore liminal states of not being so sure and give space for nourishing this limbo that has been historically so heavily stigmatised and presented as a lack, especially in the realm of (art) market-driven economy/politics, which interestingly goes back to your remark about me being an 'urgency-junkie'. Ha! Caught in my own web! Ultimately, I find it necessary to develop a custom-made toolbox of practices, machines, interfaces, that sustain this Phoenix syndrome, and can facilitate a perpetual revolution of identity.

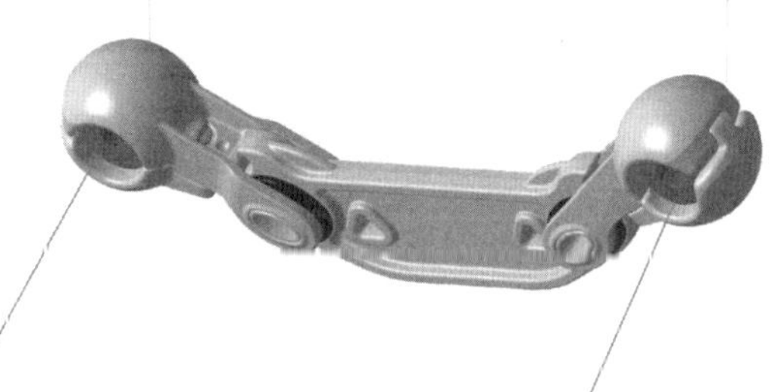

Is your preferred position the one of an anthropologist or a sociologist?

she is perhaps a pirate anthropologist
she borrows tools from anthropology to observe and manipulate social, cultural and environmental relations to question the nature, origin, and destiny of certain facets of human behaviour
she is a pirate sociologist who analyses social institutions in order to divert collective behaviour

Can the work be qualified as weird? What is your definition of weird?

a stutter in a flow,[5] a challenge in processing information
she identifies her work as a conglomerate of different ideas
a monster body (out of focus, blurry) – perhaps it can create an uncanny feeling
she welcomes the weirdness but it is not the intention nor the objective

Why are the structures that you generate 'slippery'? And what does the qualifier 'slippery' perform?
You seem to approach this 'slippery' concept without censoring its shape-shifting properties, is it your singular way to try to index things that 'don't want' to be indexable?

she finds that the property of being slippery adds a layer of unpredictability
humour
malleability
it breaks the rigid score
by using slippery tools she is practicing alternative methods[6] for critical thinking that, instead of judgmentally stigmatising, are allowing for new viewpoints, consciousness,
hopes, and actions to emerge

5. STUTTER IN A FLOW

PIERRE: In one of your haiku-like responses you wrote something around 'lightness'; indeed you have such a 'light' approach when you engage with the work and with people. But in another response you mobilise the idea of 'electricity' that seems to structure your work. What do you think of this contrast? Is 'lightness' in tension with 'electricity'?

VANJA: Perhaps in this context, we could see lightness also as...

PIERRE: ... playfulness?

VANJA: Yes, playfulness. I actually find both concepts intricately connected rather than in contrast. Maybe because I don't perceive electricity as only a two-directional energy tamed within cables and wires, but as an alive, pulsating matter. Therefore, I see a lot of potential in short circuits and jump-starts as generators of conceptual monster bodies. It can be very funny and amusing to collaborate with them.

6. ALTERNATIVE METHODS

PIERRE: In a recent presentation you did, you were shapeshifting drastically, to the point of assembling your body with a portrait of Nikola Tesla and a puppet of La Gioconda connected to a rolling metal frame and a kind of weird machine. You became the human part of a complex object or, this object was a part of your body with extensions made by layered masks and identities, ultimately creating a chimera, a monster, a monster-image and a monstrous performativity. It contained historical representations, ideas of control, representational objects, yourself and some soundtrack and, if I remember, shreds of text. Throughout the performance, the phased construction of this hybrid structure accumulated clues step-by-step so that the audience, in the end, could

What is a monster for you? Why does your work have to be monstrous? What does the qualifier monster 'organise' for you?

going outside of constraints of 'normality'
breaking normcore traps
welcoming mutations
allowing the *enhancement* and diminution at will and their switching in-between
allowing the hybrid, undefined, queer, to exist, express, be
operating beyond binary
becoming undone
allowing the fluid identity to perpetually redefine
resisting fixed, sedentary, structures
merging reality and fiction and 'low' culture and 'high' abstract thinking and dark ecologies and light-hearted milieus and costumes and sci-fi povera sculptures

contemplate (and understand?) a completely crazy object. You have a taste for monstrosities, for assembling (apparently) incoherent parts, but also for monster-tools. You don't end at representations just for the sake of hypnotising the audience, your monsters are invitations for practicing vision through them in order to reconsider reality. Like telescopes or microscopes or lenses, they pose ontological and epistemological questions because objects and subjects are not classically separated, grotesque and theoretical materials are dialoguing, and you surprisingly handle and define a bizarre idea of space. I feel invited to reimagine what the limits of the idea of space are, what the difference between real and fiction is, what time and memory are made of when layers of history are recombined and what the correlation between dreams and the institution of the so-called real could be. I feel invited to recalculate, to reconsider what I think is real. Do you think these monsters can possibly operate as filters? Do you end up with hybrid monsters that can be instruments for (re)-vision?

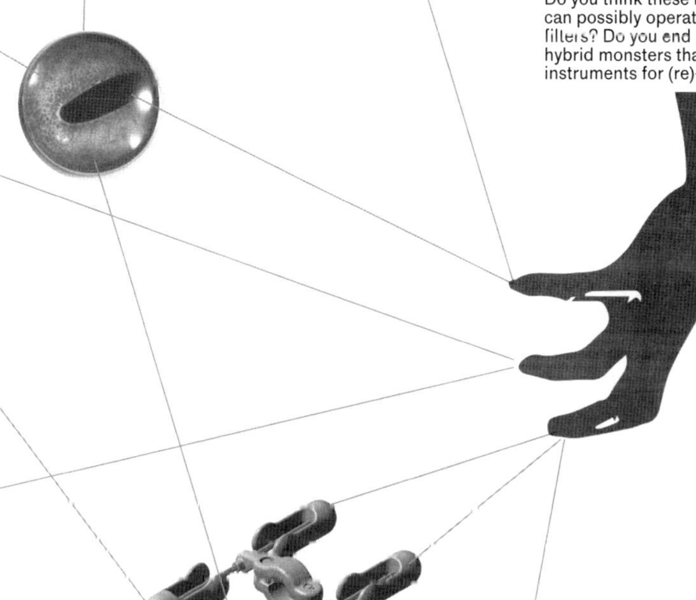

What role does power play in 'your' work? How do you embrace the energy of 'electricity' and 'power' and conduct their potency?
How do you embody – in your own words – the alternative/alternating current of new senses, of new organs, of an expanded perception of intelligence?

power within her work has an ouroboros-like movement
power, or more precisely, the lack of it, being stripped of it, (repressed, disempowered, marginalised, censured) is the ur-stimulus[7] for performing her research through her ministering practice she channels power
she opens a space for exercising power
in some instances power borders on control and authority
one-directional power[8] is not sustainable
pulling the plug
her apparatuses channel the capitalistic-driven self-optimisation techniques and tools, and the imperative for absolute productivity
the (absurdity of the) tools explore/question the idea of the promise/cure/easy fix /3 things in 1/model + 5000

7. UR-STIMULUS

VANJA: My monsters operate as filters, yes. But, they also have a part-time job working in a socio-political spa. The monsters do become instruments for critical viewing and also for re-imagining. But if I may be frank, deep down I feel I was indoctrinated by teleshopping-self-optimisation strategies and their DIY tips on becoming a more effective member of society. Somehow, I'm still deeply impressed by all those conglomerated objects, for example, an iron, a phone, and a lamp in the same body. I find them astonishing. I mean I am affected by their creative potential and at the same time paralysed with fear by their ability to adapt so quickly to the frivolity of consumerist desire. This constant quest for blind spots within an already oversaturated marketplace and the creation of commodities that have multiple functions and that hold a promise of solving all of your problems with just one click, those perhaps, were my ur-monster bodies. They definitely changed my way of looking and acting.

8. POWER

PIERRE: 'Acting'... you mean?

VANJA: Acting...

PIERRE: Behaving like an agent... affecting... effecting... acting out... AGIR!

VANJA: Yeah, yes, yes.

PIERRE: So by giving space to the object's agency, you think you can contribute to stimulating the viewer's agency?

VANJA: Precisely, yes.

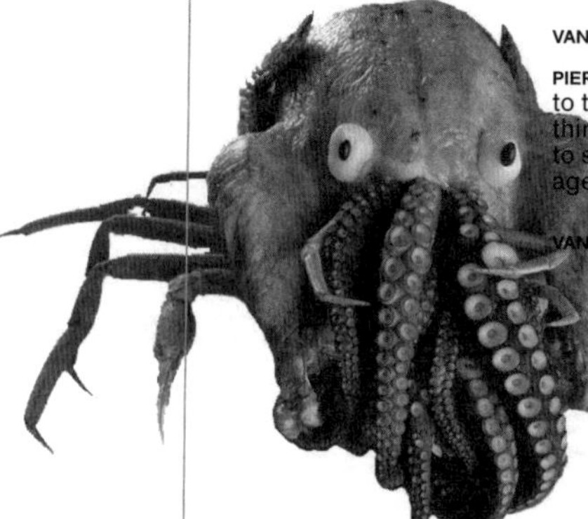

You use the term 'potential vehicle' to define the last object-tool you created, what does this vehicle transport and where does it take the audience to?

she relates potential vehicle[9] with potency – having power/latent quality – but also with possibility in a speculative sense – projection/belief – she enjoys the limbo in between
placebo effect

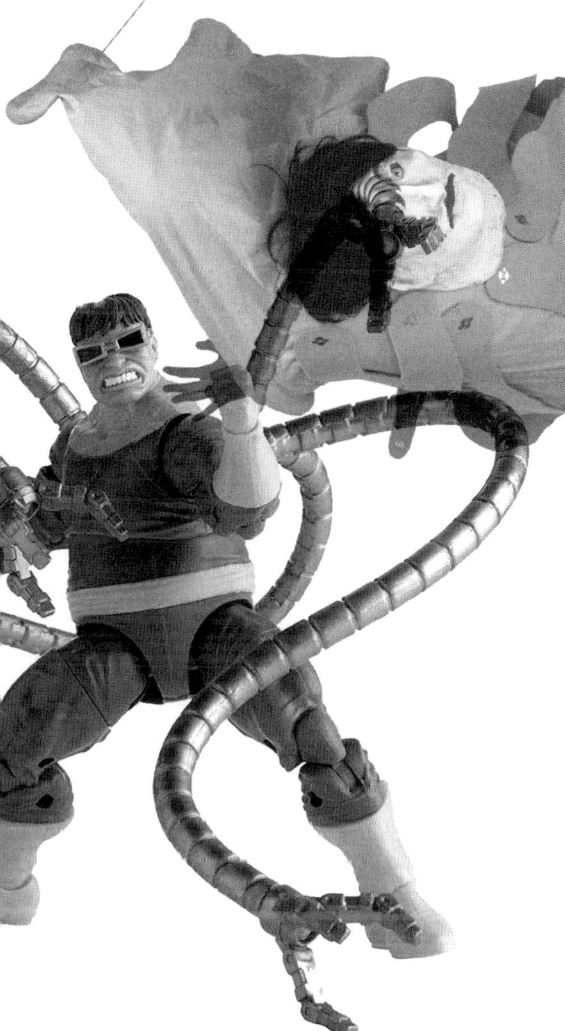

9. POTENTIAL VEHICLE

PIERRE: We have not discussed one of your expressions, 'the potential vehicle'. We could also talk about 'knowledge'... You seem to find it pompous to define the aims of your work as potentially producing knowledge. You prefer the qualifier 'survival strategies' instead. You could also elaborate on the word 'slippery'. You define 'slippery' as a 'portal to the unknown'. This is an additional quality for the ongoing construction of a liquid identity. You seem to think it should be 'slippery', a bit like a gel, a gooey substance... Not just a liquid identity, but a viscous identity that resists being grasped. A bit like cornstarch reacting with water...

VANJA: By bringing together the potential vehicle, survival strategies, and a slippery substance, you are summoning the Blobject! It's one of my favourite non-human collaborators and I'm both love-struck and disgust-infused by it. Morphologically speaking, Blobject has the coherence of a solid, but the amorphousness of a liquid, empirically it's a soft, gooey, oozy, slimy, slippery field of experience, and socially, it is completely dependent on its contextual constraints. As you've said, it does resist being contained and grasped. Since the word 'blob' appeared for the first time in the fifteenth century as an onomatopoeic expression for 'making saliva' or 'spit bubble', it has been perpetually transforming, mutating, and along the way creating multiple histories and fields of action. Therefore, when my yes-human collaborator Dieuwke Boersma and I were invited to contribute to a conference on the-role-of-art-and-critique and the rise of right-wing populism, the Blobject felt like a perfect vehicle to address the entanglement of the issue and a complex toolbox that could speak (non) sense to this slippery abyss of banality. We constructed the Blobject as an object-to-think-with, an evocative object that poses questions by taking seriously the slime and all its disgusting flows as a catalyst for encountering a radical Other(ness).

Working in collective environments crowded with processes developing artistic practices and research, how, in these circumstances, are singular ideas generated and what consequences do they have on the collective?

in collaborative environments, she
attempts to be as receptive as possible
she allows for bi-directional contingency[10]
perhaps it is a conditioned reflex
to lose the 'hers' comes as a relief.

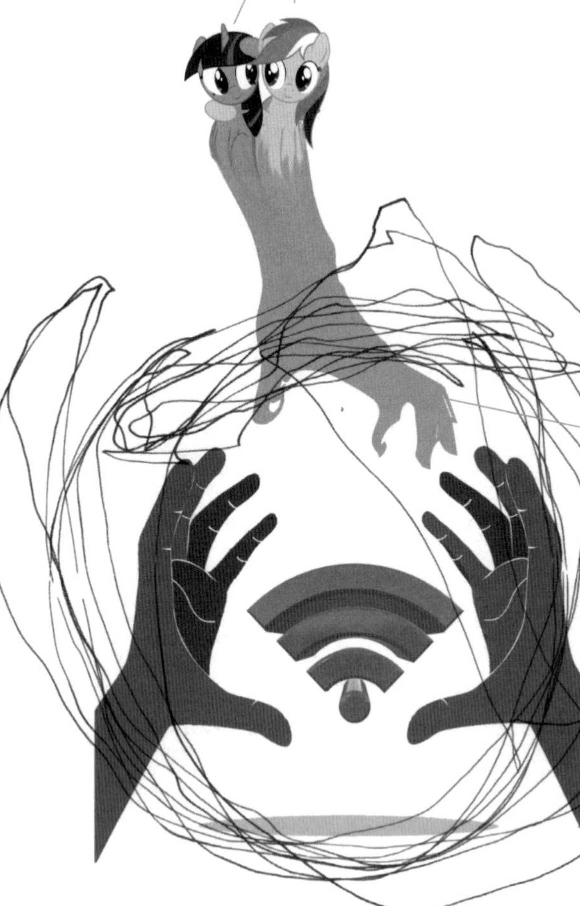

10. BI-DIRECTIONAL CONTINGENCY

VANJA: But, we were talking about the potential vehicle. The etymological root of 'potential' comes from potency, to exercise power, but potency itself has a layer of speculation, of belief. Therefore, there is also the possibility of failure. I want to invite the practice of experiencing the object without being sure of it.

PIERRE: Let's further discuss the question concerning the notion of vehicle but as a pharmakon. You stated something like, '... the vehicle is a participatory platform through which we can collectively reflect on how past modes of existence can be used as a resource against the emphasis of the present'. Could you expand on this idea? Does every object you make actually transport that, or transport like that? Previously, we were referring to these complex objects as lenses and also as supports, but they also seem to function as therapies/medicines. Are all your vehicles/objects therapies/medicines? Are all your vehicles actually... ambulances?

PIERRE-VANJA: Hahaha... (laughing)

VANJA: When I wrote that, I was referring to the last machine I built. It is a gyroscopic three-dimensional inception labyrinth that functions as a past life therapy machine. This machine was developed for the specific context of 'School of Waters' a biennale with a conceptual framework of reasserting the history of the Mediterranean area, starting from its waters. So yes, in this environment the machine really did become a remedy for dealing with eurocentric interpretations of the Mediterranean area, and with the surround-system (and experience) of the divergent claims, cultures, mythologies, wars, tragedies, and so many levels of colonial exploitation of the land

and of people. Through the activation and use of this labyrinth-object-tool – driving a ball through its multidimensional orifices – me, and other people who were using it, were able to explore the resilient potentiality of polyvocal communication within a spirographic time frame.

PIERRE: Maybe you are a female version of Captain Nemo? Captain NemA!... In fact Jules Verne is a sort of disgraceful father... for Raymond Roussel, of course, and surprisingly enough for Gilbert Simondon as well. One day he was asked about his primary inspiration, he replied without hesitation that it all began with reading Jules Verne. Perhaps you have a kind of Jules Verne spirit too? Without the sexist and racist side... Have you read him?

VANJA: I recollect borrowing *20.000 Leagues Under the Sea* from my primary school library, and the cover had a lot of tentacles painted on it. But it is funny because Nema in Serbian means 'there is no/doesn't exist' and also 'mute'.

PIERRE: Captain Nema.
Captain silence.
Captain nobody.
The Captain
-does-not-exist...

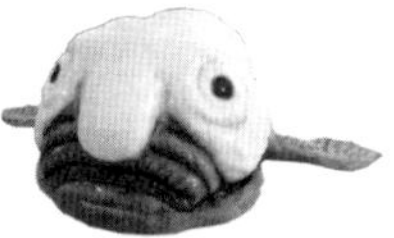

We reach the centre of the labyrinth and retrace the same path out.

Isabel Burr Raty
Adrijana Gvozdenović
Sara Manente

Not in the Mood

The block 'Not in the Mood' unfolded from the 3rd of May to the 31st of July, 2021 as part of the a.pass postgraduate programme. The curatorial team was composed of Isabel Burr Raty, Adrijana Gvozdenović, Antye Guenther, Sara Manente, Rob Ritzen and Sina Seifee, who were previously Associate Researchers at a.pass Research Center.

The following text is divided into two parts based on two recorded conversations, reflecting upon the block curation. The first conversation took place after the first week of the block, and the second conversation was held amongst the curators at the end of the block. The group of curators have decided to speak in this text from the first the person plural – as a 'we' – catalysing the experience through one voice, to represent the plurality of the body composed of tentacular parts that they created together, or rather: that they came to be, in the process of curating.

PART I
COLLABORATION/FEEDBACK AS A PROPOSAL

Curating a block prolonged the dynamic of working together which we had developed as a group of Associate Researchers during Cycle I of the a.pass Research Center (2018-2019).

In March 2020, during the first lockdown in Brussels, we wished to catch up with each other, bringing up the awaited topic of feedback to the institution on our individual and collective experience at the Research Center. We set up the first online session that became feedback to ourselves, as well as feedback to a.pass.

As Associate Researchers in a.pass, we got to know each other's differences, to enjoy each other's practices and company. During that time we developed a collaborative dynamic where we responded to each other continuously – when we agreed, but also when we didn't – without consolidating the differences into one position. A dynamic that was not about devoting the shared time to our individual researches separately, but finding shared proposals and learning from each other within them. The desire to do something together came from this intensity that we still held, as well as from a need to stay in touch and to continue learning from each other.

Our feedback became a proposal when we recognised that what we were missing in the research programme could become a generator for different practices within the institution.

The Research Center had been established in parallel to the post-graduate programme and we agreed that during the year that we were there, there could have been more interaction between the two. This led us to rethink the overall roles in the institution itself: What is a mentor? What is a participant? What is a curator? What is a workshop facilitator or a guest artist? ...prompting a proposal where each one of us could shift between all these roles. This opened up new questions: What does it do to embody these different agencies? How do they inform one another? We also realised that we have something particular to offer. By acknowledging our different interests and practices we could function as a curatorial group, without denying the individual positions within it.

CURATING: RESPONSIBILITY AND AGENCY

As former participants and/or Associate Researchers, we understand curating at a.pass as a structural proposal for a particular approach to teaching that provides tools and creates a context for collective learning. The aim is to create a positive educational environment that *also unfolds from the bottom-up, creating different geometries of togetherness.* Picking up on this 'non-top-down' approach and learning from Femke Snelting's reflection on a 'non-horizontal condition', (in which she states that the idea of the circle can be misleading because we are not all at the same distance from the centre),[1] we felt the freedom to propose an experimental way of curating a block. As a group, we would all produce, programme, mentor, give workshops, participate and take care of the space. We would respond to each other in the experience of embodying the many roles. The ability to switch sides within a pedagogical process would strengthen curating as a collective learning practice.

(NOT) IN THE MOOD

We were accountable for the possible mess that our curatorial proposal might create and took the responsibility that came with it. Being a group of six, and with all our different perspectives, it required a lot of time and attention to negotiate between our capabilites, needs and desires. Furthermore, we had to find a way to

1 An idea introduced to us during a workshop led by Femke Snelting on geometry of togetherness (see her article, 'The Eternal Network: The Ends and Becomings of Network Culture", edited by Kristoffer Gansing and Inga Luchs, *Transmediale*, 2020) during 'victories of the suns' in Zsenne ArtLab June-July 2019.

hold the multiplicity of our curatorial proposal and the different research universes of the participants in one block. This is when we decided to think of 'mood' as the conceptual theme, a glue that would temporarily keep everything together, giving us the possibility to practice fluidity between the many different roles.

As a result, we developed ongoing practices, workshop proposals and reading sessions that were oriented towards setting different moods for the block. Additionally, our intention with adding Not in the Mood was to think about the agency of moods in artistic processes and to question what these could add to contemporary art production if they were more acknowledged. Or perhaps to exercise how 'not being in the mood' generates tools of resistance within a 'professional' scene that also happens to be pierced by certain principles of a neoliberal economy.

'NOT IN THE MOOD' AS A SET-UP

Concretely, during the Opening Week, Sara Manente led the first collective practice called the 'Washing machine', an associative game about 'obsessions'. Throughout the block, Isabel Burr Raty offered the 'Depository cat', an ongoing practice and interactive space, where participants shared their research in the form of treatments in order to '(de)particularise' affects in creative processes. Likewise ongoing, Sina Seifee took the role of 'PR' by interviewing the participants and publishing regularly online as a different form of mentoring, fabulously speculating what their matters of care are.

During the first part of the block, Antye Guenther facilitated 'Oh so serious', a workshop testing strategies for de-professionalisation in artistic research practices. Adrijana Gvozdenović and Sara Manente hosted 'Nail art affects theory', a series of reading sessions about affect theory while doing each others' nails, playing with the idea of mentoring as a beautification process, talking about 'what makes us happy' and 'why do we feel like we feel' (Sara Ahmed).

During the Halfway Days sessions with presentations and feedback, we set forth to work from stereotypical figures of mood: reflective (analyst), lighthearted (imitator), suspicious (detective), cheerful (groupie), whimsical (overthinker), ominous (diva) and gloomy (contrarian).

In the second part of the block, Rob Ritzen, in collaboration with Steyn Bergs, conducted 'The labour of laziness' reading sessions, proposing to think of laziness as a lateral form of political agency for artists and art workers, as a way to avoid self-exploitation.

SPACE

We took 'mood' as the umbrella term to look at the collective working space as well. We agreed on the spatial elements: a net, an inflatable cat, a dance floor – keeping in mind that a variety of practices would interact with and activate those differently. The idea was to treat the space as a character, as a subject, that hosts or triggers a moody playground for research. For the reading sessions, Rob invited artist Sofia Caesar to install an interpretation of her work 'Unrest', a 6m x 4m hanging net. This kinetic and stretchable device, that we thought of as a giant hammock, imprinted laziness into the space.

At the same time, Isabel looked for a big, seductive and inflatable object, which would invite the participants to join her ongoing treatment and depository practice. We collectively decided on a giant inflatable cat that unexpectedly created a feeling of comfort. Together with Steven Jouwersma (scenographic and technical support of a.pass), we installed the objects and worked on a playful way to place them, bringing in a dance floor as the third spatial element, which invited everyone to liberate mood by moving the body in space.

FINANCING

Together with Joke Liberge (production coordinator) and Michèle Meesen (administrator), we administered the budget in a way that reflected how we were going to work together, deciding to be paid equally. The collaborative work we envisioned was not easy to express within the financial structure of a.pass, where there is a structure in place and a fair payment scheme. This limitation brought some realism to our initial ideas. How could we distribute the money equally if we were not all doing exactly the same amount of work? In particular, not everyone was offering a workshop and mentoring for an equal amount of time and we also wanted to be present in each other's workshops and reading sessions.

We had to figure out a system that could translate those constraints into our proposal of equal pay, as well as protect ourselves from self-exploitation. So, we adjusted our plans and the frequency of work to the overall budget reserved for curating the block. We knew that the minimum required presence in a.pass is during the three common weeks of the block and therefore, we built our schedule around that. The structure could be simple, but it was a dissecting endeavor. We were wondering how to be sure we would do the same amount of work for this proposal. Fortunately, it was previously established in our group that we trust each other 'almost blindly'.

PART II

This part functions as a report of what happened with previously described intentions and expectations, how the block proposal influenced our practices, but also our private lives, what the wishes and desires are that stayed unfulfilled, and perhaps most importantly, what this process taught us. We continue writing from the first person plural, to further represent the shape that 'we' took, acknowledging and accepting our different individual experiences, contradictions and disagreements, as parts of our tentacular curating body.

COLLABORATION/SUSTAINABILITY

There is an aspect of cheerleading to curation, getting excited by people's proposals and ideas, which we intentionally embraced, knowing that this might not always be a critical relationship. Furthermore, having the opportunity to navigate from being a.pass participants and/or Associate Researchers to being those who can take care, organise, mentor or advise, brought different kinds of responsibility, which extended and enriched our artistic practices. Surprisingly, the same questions we raised throughout the block (deprofessionalisation, the labour of laziness, affective economy) cross-pollinated the process of curating with our individual working habits and entered our private spheres.
Even though we might know how to set up conditions for working together, we are not always easy to collaborate with. Nonetheless, the collaboration model that we set up (equally shared budget, working hours and responsibilities) gave us the opportunity to truly embody generosity towards each other, in terms of understanding and giving the space for different rhythms and ways of doing – to the point that sometimes we all wanted to be the one who goes outside during a break to stand next to the smokers – not to smoke but rather to participate in the conversation. Then we noticed that it's not a break but a curatorial programme unrolling, and that there are only six of us discussing it.
On the other hand, throughout the block, a parallel chapter opened for us where 'resisting being overworked' became central. Hence, procrastinating work on other projects and postponing answering emails provided time for process integration and joyfulness. This made it clear that we need to prioritise the creation of other structures of appreciation for artistic effort and work in the future.

MEASURING THE PRESENCE OF SIX

Having a curator with six heads, carrying on an educational programme with content that intentionally escapes solidification, implies fragmentation and continuous moments of collective reflection. Perhaps also a full-time presence in all the activities. This was practically often impossible, as it would have meant extra working hours overrunning the curatorial budget limit. A curatorial ideal was to be able to be present in every collective practice proposed, to work in the space more often (e.g. in the evenings), to get even more involved, transparent, intense, to see the whole performative spectrum of 'mood'. In other words, the conditions for performativity demanded time and work that were beyond our reality.

That said, the tentacular curatorial body allowed us to experiment with and add to the a.pass horizontal-learning approach by spreading responsibilities in the exercise of changing roles. As curators, we participated in workshops and reading sessions led by one or some of us, which proved to be a challenge, as it demanded a certain mode of suspension of excitement and discussion in order to keep this space primarily for the participants. Conversely, adding the mentor role to being a curator offered the opportunity to meet participants during collective undertakings, renovating the individual mentoring approach by having a much earlier and deeper insight into the participant's research/practices.

TO WORK WITH 'MOOD'

During the first conversations when we were planning the block, we shared the different practices we would like to offer. While trying to understand what would be and which conceptual frame could hold them, moods and affects (especially negative ones) were recognised as common denominators each one of us could contribute to. To situate 'mood' in relation to artistic research was exciting, as there is a generative potential between mood and knowledge production, mood and collective learning, mood and productivity in general.

'Mood' was not the topic but rather the methodology, a filter we worked with and through, proposing several collective learning practices with specific angles to the subject. We recognised that a.pass already nurtured the approach that allows 'moods' to manifest themselves in the artistic environment, specifically within a collective learning cosmos. Our intention was to take this permission further, creating proposals that would motivate the participants to co-create their relationship with the subject.

We believe that to work with ‘mood’ means to create conditions for (at least temporary) affiliations to emerge. Besides sharing discourses and experiences within different theoretical frameworks, we also talked about our private lives, personal economies, management of time and desires that get produced by and at the same time produce our artistic practices.

What are you up to? What are your obsessions? Are you paranoid? Why do you dress like that when you go to an opening? How professional are you? Can you drop it all and be lazy? What aspects of your research, dreams and intimacy need treatment? What kind of treatment would it be? Are you in the mood for doing nails? Can a theory be considered through the beautification process? What if...?

Philippine Hoegen
Lilia Mestre

(No) Safe Space?

A Conversation with Peggy Pierrot

INTRODUCTION

As I cycle up the hill of Delaunoy Street, coming from the centre of Brussels and heading into Molenbeek, I fall into an old pattern from when I was a participant at a.pass, which is to hope that a car will want to enter the building, called De Bottelarij where a.pass is housed, just as I arrive. That way I can dash in illicitly beside the car through the garage shutter instead of stopping to huddle by the pedestrian's door, waiting for someone to buzz me in. Today I'm lucky: slow down, wait for the big door to roll open – it's like the building is opening its mouth – accelerate, Whoosh!

Through the courtyard, past the many other organisations and initiatives housed in this large building, up the wide metal stairs and past the RITCS theatre students gathered on the steps to smoke. Through the 'alarming' door (it always shrieks when you go through) to the a.pass office space on the third floor.

Michèle Meesen opens up, she's been the pillar of a.pass' administration for many years, but today is her last day. She has chosen a new horizon, but just before leaving she's still busy and preoccupied, especially because she is trying to help one of the a.pass participants who is battling the beast of Belgian bureaucracy for his student residency permit. We come back to this topic later on, in the conversation with Peggy Pierrot and Lilia Mestre.

Lilia and I have invited Peggy Pierrot, who is a pedagogue and teacher in media theory and human sciences, for a conversation. We want to talk about pedagogy, about alternative education, and to see how she positions a.pass in that discourse. And we specifically asked Peggy to talk about the ethics and pitfalls of alternative education, because she was engaged with a.pass in a moment when the authority and responsibility of the curators in the programme were being questioned. This challenge revealed the fragilities of the a.pass structure in dealing with conflict and led to some important changes that better support the political necessities of the present times, such as the engagement with a code of conduct and the creation of a Participants' Assembly.

Peggy bursts into the space triumphantly waving her key-card, which she still has (and now dutifully hands over) from the time she co-curated a block at a.pass, two years ago at the time of writing. A 'block' is a period of four months of which three are intensely programmed, and the last is a month of self-organisation. This division of the year into three quadrimesters is the set rhythm of a.pass. New participants can start at the beginning of every block and others finish, a participant does three blocks in total and has the possibility to take a break of one block if the need arises. Each block is curated by one or more 'curators' – who may be artists, researchers, academics, writers etc. They think together with the artistic coordinator about the pedagogical approach to the block, the thematics and the programme, and propose and co-create with the participants a structure in which participants will work individually and collaboratively on their own research in response to, or through, the lens of the proposed themes.

Connecting to Michèle's story about the student's struggle for his residency papers, Peggy remarks: 'People are in really difficult situations sometimes, and I think a lot of schools have to deal with, and prepare for this now. For so many educational structures the situation is becoming overwhelming, not just because of Covid times, there is precarity all over. And it's a huge added task for the administration and support staff of, indeed, helping people to navigate very complicated visa situations for example'. The statement is confirmed by Michèle's concerns of the day.

BLOCKS AND CURATORS

PH: So Peggy, you curated a block at a.pass, perhaps we should first delve into what that means and what it does?

PP: I find the rhythm of the blocks, and the way they are organised in time and content, really inspiring. In fact, I introduced it in another project I was working on: Les Ateliers des Horizons in Grenoble. I find it interesting and fruitful – also, the fact that you can skip a block so you can take time off to process what you have been working on in the blocks before. And perhaps most importantly, this structure makes it possible for people who are already professionals in whatever field, but who face a time where they need to rethink what they were doing, to participate. For me, when I worked at a.pass, I really saw how you can see the artist as a worker and the artist's work as a work, which is like any other work. It needs training, and time to think about itself and to study its own structure.

I find the basic timeframe of the organisation really interesting, because of what it brings the participants in a.pass. It permits an intensity, which sometimes people can have difficulty with, but when you're in your adult life, you might work to pay your fees or to pay your rent, or you're an activist or you're unemployed, but that's also work, and when you take time to train yourself, going 'back to school', then you cannot be completely free in your time – you're never out of your life. In a.pass, the way the weeks are organised, and the rhythm of three months' activity and one month for yourself, plus the possibility to skip a block as a way of taking a break – it makes the combination doable.

PH: And how about curators?

PP: I wrote down in French that participants in a.pass come to *'se nourrir aux obsessions des curateurs'*: to feed off the obsessions of the curators. Which doesn't mean that these are imposed upon them. The curator's interest, practice and field of expertise are brought in and the participants are asked to engage in a programme around a particular concept, discourse or subject from that. These proposals can function as fruitful perturbations for participants, in the sense that when you want to learn something, sometimes you think you want to learn one thing and actually the fact that you are confronted with something that is not expected makes you realise that maybe you need to learn something else. But of course, the same applies for the curator: sometimes you have an idea of what you want to offer as a work basis for the participants and then it just goes somewhere else entirely.

LM: Indeed. As a curator or as a mentor you are also learning, you don't have a passive role, you really have to be open to being a researcher yourself – both in terms of content but also communication and ways of being together, of taking care. And this is very rich, I think, for a curator.

PP: Yes, there's also a lot for the curator to do in terms of support and making things possible. What we're talking about here is a pedagogical framework, because it's really the pedagogy that makes it possible, that gives room for improvisation, room for critique, room for dialogue, which is essential for it to work. It's a pedagogical choice. What that also implies is that the question of learning is shared between people who have some kind of organisational position, and the participants. And this is another thing that I find interesting and specific in a.pass, the fact that pedagogy is everywhere. Actually, it doesn't stop.

I remember all these times of cooking together for example, or going to PAF[1] together... there's these intense

1 PAF (Performing Arts Forum) is a place for professional and not-yet professional practitioners and activists in the field of performing arts, visual art, new media and internet, theory and cultural production, who seek to research and determine their own conditions of work. PAF is for people who can motorise their own artistic production and knowledge production, not only responding to the opportunities given by the institutional market. https://pa-f.net. Since its beginning, a.pass has been going to PAF three times a year, at the end of each block. Participants, mentors and curators travel together for a week of research presentations and feedback.

days that start at nine and maybe stop at ten o'clock in the evening. Even when you are taking a break, it is still in many ways, part of the whole pedagogy.

PH: What do you mean exactly by pedagogy?

PP: In terms of pedagogy, I've been interested in the history of the libertarian view on schools and the history of popular education,[2] but I can also refer to the classical Socratic dialogical practice, because all of these subsequent approaches are fuelled by it. This is what I mean by pedagogy is everywhere: this mind-set in which you are trying to make things happen by asking questions and opening up possibilities. For me, it's not only about research in this educational context, the research is the consequence of the pedagogy. I think the framework, and the way the different curators and the mentors ask questions to the participants is the pedagogy that will bring forth research.

PH: But your point seems to be also that it's not only the curators and the mentors that are posing questions but also the participants themselves, to themselves and each other, or to the curators.

PP: And this is also why I think it's not only about the research in a.pass, it is the general pedagogy of the programme that is also what's being worked on, in my opinion.

LM: I agree. And for that the informal needs the formal. For being together informally to become meaningful, it needs a formal structure. Then these concerns and commitments can continue, can resonate. Because there's the framework... it's not that you go off and make your work in isolation, you're doing it within this environment.

PH: What are the conditions that are in place that create that bubble of ongoing learning?

PP: Well, one thing is that you never have a group of people that are completely new to the programme. Because of the system of blocks, new people are joining every four months and there are always people present for whom it's their 2nd, 3rd or 4th block. So, when somebody new gets in there are

2 That history encompasses a wide range of thinkers and practitioners from Godwin to Pelloutier, Francisco Ferrer, A.S.Neill, and so on. It also includes *enseignement mutuel*, for example.

others who are already in it, who can take the new ones in. And that is important because when you just arrive you have to get used to the way questions are asked, to the way it works. You get socialised to a.pass in a way, in order to be able to get involved in this practice of doing research in a collective environment with particular ways of working. So, the participants themselves are mentors for the new ones, introducing them to these sequences that are shaping each block, the programme culture and practices etc.

COMMUNITY OF LEARNING

PP: When we were preparing this conversation you were saying, Philippine, that a.pass is often perceived from the outside as a sect (laughing). Well, for me it's more like a network of learning because it starts within the programme and continues after. And for me, as I told you the other day, seeing this as a community, as a network of learning, or constant learning, it's something that I find positive, not negative like a cult. Because it's more something that has to do with co-education, learning together, and ongoing learning in fact, because when people have been to a.pass, those who want to stay connected to the framework of a.pass can, and are still learning. At some point, they might be a curator or they join the Research Center or... So for me, it's more something that the framework permits, this kind of network of learning that is at the core of a.pass. It creates dialogic relations between the organisers – the people that allow the framework to work – and the participants who can also be part of the pedagogy itself. So, when I say: 'a community', it's about having this kind of dialogical relation in terms of pedagogy.

(NO) SAFE SPACE: CRISIS AND CODE OF CONDUCT

PH: Peggy, in that same preparation of this conversation you said, 'a safe space doesn't exist. You put yourself at stake, just by coming to the institution'. And this was on the one hand, to say that a group of people coming together always comes with problems. But it was also about the role and responsibility of the institution.

PP: Well, I was talking about intensity before. And the fact that, as I understand a.pass, part of it is about putting yourself in an uncomfortable position so as to change something. For example, you're a writer and you want to confront yourself with the question of performance. This is a big step and this is somewhat uncomfortable. And you will meet people there that have completely different practices and come from different fields, different kinds of social backgrounds, and you're all together in it, you have to work together. And then you have the curators and the mentors and everybody's asking you questions all the time. And it takes time to say 'okay, no this is not where I want to be, this is where I want to be'. Especially if you come at a moment in your life where you need to change something about your practice. So, this is uncomfortable and it makes people fragile. And I don't remember your question (laughing)...

PH: Well something that we've talked about a lot in the past years is this idea that, especially in more alternative or experimental types of educational institutions, where you don't have all the traditional bodies in place that can be brought into motion when things go wrong, and especially in an institution where there is also an ambition to be horizontal – whilst of course there is always hierarchy – there are weak spots, or there are blind spots. How do you see that?

PP: If you don't want to be authoritative, the space for challenges should be everywhere, not only with the participants. We know that the world is not safe, but we are in the classroom, and we expect it to be a bit different. We have the expectation that things will be different than in other places. So, yes, when something bad happens, it's even worse than outside. So, for me, this is really clear, you need tools in place such as a code of conduct to hold the safeness of the space as much as possible.

I think the negotiation is the most important thing about a code of conduct: to have a base for a discussion, but to make it something that is always... in French we say: '*quelque chose qui est toujours sur le métier*'. That is always in the making. Because of course from one group to the other, there will be different people with different ideas.

And because it should respond to the needs that are present at the time, that can mean, for example, that I don't always understand the need for everything in it, but I can still do it. Sometimes we don't agree, but if there is a need to respect certain things you have to do it.

PH: And pedagogy is also there, right?

PP: Yes. When we say, pedagogy is everywhere, then being able to do things that you don't understand but that are needed by some others – yes, it is something that we all need to learn.

LM: It's also about the practice, right? Indeed, a code of conduct isn't something static, I find it important to discuss it, read it together and question it, get feedback on it. And when things occur, to talk about how we are dealing with the situation. To open up to different voices, right? And this is a challenge, because we are all so used to silencing our fights. So how do you create that space in which disputes can be discussed and different perspectives are voiced?

PP: I think with all of these kinds of topics the difficulty is to be able to make your point, but still stay open, so stay in the place that makes discussion possible. But to address it, at least find room to talk about it is the minimum that we can do when we're involving ourselves in this kind of radical progressive pedagogy. Because if we don't, then we're failing.

PH: So how do you do this, what makes this space of exchange and learning from each other possible?

LM: One year ago we started the practice of the a.pass lexicon on the a.pass Kitchen[3] collective writing website. This practice enables a look into the vocabulary we use at a.pass and to introduce new terms that are urgent for the group. It has been an important tool for collective discussion and updating/resetting of the programme.

PP: There is this group of activists in Brussels – Thierry Müller, Olivier Crabbé and David Vercauteren – who made a book called '*Micropolitique des Groupes*' based on the practices of different groups like '*Collectif sans ticket*,' and others. It's like a guide on how to make a group work and to work as a group. It's not a set of rules that can be applied everywhere but there's one thing in it that I think is always helpful, they call it 'taking the temperature' right before starting. It's like, 'How do you feel today? What is your energy?' Sometimes you need to do it every day depending on the group or the moment, sometimes it's just once a week. In terms of code of conduct, it's not something that you can capture there, but it's important, it's about paying attention to how the group is feeling: the mood.

---

3 kitchen.apass.be

I remember the day during the block I co-curated that there was this huge conflict that occurred just before I arrived. When I came into the room, I knew there was something wrong but I didn't know what was happening, and I asked but no one could tell me, it was too fresh. They couldn't say anything but it was there...

In artistic work, it's quite particular, I think. People are at stake with their whole body, all the time. I think it's true in many types of work actually, in a lot of different kinds of human activities. But the fact is, that it has so much to do with who you are in your artistic work and in this kind of training. So there, of course, the mood and the small things... you have to pay a lot of attention to it, because otherwise it cannot work.

PH: The block you're talking about was called Zone Public. During that block, there was a strong breach of trust between the participants and one of the curators, which included them lodging a complaint. This episode brought home the urgency to address the position of power of the curator and mainly made clear that a.pass didn't have a system to deal with conflicts and situations of power abuse. It was a really important moment for the organisation to think together with the participants, staff and board about what tools to implement to support everyone involved. Peggy, from your perspective and in relation to what we are saying, how do you look back on that moment?

PP: The block was about publication and making public. Which comes with questions of recognition. And I think now that we're talking about this, that we should have been more careful about the temperature of the group, because we the curators, had needs and practises of making public that might have been confronting for the participants.

LM: Publishing has to do with exposure. Of course, we are exposing ourselves constantly but here it's pushed forwards, it's not a secondary thing in the research. And because that work is so related to who you are, it needs more care. Making yourself public means that protection is needed to enable publishing, it needs barriers around certain things.

PP: We were addressing what it is to be productive and to make public, not only in the sense of a publication but of making public more generally, which also comes with the question of recognition through making the work public.

And I think the way we did it didn't acknowledge the fact that this was a vivid, sensitive issue for some of the participants. I think in retrospect that, maybe, I'm still not sure, we didn't take the individual positions and needs into account enough.

Kate Rich

Administraart

On Tues., May 9, 2017, X wrote:
At a.pass as well, we are shifting things around. There is another attempt to finally realise the idea to invite you for a workshop with the team about your approach to administration of artistic places. Would you still be up for engaging and sharing with us your perspectives and practice? There are not many dates possible, but as I'm curating the Research Center this block, and I'm looking at institutional impulses and their psychostases, it would be great to be able to realise this block!! Would there be any chance that you could come over for two days in June – if possible, the 19th and 20th?

Preliminary sketch for a workshop on administration at a.pass:

Day 1 – Organisational portraiture. Thinking with diagrams of organisational form: programme, practice and administration. How does this fit with a.pass programme & theoretical concerns?

Day 2 – Hypotheticals and practical applications. What would it mean to map a.pass teaching/research practices onto its administration? The reverse? To imagine 'administration' as an a.pass block or research strand?

In May 2017, I was pleased to receive an invitation to deliver a workshop – not in the programme of a.pass but in its infrastructure: to extend attention into the fabric, or more particularly the seams of organisation, the administrative structures that enable the programme to function. My notes from that workshop are carefully filed – that is to say, *lost in the shadows of time*. Accordingly, this report is assembled from afterthoughts, fragments of interviews recorded in the field, and some restless shapes that hum or move toward different ways of being administrative. As the impressions and speculations of a visitor, it will bear only a passing resemblance to a.pass. It is to be considered more of a fantasy or fairy tale, full of holes – an opportunity to think through conditions and contradictions of the *administration of artistic places* more widely, through a wild procession of allegories.

ADMINISTRATION – THE FINAL FRONTIER

In my visits to a.pass as an occasional mentor over the years, my imagination was drawn to the boundary lines that hold this uncommon space of possibility together. Its operating conditions contrast with the lurid tales one hears of life in the university art school, where a set of administrative demands and managerial styles has oozed into the teaching and research spaces, and staff resort to games of Vice Chancellor Bingo. *Get five in a row to win: adapt, challenge, innovate, care, pivot!, new normal, new university, staff exiting – BINGO.*

At a.pass, the programme remains largely untouched by such alien encounters. '*From the point of view of the university*', an agent of the a.pass pedagogical team goes on record to confirm, '*we are rather a free field*'.

I am interested in considering the firewalls, the shock absorbers of this protected territory. A spaceship perhaps, designed to defend its precious cargo from the radiation effects and cosmic detritus of contemporary education systems. So – where are the radiation suits?

VENTURING A DIAGRAM

I start with some basic geometric shapes. First, to imagine a simple shift or inversion of perspective that might also apply to other places of education and research, where the programme content – the art – resides on an inner ring while the administration faces the world.

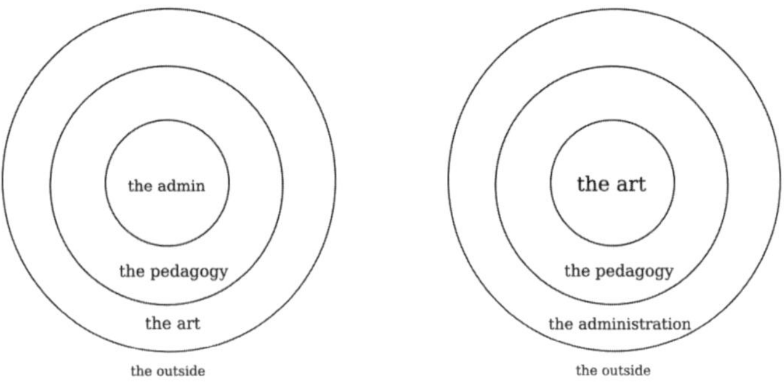

My interest in this rendering is not to model a whole system but to capture an impression of a singular entity: a portrait, not a model or a map. At the same time, its subject or sitter is not just the internal constitution of a.pass but its wider situation in the world, '*organism plus environment*' in the words of distinguished ecologist Gregory Bateson.[1]

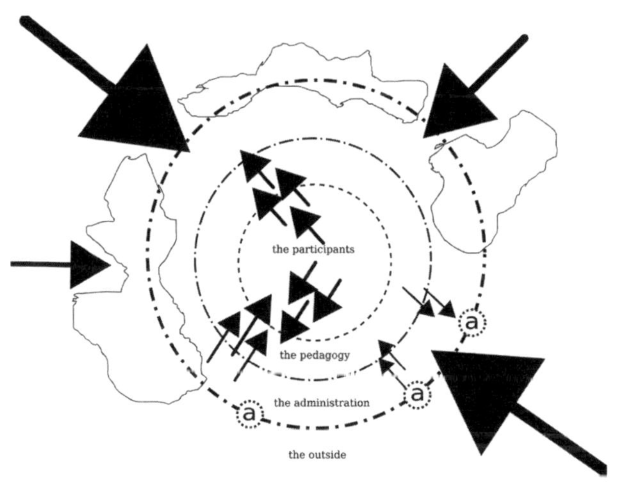

KEYS

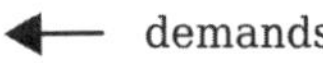

demands
administrator bodies
grey areas
----- re/movable barriers

The administration of artistic places is regularly formatted in the medium of demands. At a.pass, participants require assistance with their study visas, block curators need contracts for visiting artists and presenters, administrators need forms filled out. This internal economy is also in constant interaction with a host of entities and phenomena outside its own field: the Ministry of Education, the Bologna Process of higher education standards, the auditors, accountants and insurance brokers, the immigration controllers and the labour inspectors.

To take one perspective on the administrative layer or ring, it forms a strong boundary that protects a.pass pedagogy and practice from outside interference. *'It is the wall in which the whole project shelters',* as a member of a.pass pedagogical team reflects. At the same time, from the point of view of its inhabitants, it may be experienced as a place of osmosis and encounter, an interface.

EMULSIFICATION

For specific intelligence on how an interface between strong forces and unlike entities might operate, I turn to my own devices as an open source cola manufacturer.[2] At the heart of the cola-making process lies the technology of emulsification. The flavour oils that give cola its distinctive taste are hydrophobic, they repel water. Yet adding an emulsification agent (gum arabic, derived from the sap of the acacia tree) and applying sufficient force will produce an oil-in-water suspension in which nothing is substantively changed, except the potential to produce and even overcome the world's most powerful commodity drink from your own kitchen/workshop. Gum arabic forms the interface between otherwise antithetical substances: it 'holds hands' with the water and with the oils, enabling them to mingle, at least for a while. A catalysing entity, an essential player, yet one that is regularly overlooked in the global status and cultural admiration that cola enjoys.

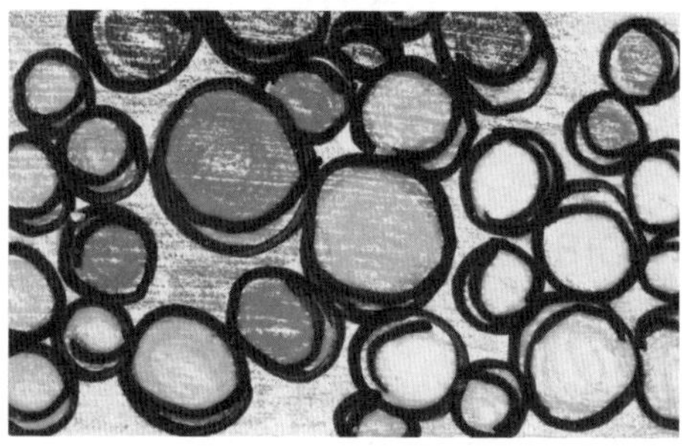

Emulsification: an oil-in-water suspension, the gum maintains the interface. Image credit: Morag Porteous

HOLDING THE FORT

I prefer to think of the administrators of artistic places as emulsifiers, agents that hold the interface between seemingly immiscible elements of art and bureaucracy, rather than enzymes. Enzymes are hyper-complex proteins whose critical contribution to food manufacturing is effectively erased. Unlike emulsifiers, the enzymes are not even listed on the food packaging. Rather they enter and leave the production space like ghosts,[3] they perform their magic of binding, stabilising and enhancing then get micro-filtered or centrifuged out, their transformative agency vanished from the end product.

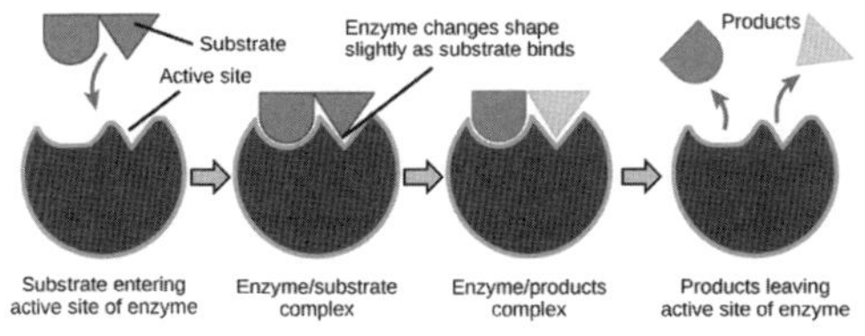

Enzyme. Image Credit: Khan Academy, CC BY 4.0

To delete or expunge the intermediaries from the frame, the elemental relations of support, as if art just appears on its own in a swoosh of creativity, is of course not what art is about. The practice of administration is integral to the arts ecosystem, not a service to be kept out of sight, filed away.

So – where are the art administrator symposia, residencies, reading groups, festivals,[4] publications,[5] superstars?[6] Or, if the tricks of the administrative trade are better not always made public, what are the underground circuits of knowledge, the administrator-led spaces and their support systems? What would be the circulatory channels, the handover mechanisms, the legacies?

Eminent anthropologist David Graeber, writing from the corridors of academic scholarship, a habitat crackling with administrative responsibilities, notes the curious lack of critical attention in academic writing to administration itself.[7] Graeber interprets this blindspot as a scholarly tendency to misconstrue what is interesting with what is important: to identify places of density with places of power, where the inverse may in fact be the case.

At the Cube Microplex, an all-volunteer run arts venue in Bristol (and my own administrative *alma mater*), the concept of 'radmin' – importing background activities of organising, processing, accounting and maintaining into the programme of events – is slowly gaining traction. Yet even there, the status and excitement of admin as a radical art form has still not entirely taken hold.

At this point in the research, due to poor preparation, the batteries of the field recorder go flat. After a lengthy search, batteries that are equally flat are unearthed by an agent of the a.pass pedagogical team. We then ask the a.pass administrative team, who locate some well-filed, brand new AA batteries in their office. The research resumes.

Maintenance art.[8] It is over 50 years since Mierles Laderman Ukeles made her celebrated move to install the work of *'renewing, supporting, preserving'* at the heart of the artistic process and yet still, we are here! Admin is almost universally bypassed as a subject of interest in research, as Graeber relates. It is also rarely considered by artists as part of the creative process. What if admin were embraced as constitutive to art practice, like learning about materials, reading up on theory or '*making visible the invisible*'?[9] Would the administrator class then appear less like protectors, combatants or providers but as fellow investigators in the field? What would it take to consider administration as also the research?

RESEARCH CULTURES

There are notable differences with the other kinds of research that a.pass cultivates, for example the particular focus of administration on problem-solving rather than '*problem-opening*', as a member of the a.pass pedagogical team described their work. Problem-solving is the habitat extraordinaire of the competent administrator. The a.pass pedagogical team set themselves up, quite reasonably, as unravellers of such instrumental logic. Given these distinctions, should we be thinking of the relationship between artists and administrators in terms of intercultural trade? Yet perhaps that concept is also a kind of mirage: to consider administration as a separate culture when 85% of any contemporary artist's time is spent on renaming jpegs. Might we instead call up the prophetic words of another celebrated artist, Joseph Beuys: *'everyone is an administrator'?*[10]

Or perhaps we could put aside the problematic binary identities of artist/administrator for a more entangled approach. For ideas I look to another, ancient protagonist of food science, the kefir grain, whose agency in making tasty carbonated beverages is second to none.[11] Neither a bacteria nor a yeast, the kefir grain is a symbiotic community of both. Submerged overnight in milk or other liquids, its transformational capacities will produce a beneficial and highly digestible fermented kefir drink, with its own unique culture. With the kefir grain as our emblem, could we imagine a symbiotic culture of art and administration, as a new area of advanced research?

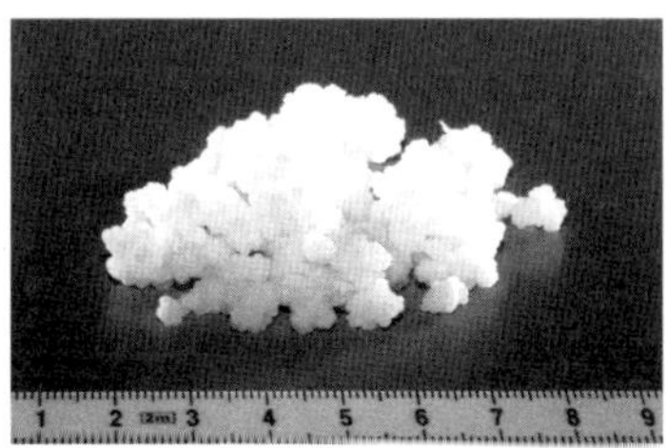

Kefir grain, a symbiotic matrix. Image credit: A. Kniesell, CC BY-SA 3.0

Can we move from the demands into the possibilities? An agent of the a.pass administration team delights us with tales from the grey zones of regulatory systems. She is instigating collaborations with the legislators and the regulators, negotiating agreements with the payroll company, legal services and formulating creative ideas for new forms of paperwork that safeguard a.pass' resilience. In this picture, grey areas[12] are not just places of hazard but their own operating field, in which other kinds of research, relations and culture can also grow.

It makes me wonder if the places of density that artists, anthropologists and other thrill-seekers thrive on, with their intricate symbolism, social dramas and poetic forms, are really missing from the work of administration, or in fact, it's just a trick of the light.

'Maybe there is something in the lack of optics in grey zones, being murky or opaque, that fills them with possibility', another administrative agent, the editor of this text, suggests. *'If the desire for visibility is about gaining power or agency, then maybe the grey zone is another kind of visibility that doesn't subject administrators to the direct light of regulating bodies'.*

It's a good point, and I briefly consider adding a light source to the a.pass administrative diagram, but it exceeds my graphic design skills so I leave that to your imagination.

ADMINISTRAART: AN UNDER-OCCUPIED SPACE RIPE FOR FURTHER COLLABORATIONS

On Wed., May 21, 2018, Z wrote:
Dear P, Dear all,

As I am the one dealing with a.pass production costs, I take the floor.

It seems there has been some confusion, or even better, three lines of communication: For me, the first being me and X saying Kate's (4th) visit was not charged to a.pass as she would be here for a lecture. The second being the Kate and P one in which P confirmed to Kate that her travel expenses would be paid for. And then the Y and P one which seems to be the one causing confusion as there were assumptions made from both sides about the logistics.

What I would like to mention is that Kate's fourth visit would not have been planned by us had we known we had to pay for travel. Nevertheless, she's here now doing a lecture and mentoring. For which all are happy!

Meanwhile, I prefer to see between P and I what to do as there is also Kate's stay to take into account. As we host tomorrow's lecture and workshop, I hope we get the time before or after to exchange a few words. I will assist during the lecture but not stay for the workshop.

Have a good evening and see you tomorrow,
Kind regards.

Z

1 Gregory Bateson, *Steps to an Ecology of Mind: Collected Essays in Anthro pology , Psychiatry, Evolution, and Epistemology,* Chandler Publishing Company, 1972.

2 Cube-Cola, *Standing on the Hands of Giants,* http://cube-cola.org

3 Frederick Kaufman, *The Secret Ingredient: Keeping the World, Kosher.* Harper's Magazine, 2005, pp. 75-81.

4 RADMIN, 2019, *A Festival of Administration* https://cubecinema.com/pages/radmin

5 Live Art Development Agency, *Managing the Radica*l, 2020 https://thisisliveart.co.uk/resources/managing-the-radical-2020; Angela Piccini and Kate Rich (eds) RADMIN Reader 2020 https://fo.am/publications/radmin-reader-2020

6 https://barbarasteveni.org/Work-APG-Artist-Placement-group

7 David Graeber, *The Utopia of Rules: On Technology, Stupidity and the Secret Joys of Bureaucracy,* Melville House, 2015.

8 *Maintenance Art Manifesto* https://artpractical.com/uploads/docs/5.4-Ukeles_MANIFESTO.pdf

9 Francis Whitehead, 2006, *What do artists know?*

10 https://tate.org.uk/art/artworks/beuys-joseph-beuys-every-man-is-an-artist-ar00704

11 https://kefirwala.in/what-are-kefir-grains

12 FoAM *Dark Arts and Grey Areas* https://techniquesjournal.com/dark-arts-grey-areas-and-other-contingencies

Part III

PLAY

It’s all about practice!

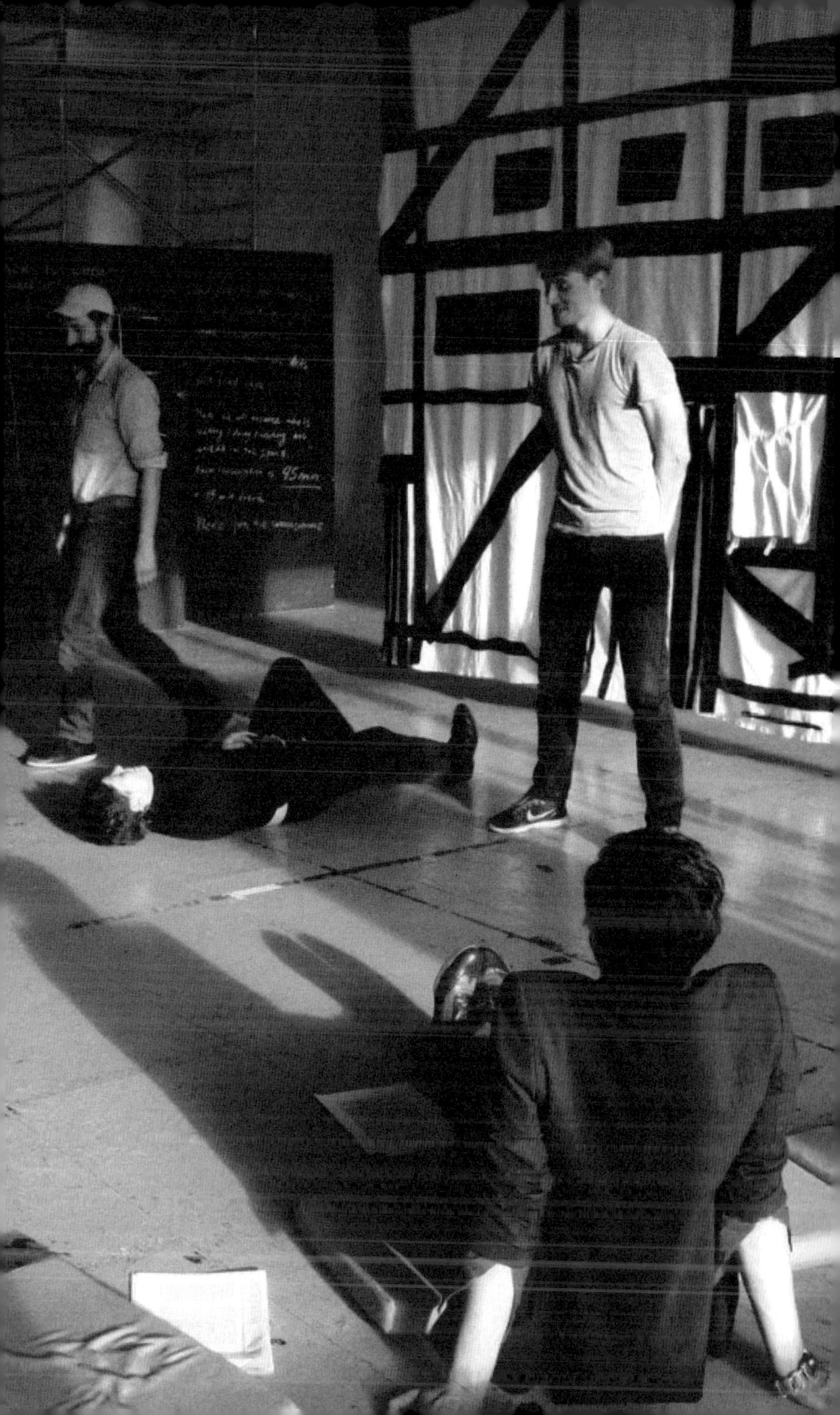

Rui Calvo

Filming Bodies without Characters

I came to a.pass with a background in cinema. Busy with notions of fiction and drama, I had one main question: How to film bodies without imprisoning them in rational discourse whilst rejecting the logic of confirmation, belonging and psychology? At a.pass, I met performers with different backgrounds that engaged in doing and thinking with me. Throughout the trajectory, I created instructions that played out in film settings without a fictional background to situate the performers, and as such do not build a character. The performers and their relationships, in front of the camera, were being constantly constructed in an ongoing situation. They received the instructions right before filming and, once the shooting started, I recorded uninterruptedly for one or two hours. The actions, lines and stories were repeated many times, perpetually rearranged and rearticulated. The production of fiction was unstable and influenced by the shooting process itself, in which the performers hovered between being characters and themselves, opening a space for subjectivity beyond identity.

CAMERA

The camera must make the intrusion of filming more noticeable:

- Enhance the camera's potential to interfere with the performers' acting; facilitating or threatening what is being produced.
- Open the possibility for the performers to experience a different embodiment by the intersection of context and camera.
- Look for (and at) uncomfortable physical responses to the act of being 'caught', 'captured', or to the feeling of being 'unmasked' by the camera.
- Keep alive the negotiation between performers, camera and filmmaker.
- Maintain the negotiation between what I see, what I feel about it, what I would like to produce.

PERFORMERS

Andrea Zavala Folache
caterina daniela mora jara
Diego Echegoyen
Flávio Rodrigo
Lilia Mestre
Lucia Palladino
Sara Manente

MAKING THE INSTRUCTIONS

The instructions must create the conditions for something to emerge, for under-narratives,[1] for the articulation of new meanings. They must have one or more of the following qualities:

- Produce repetition.
- Depend on personal interpretation according to the performer's own feelings and opinions.
- *Don't depend* on personal interpretation, opinions, or feelings; the performers do it and immediately afterwards they must process what happened, they are not protected by a character context.
- Demand attention to find the cue; the right moment to do it.
- Divert attention or shift the way attention is given to something.
- Interfere in the flow of the action and/or the narration.
- Activate an otherness ('Is it me who did it or not?').
- Demand the knitting of stories (the self does not produce fiction, but is instead produced by fiction); personal stories are mingled with instructions and move towards fiction.

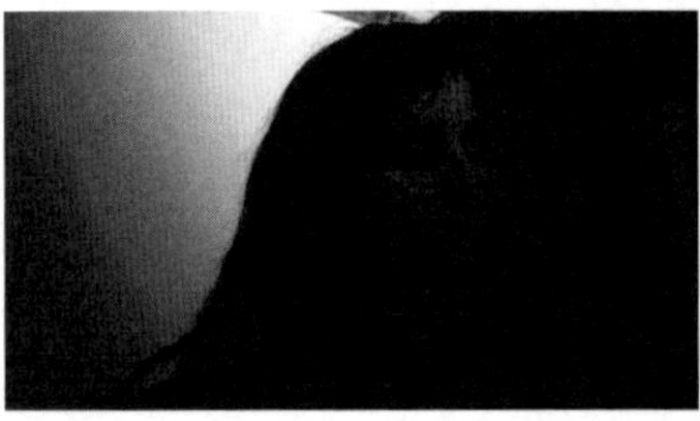
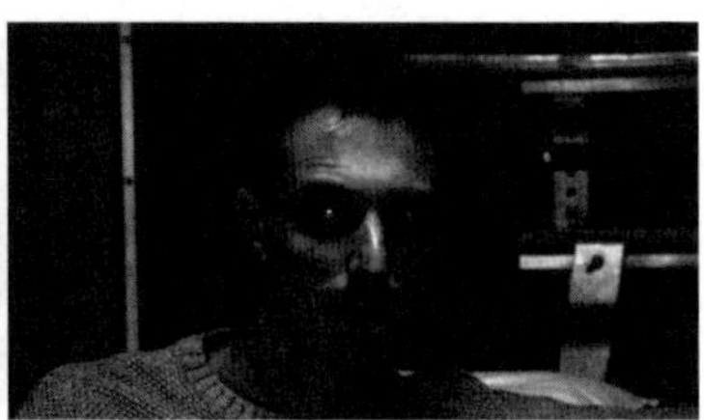

The instructions must allow for:

- Vulnerability.
- Banality: empty the image. Emotions are constructions, feelings that have become labeled and have been attached to.
- Overdramatic reactions: the banal and the overdramatic as ways of approaching the subjects otherwise.
- Impunity: because it's fiction.
- Shame: actually, it's not fiction! According to Eve Kosofsky Sedgwick, shame is 'the affect that mantles the threshold between introversion and extroversion, between absorption. and theatricality, between performativity and – performativity'.
- Contingency.
- Negativity and ways of confronting it: misconstruction, frustration, becoming defensive and feeling misunderstood.
- Opacity.

---

1 When a narrative is disrupted by the ostensive presence of the camera or by the result of instructions given to the performers, rearrangements and rearticulations are made in the improvisation, a story is no longer about one performer or one character, which opens space for under-narratives.

FILMING IS VIOLENT, THE INSTRUCTIONS ARE VIOLENT, EDITING IS VIOLENT

The way I use the camera, in addition to the instructions played out by the performers, make the violence that is inherent to filming more visible. There is violence done by the framing of bodies, by allowing the spectator to see what the performers see and also by watching the seeing, which the performers can't.
I also try to produce violent acts. As you will see, one kind of instruction is related to insulting. According to Didier Eribon, an insult is 'a way of looking me over and a way of dispossessing me. My consciousness is "beleaguered by others" and I am disarmed by this aggression'. Moreover, it is 'a linguistic act – or a series of repeated linguistic acts – by which a particular place in the world is assigned to the person at whom the acts are directed'.[2] One aim of these instructions is to produce a personal identity out of an assigned identity imposed by the social order, shaping it from within. At the same time, how much are the violent thoughts and acts already embedded in the performers?

There is also violence in the stories that the performers are asked to tell. Moreover, violence is present because none of the performers know the others' instructions, so there's a tension of not knowing who has instructions that demand disrespect or aggression, nor what they might do with them: a dynamic of glances is played-out between performers.

All this makes the performers have to admit some aggression and to move within dissatisfaction, vulnerability, exposure to the other and to the camera, ongoing rupture, misunderstanding and indeterminacy, which disrupts the narrative's causality. This is produced in the very moment of shooting and it's not just a work of editing. When I edit the material, and the context (either real or fictive) is more unclear, the cuts become more prominent; every cut becomes an ellipse and the spectator has the feeling that something is missing. The ellipse can be violent, but it also calls into question the surveilling eyes of the spectators.

---

2 Didier Eribon, *Insult and the Making of the Gay Self*, Duke University Press, 1999.

INSTRUCTIONS FOR THE PERFORMERS

SHOOTING DAY 01

Everyone but Lilia Mestre
- You cannot be the first to say something.

Lilia
- First sentence you should say: 'I realised that when you socially don't notice the violence, it is because you do it'.
- Take notes.

caterina daniela mora jara
- What are the others hiding or showing/revealing?
- Say, 'Stop that acting'.
- Always look non-stop at the one who speaks.

Flávio Rodrigo
- Always start speaking using 'I'.
- Hit the table to get attention or interrupt someone.

Lucia Palladino
- Repeat the sentence until it is understood or you are convinced that you were understood.
- When someone says something, stare at him/her for a while.

(In the first shooting, they talked about how to recognise violence and one of them told a personal story. On a train, she and her boyfriend sat in front of another couple who were a little bit older. They said, 'Can we sit?' and right after the other couple left and sat somewhere else. It felt like a very weird and violent act of exclusion. 'What does it do to suddenly have someone refusing your existence? I think it's because we are just... I mean, we are fifty years old and we look... I don't know. I think we are not... we didn't correspond'.)

SHOOTING DAY 04

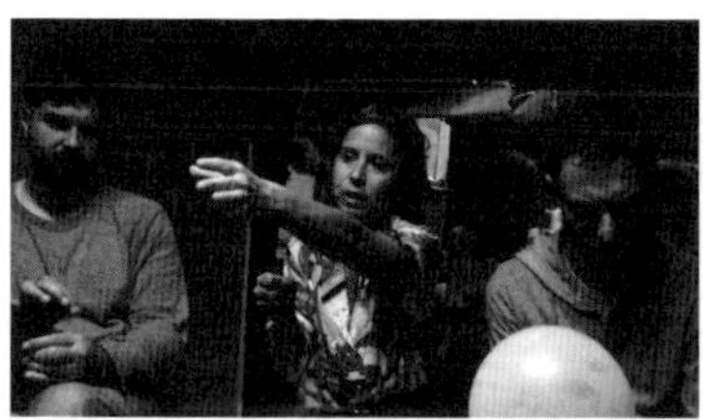
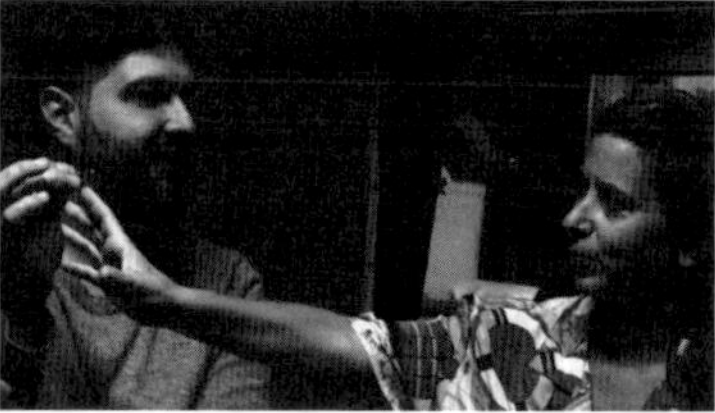

Lucia

- Tell the story about violence that you told in the first video, making only important gestures in order to explain it. Stay clear-eyed in the scene of *violence*, repeat the story giving more details, creating facts, trying to communicate.

Flávio

- Describe the gestures and behaviour of Lucia and imitate them.

Diego Echegoyen

- Ask about *the other* involved in Lucia's story, imagining this role in the story.
- Play with a balloon.
- Ask Lucia many times: 'Is it violent?'

(Lucia repeated the story while Diego was busy playing with a balloon without clear meaning in the context, and Flávio was imitating her but not concerned with the content of what was being told. The repetition, focused on negotiating the situation full of misunderstandings between them, created conditions for something to emerge from this narrative's opacity.)

SHOOTING DAY 06

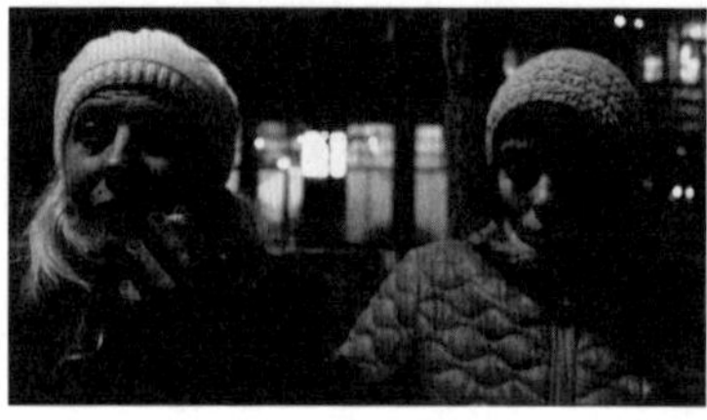
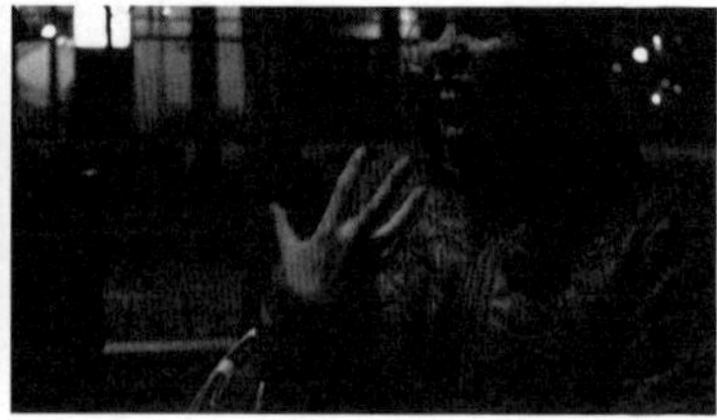

caterina
- Tell the train story as if it had happened to you.
- Touch Lilia.
- Repeat some of Lilia's words.
- Smile a lot.

Lilia
- Tell caterina that the story didn't happen the way she's telling it.
- Ask caterina to choose an insult against a woman and then repeat it.
- Describe people who pass on the streets and their behaviour.

(The train story didn't belong anymore to the performer who experienced this story. Due to this, there was a clear production of fiction allowing the performers to move more freely in an undefined boundary between reality and fiction.)

SHOOTING DAY 11

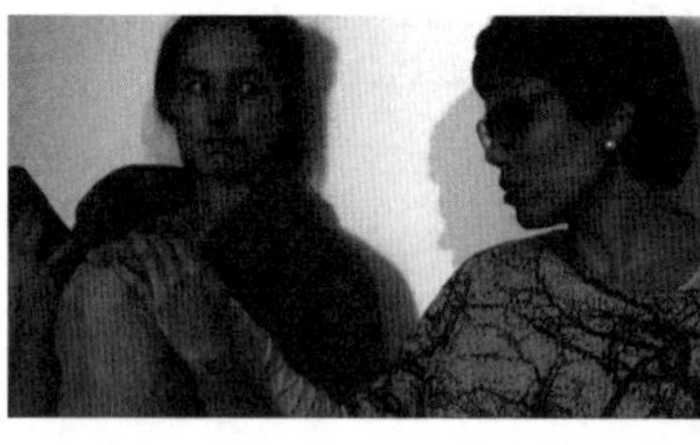
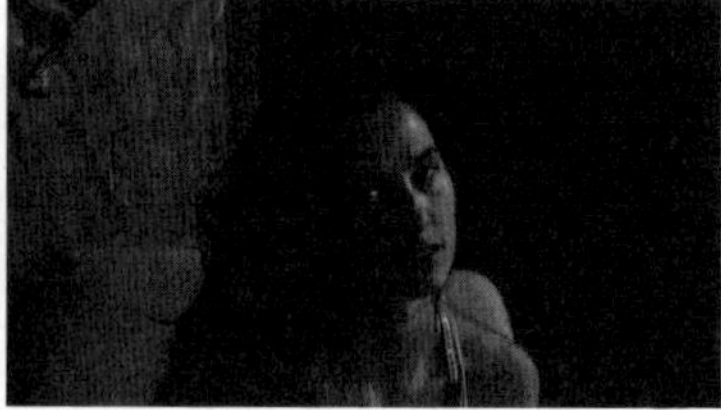

Andrea Zavala Folache
- Before saying anything, tear your clothes. Take the time you want.
- Go through the curtain or corridor and come back sometimes. In silence in the beginning and... when you can speak, you ask Lilia or cate if they're ok, if they want something to drink.

- Tell a mysterious and violent story (repeat it sometimes, trying to be understood, remembering or inventing more details around the mystery).
- Record an audio message to someone. Repeat it in different moments, trying to improve the content of the message, voice etc., (the person for whom the message is addressed should feel the importance of the message.) Say: 'Hi... hi... talk to me...'
- The first time you say something should be an audio message. Take your time.
- Ask Lilia which words are the most violent insults for her. Then, use these words sometimes when you talk.

caterina
- You cannot be the first to speak.
- Tell the train story as if it had happened to you. Repeat it, giving more details, trying to understand how it affects you.
- Touch Andrea.
- Look non-stop at Andrea when she speaks.
- You think Andrea is hiding something.
- When Lilia bends her body towards the ground, hug her and whisper some words.
- Say, 'stop that acting' when you can.

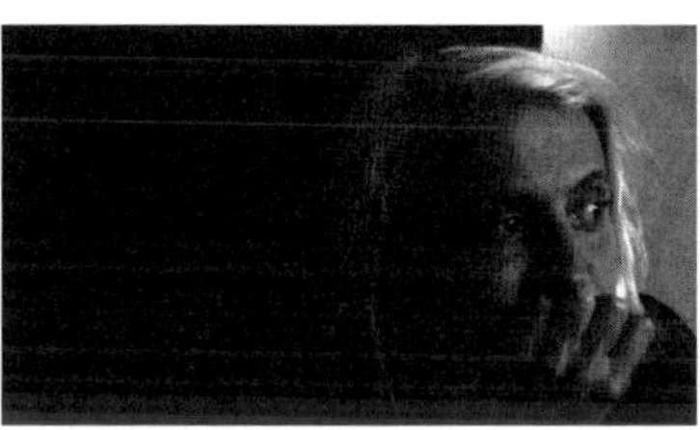

Lilia
- You cannot be the first to speak.
- Laugh whenever you can in different ways.
- When you have something complicated to say, breathe faster and rub your head.
- Pay attention to cate's gestures and behaviour, describing what they mean to you and questioning her.
- Sometimes bend your body towards the ground.
- Read the news on the table (NOT out loud). Sometimes you talk about a detail of it that stays in your mind (ex.: Why did they enter shooting? Her mother wrote to him...)

QUOTES FROM AN INTERVIEW WITH THE PERFORMERS

LM: It's about interfering, the possibility of interfering, as well as dislocating what's happening. (...) I think we are on standby and then things start to happen. There are quite some ruptures. The instructions are my guidelines to interfere.

CM: But for me the agency is more related to how much I can push the rule, how much the rule resists. My agency is kind of being as obedient as possible.

LM: I do feel vulnerable. There's nothing bad, I never felt bad, neither trapped. Neither did I want to interfere. There's something there that is supporting these actions or these qualities that you are naming. So I also feel confident that I can feel vulnerable. Sometimes I think it's needed, somehow I'll work for that, to try to be in that place of vulnerability.

AZF: Cheating is totally inscribed in the rules. I am given enough information to know I can't know all the rules. So there's an impossibility for me to know everything, you know, to hold all the information of the rules. So then there's gaps of interpretation that opens up a... Maybe that's also for the agency, a sense of being able to interpret and cheat.

AZF: If I would be an actress following a script, people would know I'm a character. So it's sort of excused in a way. And here, because part of the script is taken out or something, it's almost like I'm playing Andrea so I am close to reality. People don't know how I am playing with fiction actually; the fictions that I play for myself are not totally visible. Then that kind of unappointed fiction or undefined fiction is what is the most violent within the work.

CM: It often happens that I'm kind of surprised in my interior. It's a bit shocking because the camera is there, not far away. Depending on how this surprise is, I'm also trying to integrate it.

CM: The most violent is the editing, when I see how it's also manipulated afterward.

LM: I think it is very hard to repeat actually. Spontaneous is maybe more 'ok', you just throw yourself, let's try this. But then in repeating you have to think twice. And then I think, in a way, it's there that the work starts. Like how do you say it, and then maybe sometimes you just say it half-way... There's a lot of practice there. (...) I think it creates a certain intimacy, maybe not intimacy, but history. Like I've been there before. I've heard it before. I've heard you say that before. I'm not telling that story myself. There is something that builds a common history.

CM: [repetition] creates a condition that escapes, it's escaping from the successes and failures, another condition of doing it. It doesn't have to succeed because it doesn't have to fail. It creates a condition to navigate.

AZF: It's like a level of being hyperaware, of self-awareness, alertness maybe, surveillance, I don't think I forgot at any point that there was a camera.

LM: In a way I think it [the camera] becomes a character, there's also Rui there. It's also intrusive in a way, like, 'I'm looking at this, I'm interested in that'.

MUSLIN BROTHERS
Tamar Levit & Yaen Levi

oversized, overlooked and over the shoulder

A poetic investigation through the prisms of fear and desirability, into clothes worn in and next to correctional facilities.

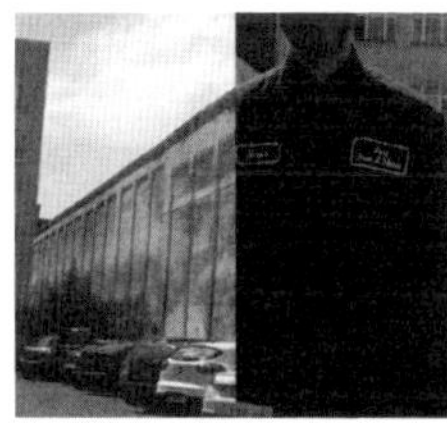

I

in the yard surrounded by weary orange
set-complet suits

and dragged feet on corben rubber black
sole sneakers,

chronicles of details,

chosen, protocoled, functional,
superstitionalised

being documented by handwritten notes
a soft story is told through protagonist
details,

fostering a docile body,

cxhibiting the proud soul: no room to
place innocent palms in pocketless pants,

illegally self-tapered sleeve pressed
against a bicep

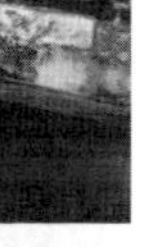

cleavages are as deep as their non-sexual
potential

one-size-fits-none pants with elastic
bands

that stretch, stress and span

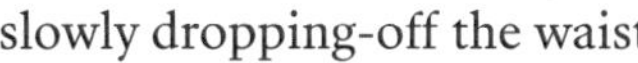

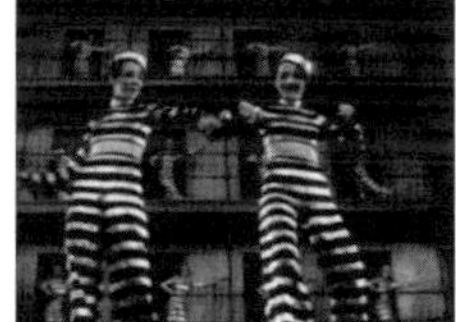

slowly dropping-off the waist

to ultimately/illegally suspend on the hips
prisons are ambivalent, speaking

the language of rationality and efficiency
when in fact they are in charge of a
ceremonial cleansing of the soul.

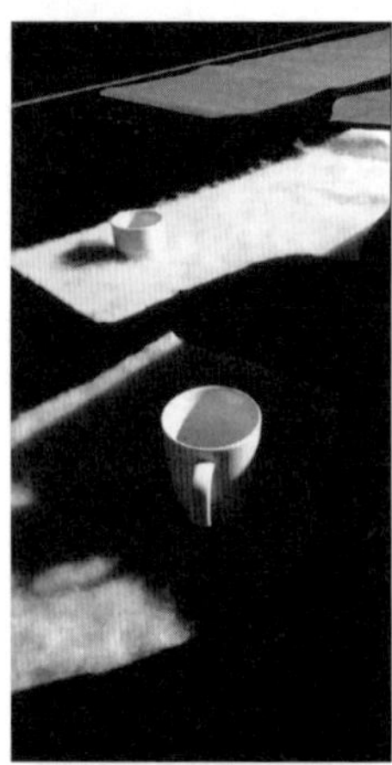

II

On the black linoleum floor dance we were,

surrounded by generic objects
white IKEA porcelain tea cup smashed
on top of uniform, reverse engineered:
taken apart and exhibited in forms of their making

uniform sewn and buttoned-up, stuffed
with foam

next to flat cuts of synthetic lining acrylan
(like an itchy cloud)

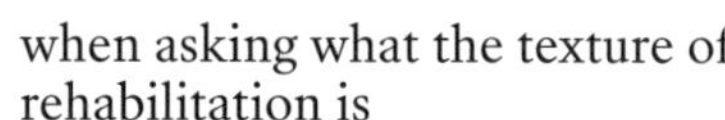

when asking what the texture of
rehabilitation is

more than a few said a porous-sponge-like
material that

can rearrange itself next to the body

restaging a limbo-esque space,

down by a ladder, all of us laid-down and gazed

at a high wavy ceiling, a projection

slowly appearing letter by letter, statements in a loop

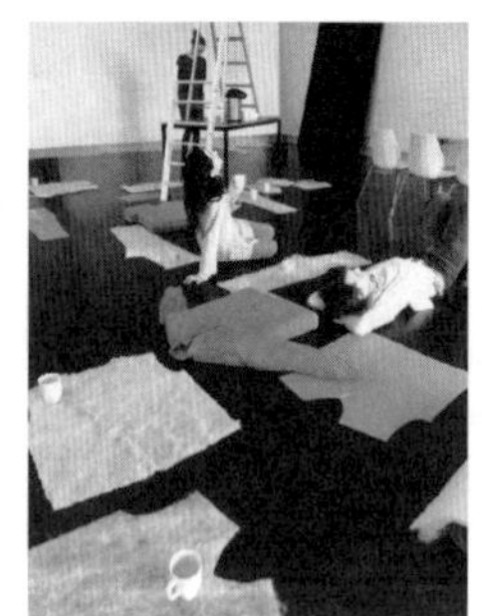

of anonymous people who are doing time
future or past were held in words of
expectations or memories

what covers will one wear on their
release day

what texture one's skin will never more

rehearsing the installation manifests
to watch the way the space makes the body
perform,
take (a)part (rearrange)

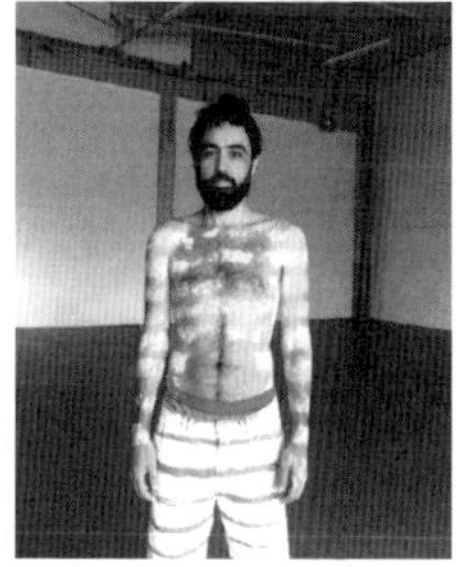

rehearsing the installation manifests

by writing the way the objects perform
for us,

take (a)part (rearrange)

rehearsing the installation manifests
by observing if the body remembers the
order of objects

manifests

axes of time and space in a dimension of
participation,

on the black linoleum dance floor we were
with shoes on.

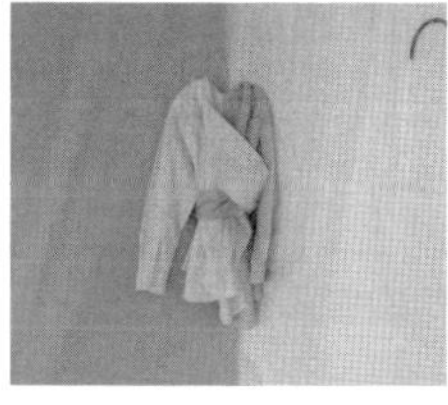

III

from the projection to the prayer book
when reading words of others, the narrative

appears in one's mind, portrayed by one's
own voice

hence, the telling of a dress' tale are retold
attuned,

whispering confessions while fitting
mending bodies and their covers at the
same time

it is embarrassing
you take off your clothes
we are close to you
we are doing our job
you need to feel correct
we touch your body

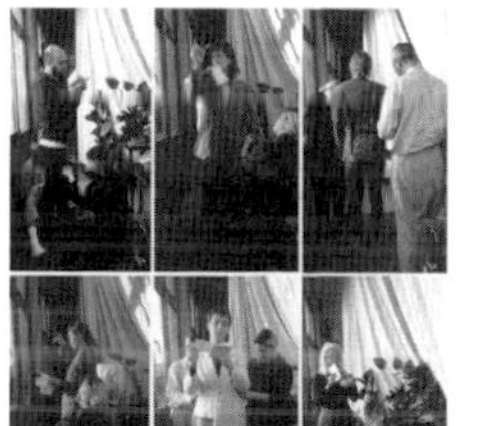

we tighten the fabric around your body

extracting a reaction

you tell us what's on your mind

we pause and look in the mirror

no… not sure…

are you satisfied, we ask, what would you

want?

but we, know better

(what you need)

let's try again

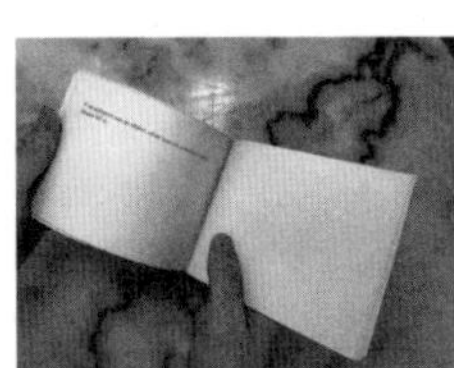

we ask you to hold still please

we snip, we trim, we cut

reflecting on what this cut reminds you of

how it makes you feel

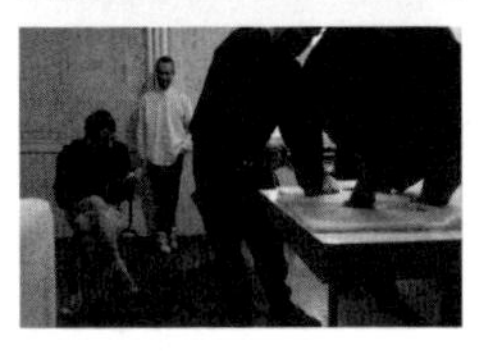

transaction has been made

we exchanged information services and
greetings

you thank us and we thank you

hoping you won't change your mind in the
coming days

you are free to rejoin society
you are reformed

IV

then all the world went under lockdown

suddenly we are/were all in confinement

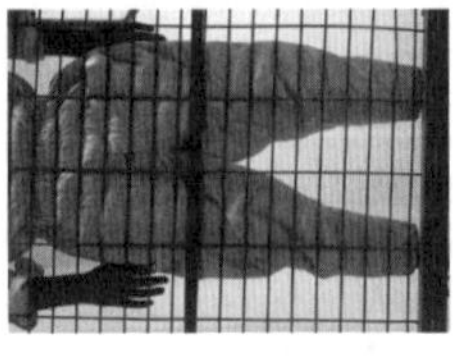

bodies and clothes and time are
distancing from societal encounters,

outlining experiences of wearing

an unchanged unwashed jersey sweatshirt

these are too convenient,

and yet, continuous decision making of
clothing is being made, all

who are seen and imagined, all who are
participating in fashion

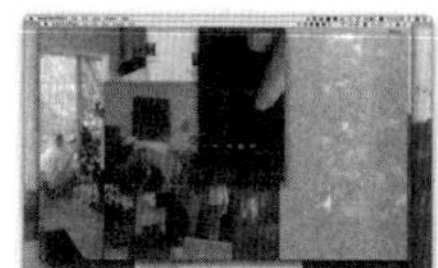

we are in collecting and assembling mode,

our screens are surveying our cells,

our phones slowly scan our skins,

our conversations direct our bodies to
reflect in a mirror

a stream of consciousness allows itself to
be singularly screencast

on broken timeline multi-layered,
disagreed,

texturised,

rewarding the mind for knowing what day
it is

digging a day's earning in the ground,
reserved 'could haves'

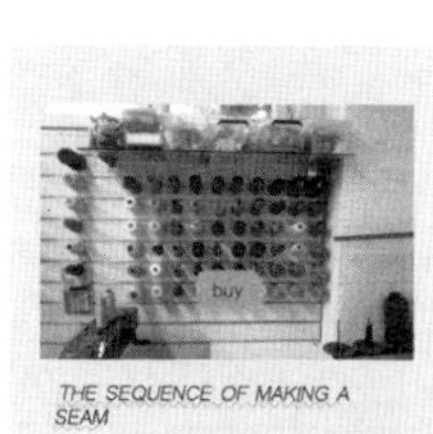

THE SEQUENCE OF MAKING A SEAM

or 'must haves'

like holes, but on the body,

trying and saving some for later,
(instinctively)

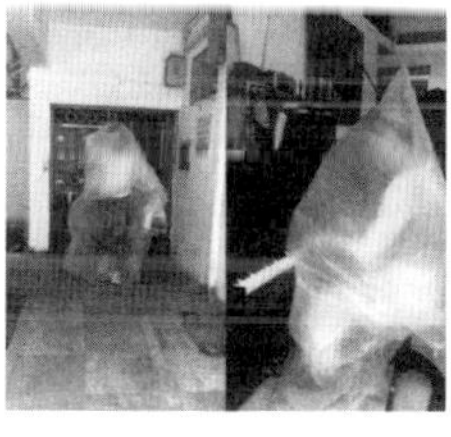

like holes, but pockets

are full with dopamine,

striding the streets in slo-mo for the
catwalk finalé.

Laura Pante
Pierre Rubio

Your Blood is Streaming, My Wifi is Dreaming

Working session on pedagogy, agency and performative matter

PR: Laura, today will be our first official working session. We will follow the same procedure as with Sina Seifee and Vanja Smiljanić. First of all, we will focus on the short text and the list of questions that I have written and sent to you. Then, you react? These two texts set out some of the points I have been thinking about in relation to my work in a.pass and the participants' projects. It is the first step towards a conversation between Sina, Vanja and your objects of concern, a dialogue between yours and my goals, our singular modes of artistic research and curatorial practices, our technologies, our historical references, between the questions we ask ourselves and the problems we encounter.

LP: All right, then. Can you read your text and the questions out loud? I'll take written notes and then I can answer you.

PR: Ok, I'll read, but I'll also comment from time to time to start connecting with your work or some situations you have experienced at a.pass.

LP: Let's go!

PR: First the short text. Actually it's not really a text, it's more an assemblage of keywords... I will read: *'In a.pass, I have been busy with proposing a series of collectively structured co-learning environments which reflect on the multiple artistic research projects (developed in this context of collective work) as non-stable and non-autonomous operative and performative complex objects'.*

Laura, this first sentence is about the proposals that I put in play as 'curator' at a.pass, but it's also a tentative definition of how I 'read' research and artistic projects. In fact, I did propose structures that sometimes looked like a school, sometimes like a radio, and so on, as fictional environments for displacing the participants' projects slightly and to reflect their non-stable nature and their transformative complexities. I thought that complex transformative objects needed complex displacing contexts. I believe that individual projects, whether research and/or artistic, are complex arrangements of energies, information, forms, statements, and so on... and they are always in process, able to change. And if they are changing in themselves, the artistic research projects also have the capacity to operate changes of the context in which they are developing. Thus, I thought I had to propose contexts for these possible inter-changes to happen, to be noticed and reflected upon. Will that resonate with your work, Laura, in any way?

'What kind of code is embedded in your language? What kind of code is there in your dance? What kind of code is written on the dark side of your interface?'[1]

I go on: *'Within these collective environments, artistic research projects were identified as also possibly individuating principles and considered to be generating new epistemologies, taking and giving shape to a general intellect that feedbacked upon itself.'* Laura, for example, I believe that your party-like installation-performance *No House No place No Space*, created an opportunity for us to individuate ourselves differently than if there had been no party at all. Your project/event created some conditions for a part of our identities, our subjectivities, or our construction-as-individuals, to be re-routed in a way because your 'party' was part of a collective intellect-in-the-making that we were part of as well. This 'general intellect' was influencing us as much as we were influencing it. Do you play, Laura, with the notion of general intellect?

I continue: *'Through different slightly fictionalised forms that were always collectively organised, the individual artistic research was activated as generative fields for creating experimental tools, different modes of knowing and interfaces for collective learning and apprenticeship. The apparatuses thereby developed a form of resistance by questioning capitalist standards of art and research production, namely commodification, individualisation, disciplinary determination and hierarchical structures.'* For example, if everybody is given the opportunity to teach, then everybody is considered potentially as a master and the teacher's position does shift. And if everything is in a process of exchange and gift, then there is less to be acquired and privatised. Or, if there is a space of attention left for transdisciplinary 'objects' that are ungraspable or difficult to grasp, then the labelling obsession is diffused. Echoing that, Laura, I wish you could tell me about the different political and ethical standpoints and consequences of some of the five different performative situations/events that you proposed in a.pass.

Then: *'The pedagogical and research environments I proposed in a.pass emphasised transindividual mediations and operated as communication fields between artist-researchers-individuals-as-milieus and their projects and...'* I pause my reading here to point out three keywords that are important: 'mediations', 'communication fields' and 'milieus'. How can projects be considered as complex milieus that are interlinked and have transformative powers on each other? As an example, again, your 'party' was particularly complex, and particularly enjoyable for me to attend as you and your team proposed a transindividual critical communication field which was a challenging multi-layered and intricate structure.

LP: It was a response to the thematic you proposed: to reflect on our projects through the notion of interface.

PR: Yes, there were a lot of interfacing methods and modes of interfacing in the 'party'. I am interested to know what your specific relationship was with the notion of interface in the work you have developed at a.pass and how do you understand it today.

I go on: *'...communication fields between artist-researchers' projects and the collective milieu that they collectively formed to actualise their works' potential in tension with possible cultural changes'.* So, Laura, it is also about constructing another future, no? A political positioning aimed at proposing other forms of being together, other modes of relating with the environment, other cultures of collaboration... Are the participatory art forms that you propose future-oriented, and what is your relation to the present and the past?

And the last sentence: *'The concepts animating the structures were also methods'.* Although this has become second nature in artistic research and in the human sciences now, bringing into play concepts and methods as potentially the same thing is not obvious. I think it should be looked at more closely to understand the consequences. Laura, I believe you have things to say about this. What is your formula for articulating concepts with methods?

---

1 All bold quotes are by Laura Pante from two participatory events/performances she organised at a.pass in 2018. *No House No Place No Space* (performance text) and *Screenshot* (communication flyer).

'What degree of propaganda is contained in the production and use of body images to which we are subjected by our exposure to digital and media virtuality?'

Now, let's read the preliminary questions that I shared with Vanja and Sina as well. I will read and also comment in the same way, to start bridging with your work/ propositions.

First question: *'In a collective environment, crowded with processes developing artistic practices and research, how is an individual idea generated and what consequences does it have on the collective in return? And what is the nature and power of feedback, in the context of artistic research, when information is individually but also collectively developed?'.* In other words, Laura, how does information loop from your point of view?

Then: *'What are the genealogies of generative processes that constitute information that is in turn constitutive? Beyond the intention to fabricate, that structures an individual project, what is the role of the singularities necessarily produced by chance through encounters in a collective environment?'.* For instance, Laura, you decided to build up a form of 'party', that you named *No House No Place No Space*, but in the meantime, you met Elen Braga. By chance, Elen Braga and her work were there, interacting with others within your 'party' project. It was totally controlled, and also not controlled at all, because there was a random factor that was part of the composition of these circumstances. So what is the nature and function of randomness for you? When and how does randomness operate beyond your intention to fabricate?

LP: Ok...

PR: A more speculative question now:
'If random encounters are not only the cause of the becoming-project of a research, because the individuation process of this research is not a simple effect of these encounters could we then say that the research project is also a milieu and an agent of the encounters?' For instance, could we say that your research provoked the singularity that was the collaboration with Elen Braga for the 'party' event? It's not only that you met Elen Braga and it became a singularity that affected your project, but you or your project was compatible enough for Elen Braga to become a possible operating singularity. Your project created Elen Braga as a singularity as much as your project was influenced by Elen. This sounds a bit science-fiction but it is also very pragmatic.
I believe this is how things happen in collective artistic and research contexts. What exactly are the inter-activities and inter-dependencies of your ideas and projects made of? How does that work for you, Laura?

Then, the last batch of questions around the issue of artistic research generating matters and forms: *'At the level of projects themselves, what are the implicit forms contained in their very materials?'* I have to explain that a bit. Laura, imagine you want to kill some animals because you need to eat. You have to fabricate a bow. Not all kinds of trees will provide the appropriate material, there is a specific kind of wood that you need to get for the elasticity that is required for a functional bow. So you need to discriminate and find the tree in which you can fabricate a bow that works. So, in the matter of that tree, the form of the bow is already there. The matter is not inert and passive, it contains implicit forms. So, if we fold this model to the participatory forms of research/performance like the ones you generated at a.pass, what are the consequences? For example, if we take *No House No Place No Space* – the 'party' – not as a form but as a matter, which implicit forms were already there? Convivial encounter? Crazy dance party? Delicious collective dinner... Joyful entertaining event? These were some of the implicit forms generated by the material 'party'. What kind of a relationship did you develop with these to achieve the final form of the event? It was called a 'party' but was it really a party? We danced and ate, yes, but we were also a bit puzzled by the event's structure, we were invited to think, and so on and so forth... Did you resist the implicit forms that were contained in this party-as-idea?

LP: You go too fast! I write notes at the same time... What is the last batch of questions again?

PR: Sorry, I over-commented maybe...
The last questions are: *'Which implicit forms are generated by forms of research considered as non-passive materials?'* and *'What implicit forms are generated by artistic practices in the form of conversations, databases, workshops, convivial parties, rituals, meals?'* and *'How do artists and researchers position themselves towards these implicit forms?'*
and that's it. The reading is over. I'm throwing these questions at you like a bottle in the sea. How do they resonate?

LP: I wrote down some points so we can go through them. With some distance, what I was busy with during my time at a.pass, is getting more clear and at this moment I am working on a PhD, so let's see how all the elements I would like to talk about could possibly gather into this dialogue. So, following the first question about the generation of ideas in collective artistic research environments and their consequences, I wrote down: '*institutional critique*'. My attitude was one of an institutional critique of the very possibility of a collective environment and a destabilisation of any tendency to define a specific methodology, or better, a specific style. Then, around the second question, about the nature and power of feedback, my work in a.pass was similar to the description you gave just now when elaborating on my proposals. I am very much into feedbacking and how information creates loops. The practices I'm looking for are written in a way to contain the possibility to build up a feedbacking process. Not a postponed feedbacking process, but rather one where the feedback is within the practice itself. The practices I am looking for are a sort of feedback actually, and it implies technique. It questions technique as well but it depends on the language chosen and how the practices are structured. We will talk about that later, ok? Then, about your question of genealogies of generative processes constituting information, I have a remark. More than genealogy, I am now developing a concept of a cycling epistemology and this is what I was generating at a.pass already. Cycling epistemology is the name I give to the movement and structure of the type of practices I have developed. This name prefigures a metabolic behaviour of the practice itself that begins and ends at the same point at the same time, as if it was spinning on itself generating a recursive loop. I was building up this idea of a cyclical epistemology when I literally built up a bicycle. It was a pedagogic and didactic first experiment of the cycling epistemology.

‘The bicycle machine functions as a mythological machine, that is, trains the body to produce the necessary energy to bring into view an image and shows the mechanism of its own production in terms of both aesthetic and political experience’.

PR: This idea of challenging the knowledge order and the linearity of time through the creation of ad-hoc technologies, makes me think of the pedagogical proposal ‘A Blind Graft’ that you performed in nature, using the mask-with-one-eye. It was a very interesting pseudo-technology because it was a technology of the senses, a technology of vision where vision was suppressed or displaced. How to see nature without seeing it? That was an interesting paradox. By the way, you presented, during your time at a.pass, different iterations of your relation with the idea of nature. The mask, the clay objects, the volcano… In fact, you do relate with natural elements and natural forces. You are not completely digitised yet!

LP: No! Hahaha… The problematic relation between nature and culture is quite an issue in my work. Often, I refer to the ‘archaic’ as well but always in relation to the artificial. The ‘volcano party performance’ – *No House No place No Space* – was an attempt to build an artificial nature. And, through the development of the 2D research process – my initial focus on the agency of images, body performativity and the apparatus of spectatorship where I started questioning the degree of propaganda we are subjected to through the exposure to corporeal images on digital 2D screen devices – I also posed the question of how image technology developed in respect to its suspected origin.

'Have you ever seen a real volcano? I mean... an active volcano? It is artificial as only nature can be'.

For example, what is photography actually? It is something about light, a light that, at first, was printed into a stone. A camera obscura that the prehistoric humans probably already used... This notion of cycling epistemology is something that, for me now, is important because it contains the idea of recursivity, that you were mentioning, and of repetitions and loops, but it is also a composition mode coupling practice and feedback. The last time we spoke together, I also mentioned the notion of 'emblem' because of my ex-a.pass colleague Maurice Meewisse's Babel Tower proposition I found installed in the a.pass studio during the 'volcano party' which – oh gosh! that tower was probably the artificial volcano! – created a fertile circumstance. 'In these circumstances'... around the tower, I placed a performative cycle, a practice, a party that ended up at dinner, actually at the end of the night. The position of the elements were like a mandala, an emblem... and actually, that composition was operative because it was also a technique and a technology. What I think I was traveling to or training for whilst I was at a.pass was a way of composing elements through epistemological cycles as general principles. The outcome has a plastic and concrete form at the end, it can be a party for example, but it can also be an object, or another form, it is built-up on circumstances, it is temporary and collaborative and it is often auto-ethnologically reflexive and it looks like a practice which starts to reflect on its technology or language. But, in the end, I consider those forms as alchemic drawings, or blueprints that make you understand and experience the metamorphosis that you were introduced into sticking on them. It's a kind of choreography because it is dynamic but it's not a choreography, it's more a composition, or better, an architecture.

PR: How did you first conceive of the idea of the cycling epistemology?

LP: I was thinking about experimental pedagogies and about ideas that are related to some of the issues you are pointing at in your series of questions and that we talked about in previous conversations – design, information, technology – but I was focussed as well on the very specific modes of designing by some architects and designers.

PR: And what about the idea of alchemic drawing through which you qualify your form of pedagogic performances?

LP: I'm searching for modes of composing the space and time of the event in a chemical way, as if we were in a chemical laboratory. It's like a machine reacting to added elements, chemical elements that provoke transformations, or reactions like a feedback produced by the very machine. But back to the idea of the cycling epistemology as didactic and pedagogical, I don't consider it as a methodology but more as an occasion and it is as well a site to question methodology.

These 'drawings' or 'blueprints' are not instructions. They are operative but not as instructions and they don't 'instruct knowledge'. I refer now to contemporary allographic modes of drawing, using computer softwares, when you learn from and instruct the machine at the same time. You produce – literally design – but you are produced as well. I create auto-reflexive and transformative situations that can be experienced from different space/time points of view – perspectives, roles and identities and materials. I try to create multiple possibilities to generate singular responses of spectators/participants and I often activate the issue of 'producing-being produced' in one-to-one experiences where I combine elements and concepts that link nature, culture, science and humanities. The focus of the collective eye at issue here is a blurred embodied field of political relations between representation, body, technology and power. In order to activate this area of research I ask the spectators/participants to engage with a specific situation through the exercise of a body technique presented as an affected and autobiographical device (due to my identity as a dancer with a technical body) to practice and question the entanglements of one's body and technology for example. But the cycling epistemology I am busy defining and constructing is actually also a reflection on what the a.pass environment demanded of me as gestures of making public. With the interactive events I proposed, I problematised the moment of 'making public' in relation to the act of sharing practices through studying some choreographers' language constructions used in dancing and training. For me, a practice resembles a stone in which concepts and body experiences are sedimented into ungraspable, or non-instructed, forms of knowledge. It is for these reasons that I think a practice could be a technique which embodies different consistencies of care and justice and creates a vulnerable space to question the ways in which we embody elements of the institutional, and eventually public discourse.

'I am looking for a kind of depth with a dimensionless dimensionality – a mirage/a surface /an image (?!) – a kind of diversion. This depth is that of a vision that burns (flattens) the object of vision itself, the conceptual model, and explores the wonders of a mutual and inorganic/disembodied corporeality'.

PR: You make me think about the etymology of the word public so that I can relate to ideas of 'making public' and the way you challenge them. The starting point of 'publicus', the origin of the word 'public', is 'pubes', which designates the hair that marks puberty, hence the meaning of adult male population. But in Latin, there is a superimposition that links the family of 'publicus' to 'populus' – people – whereas the origins of the two words are in fact independent. 'Publicus' designates that which concerns the people, hence that which concerns the state, and is opposed to 'privatus', which qualifies the private domain. The verb 'publico' means to make public, to render available to the public, hence to confiscate. I link this sense of publication-as-confiscation to publicity, in the sense of advertisement and all the means employed to exert an alienating influence on the people/public. Isn't 'making public' always-already an alienating mode-of-construction of an advertisement? You mentioned before that we are produced products, are we also advertisements?

LP: The question of when the body became (a) public or an advertisement of the body itself, a representation, interests me and was posed through *Screenshot,* the bicycle performance that I presented in a.pass in 2018. We are the engine that builds-up images and builds-up bodies and we feed a (vicious?) circle through ongoing repetitions. We feed a machine. *Screenshot* was an epistemological practice and a pedagogical situation to problematise and complexify the machine body-image-publicity issue.

PR: During this one-to-one experience we could embody – literally by riding the bicycle/machine – a criticism of how the body is instituted in Western culture today and share a reflection of yours on the digitalisation of bodies through image-making technologies...

LP: Exactly. I am very interested in investigating how the modern body was determined historically through its relation to techniques and technologies and their continuous development. But I am also interested in other features of an expanded body that have always been part of feminist practices for instance. This other body is present in my work through the question of intimacy, that I play with as an element of resistance against the advertised body. In *No House No Place No Space*, for example, this tension between intimacy and publicity was one of the structuring elements of the performance. I wanted to create non-stable images... Iconic bodily memories were also at play, such as the figure of Jane Fonda, to trigger a reflection on how our memory is shaped by worlds of images that we keep reproducing and to which we are subjected.

But I have other notes on your question around the type of information that can be generated collectively in artistic research contexts and specifically at a.pass. My choice to work with artists who often don't follow the privileged institutional mode of production is a minoritarian way of practicing collaboration. My performative pedagogical propositions seem to be participatory but they are not, they question the nature of participation. They don't teach, they don't instruct... 'nature' doesn't teach you anything and does not pass any instruction manual. In terms of types of collaboration:

I experimented at a.pass with different modes of production or reproduction actually, and this idea is important now, especially in the context of the COVID-19 virus pandemic. An idea of producing through being pregnant with non-human and human collaborators alike and from hosting collaborations to being pregnant of these collaborations...
I believe it is my speculation on transindividuality today.

'Different from perspective, orthogonal projection is a particular projection represented by a function where the measurements are unchanged in their proportionality. There is no interpretation but a translation on a background, a space of mediation. It is a mirroring action, a centripetal movement, sculpted flat on a disembodied virtual space'.

PR: In relation to your idea of reproduction, let's go back to a question I asked you in one of our previous conversations: you are not the same person you were at a.pass, but maybe Laura-of-today was already here in 2018? And is Laura-of-today still pregnant with a.pass?

LP: When I went to a.pass I entered a habitat. A habitat is an environment and this environment is a performative artificial nature. This artificial nature is a pedagogical 'institution' that is built around something that is, apparently, invisible. This invisible thing is – as you say Pierre – a transversal informational performative matter. This matter is made of pedagogical projects where we don't know exactly what we are transferring to each other. I entered this transference area as a dancer and I have changed along the way. On this path, I found the cyclic epistemological system. Why I encountered this system is a bit of a mystery but what a.pass enables is that you can work inside this invisible plane of projection where you can think of structures and not only reproduce existing ones. Still, a fundamental question remains open: What kind of information are we exchanging when we do things together?

Today, I was reading an interview with Anne Carson where she calls her husband the randomiser. Your questions make sense in relation to the story I wish to tell through a randomising effect.

'Your Blood is streaming, my Wifi is dreaming'

PR: It is like the bicycle-machine randomly selecting images in your *Screenshot* performance. But, how do you translate chance in Italian?

LP: Chance? Like by chance?

PR: Yes. What is the name for the dice game in Italian?

LP: Ah! You mean: '*giocare a dadi*?'

PR: In French it's a '*jeu de hasard*'...

LP: Ah, more broadly: '*il gioco d'azzardo*'?

PR: But you don't use *azzardo* for randomness, you use another word.

LP: Exactly. For randomness is not *azzardo*, it's *casualità*.

PR: *Casualità*, that's it. Randomness is not chance.

LP: 'The randomiser has no chance', that's the title of our next film Pierre! You are funny (and I love you).

Anouk Llaurens

The Breathing Archive

In 2013, I started research on poetic and polyphonic documentation. My initial question was: What if improvisational dance artists apply their perceptual, motor, mental, and composition skills to document their own practice? I was interested in creating and encouraging documentation that emanates from an embodied consciousness so that dancers' empirical perspectives have a voice in the creation of dance archives and dance history. Also, what kind of documentation could emerge from our protocols?

I chose to document movement practices that I had learned from Lisa Nelson's Tuning Scores, which address 'hand-eye coordination', like: 'Follow your hand with your eyes' or 'Play with your hand entering and exiting your visual field'. Hand-eye coordination is unfolding during the first year of our life. It is necessary to execute the simplest action like taking a glass, opening a door, putting on a coat, writing, drawing and filming. It is also the foundation for language and conceptual capacities. Through my documentation research I wanted to question the separation and hierarchy between matter and idea, body and mind, making and seeing, intimacy and distance, in an attempt to get rid of binary logic.

The practical research process led me to the insights that living is an ongoing documentation practice and our perceptual apparatus, an embodied documentation technology. A document can be an abstraction, a removal from experience, and the experience itself. The research chooses to investigate the notion of *lived experience as document*. It does not focus on producing material documents about dance like pictures, videos, drawings or anything else, but produces *live documents*: poetic documentation practices that are collectively embodied and performed.

One of these 'live documents', *The Breathing Archive*, was developed in the frame of a.pass' postgraduate programme, and in response to this particular context. At a.pass, I had many conversations with my peers and mentors. *What is your research?* was the question that I kept trying to answer. During this conversational practice, I noticed that each time I was presenting my research, my interlocutor was responding through her own interest. If I would talk with a person that had an interest in neuroscience, the research would be defined through this filter, or if I would talk to a former designer, suddenly the A4 format of the pages became significant. The answer to *What is your research?* became the multiplicity of what people could see in it or what triggered their attention during our conversation. I recorded most of the conversations and transcribed some of them. The collection of the possible versions of *What is your research?* became the postgraduate archive, a kind of polyphonic theory of my research. I printed some of the conversations on A4 pages, gathered the pages in a tote bag and set up a developmental score to play and edit the archive collectively. The score takes breathing as a ground to activate all layers of perceptions from touch (hand) to sight (eye). It opens players to a receptive experience of their surroundings and induces an attentive presence that favours the emergence of a poetic experience made up of the sensations of paper, flesh, sounds, words, images, table, colours, smells, emotions and thoughts.

March 2021, in response to a.pass' call for contributions to this publication, I invited long-term collaborators Sonia Si Ahmed and Julien Bruneau to play the archive with me. I have recorded and transcribed our practice and selected fragments from the recording. My contribution is composed with layers that are organised from the most intellectual to the most material one, in analogy to the layers of perception that composed the spectrum of the senses, from sight to touch.

Reading this text is like peeling layers to access different types of experiences, from the analytic to the poetic.

The Breathing Archive invites players to collectively edit an ephemeral document that is contingent on the present conditions. The core action of the practice is to crumple and uncrumple printed A4 pages. This simple action, performed with care, wishes to send us back to the most basic of life's movements, like the movement of cells breathing and the heart beating. Players are invited to pay attention to their own breath as a continuous support for their action, before crumpling and uncrumpling the pages. After an immersion with closed eyes into the materiality of the paper – its sounds and smells – the eyes open and the players let their attention be called by this or that fragment of text, some of which are read out loud, in tune with the overall space. Throughout, breathing is a ground that induces an attentive and open presence that favours the emergence of a poetic experience made of sensations of paper, flesh, sounds, words, images, colours, smells, emotions and thoughts.

00:00:11

...close your eyes and... pay attention to your sensations... the sensation of the body... the sensations of the environment... what is touching you?...what are you touching in return?...

00:02:36

... become aware of the movement of your breath... its amplitude, its rhythm... inhaling, taking oxygen from the room... exhaling, getting rid of waste that the body does not need... listening to the space of resonance after you inhale... after you exhale...

00:04:36

... pay attention to your hands in connection to the whole body... use them to explore the environment in front of you, the table... the pile of papers... other hands that you meet on your way... breathing, opening the pores of the skin, ready for encounter...

00:10:25

... when you are ready you can start to engage with the action of crumpling and uncrumpling the pages... folding and expanding, connecting the movement of the pages with the movement of your breath...

00:11:36

...pay attention to the sounds of your actions... how do they affect the whole body and the collective space?... tasting your sensation, and the resonance of your actions...

00:23:52

... when you are ready, you can let your eyes open and let images touch your retina, vision is also tactile... what do you see? ...what is catching your attention?...how is light touching the paper?...

00:29:05

...become aware of the words that are printed on these pages... that are appearing and disappearing in the folds... what words are touching your retina...

00:32:26

...notice if you have the desire to read some of these words out loud to share them with the space...

00:33:06,538 -->

...what emerges from the folds? ...

00:50:03

(J): '"Les fleurs du mal" on a pile of compost...'

00:51:56

(A): 'We just watched a short trailer for, "La flamme éternelle" by Thomas Hirschhorn. Julien mentioned it when I started to talk about building up an environment as a Poetic Dance Documentation Centre. He thought that there were some similarities even if what I have in mind is more humble, really more humble...'

00:52:39

(S): 'Everything is organised, in order at the right place. Since "the poetic" happens when I pay attention to details, attention is what makes the ordinary, extraordinary; it is a door to poetic experiences... The piece of bread crust that lies under the table becomes the most incredible sculpture; people around me are composing the most exquisite choreography. Nothing has changed but I see it differently...'

00:55:57

(J): 'I want to hear the voice of dance practitioners... most of the time, dance is documented by people that don't practice dance... I am interested in documentation that emerges from the practice itself...'

00:56:43

(A): 'Elke: what is so special for you about "hand-eye coordination" that you want to focus on it for such a long period?'

00:56:56

(S): 'Abu: It is the space between the light and the day, the real and the unreal, the state of being awake and the state of dream, the life and death which we are living constantly, constantly we are passing through these moments, when the sun sets and the night begins, this is a very important moment no? The sun rises, something breaks and it's a few minutes, it's a few seconds...'

00:57:27

(A): 'Well at first it's very intuitive; touch and vision define the spectrum of the senses. Touch was considered the lowest sense, associated with matter and vision, the noble one. I am interested in deconstructing this hierarchy... if I come back to the spectrum of the senses, it is also to talk about human evolution, through the evolution of the brain...'

00:58:37

(J): 'It's out of control!'

00:58:37

(A): 'Can I confuse myself?'

00:58:40

(S): 'I am not convinced with the use of clay, maybe because it's too natural, too organic, too close to the uterus for me...'

00:58:51

(J): 'Yes, it's out of control!'

der the table becomes the most inc
nposing the most exquisite choreo
erently. Everything is organized,
opens when I pay attention to deta
linary; it is a door to poetic experience

Vladimir Miller

A Good Workshop

A Conversation with Krõõt Juurak

This conversation between Krõõt Juurak and Vladimir Miller took place in December 2020. Krõõt was invited to give a workshop at a.pass and in his function as block curator Vladimir took the opportunity to discuss with Krõõt their respective methods of working within the setting of the workshop, their approach to the labour of the artist and how to disappear as an author figure. Part of the agreement between a.pass and the artists facilitating workshops is that after a workshop they pass on a 'report' to a.pass on how their proposal worked out. The conversation starts from that.

VM: Hello Krõõt, it would be great to have a conversation about the work(shop) that you proposed. I suggested this interview format to you so that you would not have to write a report. I have the intuition that reporting would be strange in connection with your workshop and your work in general.

The last time we talked it felt to me that the way you work cannot be grasped with conventional questions of 'what did you do?' and other questions that point to productivity. Productivity is so ingrained in the language we use to describe proposals that it makes it hard to talk about proposals which challenge that concept. I am curious what you think about this? Is there a language problem?

KJ: Yes, there is definitely a language problem, I agree. First of all, when looking back at the workshop at a.pass, I don't want to be the ultimate authority on what we did and what that meant or what anyone learnt or did not learn. The workshop is proposed in such a way that it is not clear what its benefits are and what the productivity of it is. I don't want to be the one who has the last word because this is counterproductive to the other participants of the workshop. Actually, because I myself was not taking this workshop, I have the least idea about what we did or what it was good for. I would say that's the reason why I find it so strange and difficult to write reports. It feels like I'm patronising the participants' experience.

VM: I know that feeling very well. When I propose a collective space in my own work it's also impossible for me to say afterwards what actually happened. I know what happened from my perspective, but then I was just one of the people who occupied that space. Producing environments in which you then yourself enter as a participant doesn't really go along with conventional concepts of what work is or what education should look like.

KJ: On the other hand – which is at first glance a little bit contradictory – I love the conventional way of educating, I like the formal structure of a school, where one person is the 'teacher' and the others are 'students'. As a role play, I think it's brilliant. It is not an environment where everything is everything. I have a rather difficult educational past. I struggled through primary and high school, barely making it, but as I am getting older, I am almost 40 now, educational experiences have been getting better and better. And perhaps in developing these workshops I have been dealing with those educational 'traumas'. Most people come with some kind of baggage from their experiences in educational institutions and I am interested in how these experiences are still shaping the way we function whenever we are faced with a 'school-like' structure.

Since I have always hated school, workshops, any kind of educational experiences (I don't even have a driver's license), I tried to do something that a person like myself could handle. I guess that's why this workshop is anti-productivity and anti-information. The proposal could also be: wasting time together and/or separately. And here's a fun fact: statistically speaking, the main reason people take workshops is to meet other people. I think that is a fair reason. Often you don't go there to learn a new skill but rather just to see who else is there. It is hard to meet people nowadays. As a workshop leader, I try to keep this in mind, and try to make sure it isn't about me.

VM: I think we have very similar reasons for why we do the work the way we do. For me, the hardest part is to navigate the persona of the initiator. I like that you described the teacher/student relationship as a kind of a role play. It's good to try and keep it a role play because this relationship constantly wants to become a reality. It's very hard to get out of the costume.

KJ: We're so trained in believing these roles, we start to take them seriously. I always try to keep in mind that in taking workshops people learn about giving workshops. When you are giving one you learn about how to take one. I do not have a lot of faith in explanatory learning, we are animals and learn from example, unwittingly.

VM: In this workshop at a.pass, did you feel like the participants were aware of that roleplay? Did they get out of their roles?

KJ: Perhaps the idea was rather to get *into* their roles, I would think that most of them became aware of the part they played, absolutely. For example, I kept postponing this interview with you, and after the second postponement I stated that I have really good excuses. It was at that moment that I became aware of my recurring role as the artist-teacher resisting report-writing. It is tricky because we are not in a workshop and this is not as safe as a workshop would be. It is relatively safe because we are friends, but we are in a professional environment. It is more risky to come up with really good (fake) excuses.

In the workshop, I really try to create a ground where excuses and this cliché known as 'bad student behaviour' can become a practice. An artist's practice.

So many of our artistic practices are based on the so-called protestant ethic, where you have to be a good person with good wishes and of course, good products. It is all based on a moral premise. Obviously, turning that around isn't going to change it, but I think at least you can have a break from having to be so damn serious about being good all the time.

I struggle with that myself: trying to keep up the *play*. I thought it would be a good idea to be an artist so I could decide for myself what work was and what life was. At some point you notice that you take less risks because your income depends on it. Then what you do doesn't appeal to you anymore and probably it will not be appealing to anyone else either. So it is a closed circle, or a downward spiral: when our livelihood depends on it, we start to fear and fear eats fun. I think workshops are a great format to make a space for *fun*, for boredom and for doing nothing.

VM: There's a counter-institutional resistance in both of our proposals, a space to fail and miss the institutional brief. At the same time, how to do *that* properly is a narrow pathway, which is another brief. I keep asking myself how to not please the institution by critiquing it in this way. It is a matter of constant evaluation for me; what actually makes a good proposal? What am I satisfied with, what is the institution satisfied with, what are the participants satisfied with? Thinking like this I find myself mostly fighting against passing on the institutional pressure and established ideas (which we all have, everyone taking part in a workshop) of what a 'good workshop is'.

KJ: It is slightly more complex than being anti-institutional. But not very complex. In fact, it is just about making a space within the space or using it for your own advantage and finding out the problems as they arise and trying not to worry about anything else.

VM: a.pass is maybe a special case; we welcome the institutional educational experiment. These are our questions as artists and educators. To a certain degree we are on a similar side of things. We are also bored with the conventional ideas of passing down knowledge. But I'm wondering how much is at risk for you in other institutions? Do you calibrate your proposals depending on where you go, or do you even radicalise them if it is a more conventional context?

KJ: I don't know if this is good or bad but I do the same thing every time. Let's say, a very similar workshop works for nine-year-olds too. Perhaps it is a very childish workshop and I wonder if it is more unusual for a.pass, Impulstanz or for *real* children.

VM: I think you deploy a Trojan horse. You have a surface layer, a structural layer in this workshop which is able to attach itself to the institution. But within that structure it feels to me like there's a space for absurdity, boredom and a collapse of reasoning.

KJ: Right. Let's say, if you ask me what we did, I could tell you exactly: we had a nap every day of 20 minutes, we wrote in our diaries, we sang karaoke, we had a silent meeting... We knew exactly what we were doing at any given moment but for a person randomly walking in, it would not have looked like we were doing anything. For sure it did not look like we were working.

VM: There's a kind of failure of the institutional perspective which you trigger, precisely because you *can* answer to it. I appreciate very much how your work invalidates certain questions by actually answering them bluntly. It becomes clear that these are not the right questions, because they can't help but grasp what the proposal actually produces, or what it triggers, or what kind of community it develops, or how practices resonate with each other.

KJ: Actually, it is not quite accurate to say it was all anti-productivity; we had a couple of lectures, we discussed political performativity and artists' solidarity. I try to combine as wide a range of activities as I can. And since I am constantly doubting my own abilities, self-sabotage is a method, it's an important tool for me. Self-sabotage is a very common method, especially in the creative field, and I think we don't cherish it enough. It takes such a large, almost elephant-size part of our lives, I want to know more about it.

In this workshop, I gave the participants the simple task to write a motivation letter, formulated as 'What/why do you want to get out of this workshop?' I formulated the task in such a way that I didn't notice it could be misunderstood. But when I read the letters everybody was writing about why they wanted to get out of the workshop. And I was genuinely confused and worried. Do they really want to get out of the workshop? Then I looked at what I had written and understood that I had unwittingly sabotaged myself.

Then in one of these letters somebody called this workshop a 'procrastination conspiracy'.

VM: I find it interesting that you identify self-sabotage as a useful methodology to pass on. So far I have only applied that to myself. In my collective gathering workshop I talk about 'authority suicide': How to fail as an organiser when you are proposing something? When people don't know what the plan is, when there is a feeling that people are lost, my initial response would always be to panic and to try and solve that situation. I have gradually developed a higher tolerance and now try to fail, or to do it badly or to accept not knowing how to go on, in order to finally collapse this persona of the 'responsible-when-it-fails', which I bring in as a piece of the institutional structure.

It feels like you are proposing a step further, when you want to pass on the practice of self-sabotage. I am still worried that the gathering would then fall apart completely, instead of reorganising itself around my failing support.

KJ: So, if I'm imagining what you do: Is it a workshop or a project where it is difficult to say who's in charge or when it starts and when it ends?

VM: Yes, that's the attempt.

KJ: I admire people who are able to do this kind of free structure. Every time before a workshop, I think I should try that and I kind of coward out and go with a very strict structure instead. Maybe someday. But, I really admire when there is this kind of a situation where you are not sure if it is meant to be that way, is it really planned to be disorganised or has everything gone out of hand. It's risky.

VM: It is risky. It is one of those things outside of language. You can't really address it, because the only way to address it is to re-establish some kind of authority over it, to turn it into an institutional method yet again. So what you can do is to go for awkward silences and dance around it hoping that either it is a true failure and something else will come out of it, or that at least there's a kind of a meta-failure and people are kind of in on the joke. That people understand it, that it is an unspoken, unspeakable thing that has to happen.

I'm talking like it is a whole method, but actually I'm always just trying to stretch that space. I try to be aware of the moments when authority comes in, what are the performances of it, and either not do them or wait as long as possible to do them.

KJ: It would be a paradox if it would become a whole method.

VM: Yes, exactly. What we say about a.pass as a structure is that it is engaging in the paradox of creating an open space. I think somehow your work(shop) deals with that as well. We do it from different sides: through over-emphasising structure or through building down structure. But the goals are quite similar. I think a.pass keeps failing in that, because at the same time there is always the question 'Are we doing our job well?' Is there 'progress'? etc. There has to be a reason to engage in this communal project/institution; you have to want to end up somewhere in your work that you would not be able to get to by yourself.

But I'm still wondering, if we take your method seriously, if there should be some kind of a radical letting go of certain goals in this environment. Sometimes I still feel like we think too 'educationally'.

KJ: Maybe it's because I'm doing psychoanalysis at the moment that I think this is also a psychological method. You become aware of your habits and then it's not about changing them, but about playing them. Performing them and enjoying it. Don't struggle. Or struggle but have a good time struggling! We could keep having this abstract idea of open space, but it's not open and it's not space. It is rather that our filters define how we understand something.

VM: I think the playful perspective helps me too. When I'm explaining these thoughts to you, I see myself from the outside getting stuck in language loops. My wish would be to get out of them. Not in order to keep explaining and subverting structures, but to step out of it, to step somewhere else.

Here I feel the limits of a specific institutional language or culture to express spaces and proposals which are really beside them. There are some things which a particular language or particular culture of discourse cannot reach. Maybe as we said, it can only be done in a sort of unspoken way, unspoken in the sense of not using *that* language.

That thought is really fascinating for me because the way I usually proceed is through over-explaining and I catch myself thinking in this conversation that this might be a trap. I have been polishing the language of my proposals, trying to subvert them within the proposal for quite some time now. Almost like trying to build a bridge from one language space to another. It's just that sometimes I get so busy building this bridge that I don't have time for the actual work of inhabiting that space. Or rejecting the space, like the way you reject the idea of educational reporting.

Thank you for this conversation, dear Krõõt!

Vladimir Miller

From Settlement to Poliset

Poliset was developed as a workshop at a.pass about 10 years ago when a.pass was still situated at deSingel in Antwerp. When I was invited to teach there, I was looking for a practice which would allow the researchers to produce a study environment that was structured around a polycentric approach to community and practice. The main question in coming up with this workshop was for me: How to design a (self)educational environment which can be appropriated by others through re-design? I wanted to pass on the role of the workshop facilitator to the space itself, hoping that interactions and presentations would organically emerge from the engagement of the researchers with their work and with each other. But for this to happen, our spatial arrangement had to dissolve the default model of 'always gathering in a circle around a table' which would privilege me as a teacher no matter what I did and said. We all needed an opportunity to stay together but to orient ourselves away from the centre and towards our tasks and questions as researchers. Not to simply fall apart into individual processes, but to disorganise in order to reorganise in multiple peer-to-peer occasions of sharing and presentation. I took the idea of a city as a spatial metaphor (or on a smaller scale: village, town), with its distributed centres of production, politics and self-organisation, as the main model for such a space. The initial proposal was therefore called 'Settlement' to point to a mode of dwelling which is never one structure and desire, but a multitude of interacting formations. The word 'settlement' was also pointing to the key practice of negotiation (a 'settlement' marks its end in legal terms) between the social, individual, material and organisational formations which would be emergent in the space. As the practice continued to develop at a.pass and elsewhere over the past ten years, then Settlement and now 'poliset' went through different iterations, becoming a larger research project on the politics of commoning and the relationship between practice and its material/spatial conditions within institutions.

WHAT IS IN A NAME?

'Settlement' as a notion, practice, tool and place is a complicated knot of connotations ranging from a communal architectural practice, to a tool of colonial domination, to an end of a negotiation or a legal complaint process. The colonial history of settling, as aggression, genocide and appropriation of space, co-exists in this cramped etymological space with the somewhat romantic, do-it-yourself, power-reversing practice of claiming space, of making one's own support structures and collective resource management, in short: with commoning of space as a political practice. In naming my first workshops 'Settlements', I was drawn to this tangle of uneasy ethics, unclear positions, and a practice of dwelling which is at once indispensable and irredeemable. To bring the question of settling to the art institution meant to point to the fact that territorial practices are not just on its outside. The language and legacy of territory and conquest permeates into all practices, including the artistic. Using 'Settlement' as the name for this practice of reclaiming, reorganising, and redistributing space intended to stay with the trouble of what comes before and after the process of settling in; the questions of access, political structure, and resource management within research environments. How do we take, share and manage space as artists? Settlement as a name intended to point to the fact that if we think of spaces as territories, the trouble never stops. There is no innocent way of using a tool as powerful as settling in.

Out there on the streets, I could argue that the public sphere is territorialised by state interest and neoliberal public-private divides. Settling in the city, temporary settlements like Occupy, or autonomous spaces and squats are re-colonising the urban space in the name of different politics, in the name of political struggles. Within leftist politics, some might argue for intrusive spatial metaphorics if the intruder is constructed as the less powerful and the institutions as privileged within a systemic constellation. I have used that argument myself: I perceive the contemporary artist as the perpetual migrant/nomad and the institution as a place that offers itself to be a home, however temporary. Seeing these spaces as already territorialised suggests the need for counter-processes, counter-territorialisations. But beyond these strategies looms a possibility to unlearn territory altogether, to stop playing colony no matter the flag raised.

Can we rethink spatial metaphorics and find new ways of talking about the relationships that are produced at the crossing of institutional borders and try to abandon territorial thinking? Can we define institutions in different terms, not as territories at all, with nothing to guard or to fence? It might seem an inherently impossible project, against the very notion of what institutions ontologically are. In conversations with my colleagues[1] who work with practices of school, commons and gathering we have time and again tried to approach and rattle the ontologically bordered condition of 'institute'. It is hard to think and practice institutions other than as an im/material *home* for a set of practices. In another line of thinking I will suggest that one way to try to approach this condition is not to abandon the idea of home but to expand it to zones of care. What can be an institution which does not entirely overlap the spaces that it supports with the spaces that it encloses?

---

1 I am grateful for the continuous support and critical thinking of Fotini Lazaridou-Hatzigoga, Jozef Wouters, Heike Langsdorf, Adva Zakai, among many others.

Settlement and settling in are not one and the same, and a colonial settlement is not the same as *a* settlement. But they are spatial practices that claim (temporary) ownership of space. In the specific case of my workshop practice, the process of settling in happened on invitation to an institutional space that was in a widest sense state property. It seems like the fact of this invitation would purge all colonial connotations from 'Settlement', and that may be the case. But the underlying condition of space as territory still persists and I am writing this to understand these metaphorics of territory which we deploy when we enter spaces, invited or uninvited. Can the practice of settling be abstracted from its use in history? Is it possible to see it purely as a tool of self-organisation, which could somehow escape the pitfalls of thinking and acting space as territory? Or, is it useful to fall into the pit in order to realise that there is no escape and that we have to deal with the territorial questions whenever we enter and appropriate spaces?

In order to unfold this process for myself I am asking how far back do I have to go in order to understand when it was that I *learnt* territory as a way of thinking about space?

There is a layer of personal and cultural nostalgia beneath my more removed aesthetic and academic admiration of the intricacies of Settlement as a notion, which I can trace back to my childhood in Soviet Russia. I grew up in the 80s – I was 12 when Russia started falling apart around the time of transition in the late 80s and early 90s. In the 1980s, the Soviet culture, at least the part visible to me as child, went gradually from a state of total occlusion to the capitalist West, to a mad jump into capitalism and its culture, as if from a sinking ship. I went through that process myself on a much smaller scale, eventually emigrating with my family to Germany, body following where imagination and desire already had gone in the years before.

Within this shifting-while-collapsing value system, I had my own formative moment of imagination when a close friend of my father's lent me the historical novels of James Fenimore Cooper. Living in the West now in the age of the internet, it is hard to imagine the Orwellian cultural control the Soviet system imposed on its citizens. Books were a rare commodity and only approved literature was printed. Within this general scarcity, the evocative, mournful novels of Fenimore Cooper were indescribably alluring. In them I found a replacement for the collapsing ideology of communist progress that had let the Soviet populace down. In them I found that moving into uncharted territory is the story which we can keep telling ourselves, even at the time of its failure. Reading these novels along with Russian adventure science fiction, I could manoeuvre between the conflicting ideologies of capitalism and communism towards a core idea that they held in common: that the frontier, the unexplored territory and its colonisation is a form of progress. As the West was looming on the collective cultural horizon of the Soviet people, here I held in my hands its origin story (or so I thought at the time), a story soon to replace the failing narrative around me.

When I look at it now, I can see that by reading Cooper I was turning to the West in its shape as an ever lingering promise. I was shown the mythical core of American ideology as a mirage of a pristine land that is waiting to be settled on. This old promise of the colonial era arrived in my hands as a renewed promise of a West which was still waiting for me now, in my socialist present. It was a dangerous nostalgia which went surprisingly unchecked by the Russian censorship, maybe because colonisation was the one thing both ideologies could agree on – being indispensable to their global spread.

I have never re-read these novels. What I want to give an account of is not their literary and historical validity, nor the role they might have played in the American self-conception, but only of their impact on my imagination, contributing 'frontier' to my mechanics of desire in a way which I think only children are permeable to. I want to trace back the reflexive imagery that appears in front of my inner eye when I think of 'Settlement'. I am asking myself why I see an empty grassy plane and a caravan of people arriving on it. I am asking myself why settlement for me is the moment they stop, disembark, assess their surroundings and [time jump] build houses, settle. Before I can untangle myself from the word, or in order to untangle myself from it, I want to see this image clearly as a process of transition of one socio-material formation to another one, from being on the move and moving one's own support, to being held by an immovable structure.

Later on, after migrating to the West myself and much later after that, when it was time to name a practice of gathering and working together in an arts education institution, settlement seemed sufficiently removed from this nostalgic underpinning, to become a word that describes what comes after migration. A verb-noun, an action made manifest to show the relationship between community and its architecture as a process of managing and organising resources, negotiating, working together and apart. The settlers as commoners who build communal and private spaces, spatialise and organise around common desires, skills and abilities.

Reimagining the institution as a space to be settled by the artists and researchers felt empowering. I myself was a newcomer, not only by origin, which I have somewhat successfully already assimilated away from, but a newcomer to large institutions like deSingel, or educational institutions like a.pass. It was clear that this was a performative game I was playing with the institution, and I was already invited and could extend this invitation to others. I wanted to push the limits of this invitation and claim some ground for myself and my fellow researchers to ask where is the place for our practice within these institutions? Not coming from a Fine Arts practice and not having had an atelier at my disposal (like most of the participants at a.pass at that time) I simply wanted to know whether it was possible to have a large hall for three weeks to ourselves without necessarily making a show out of it. In other words, how could deSingel and a.pass support actual research practice by sharing their resources with us?

Ten years ago, I was not yet thinking about decolonial practices and still cannot claim that this was a decolonial practice, as decolonising institutions is an entirely different process. If anything, this project was a *counter*-colonisation of institutional space. We, artists and workers in education are forever migrants within the institutional territory, looking for spaces and resources, looking for a wall we can drill into without asking permission first. We artists (even those who are asked to contribute), are assailing institutions in perpetual conquest and the institutions are graciously accepting this game from time to time. We are othering institutions as territories, and no matter our politics, this othering precedes our encounters, unless both artists and institutions can find a politics which are not built upon this initial divide within an ontologically territorial conception of 'institution'.

Naming the practice Settlement seemed to reflect the two dynamics of communal negotiations: that of setting up and that of claiming some space from the institution. Only much later did it occur to me that I was recreating my own process of migrating to the West, and possibly the received imaginaries of my childhood with it. I have read somewhere that we recreate our traumatic experiences until we solve them. My own critique of 'settling in an institution' is that its simple 'us vs. them' rhetoric lacked the same relational complexity it was trying to introduce into the question of space-making and claiming. The actual process of setting up, from the beginning of this practice, has always involved many conversations with institutional supporters and was premised on invitation. And while I as a guest tried to challenge the invitation to a breaking point by extending the rights of the host to all who would be involved, it was always a process of advocating and convincing rather than of taking over.

MONOTECTURE/POLYTECTURE

Moving away from 'Settlement', I became interested in a particular distinction that emerged in my research as a helpful tool for understanding spatially self-organised gatherings. Like many before me, I took the word *architecture* and tried to disambiguate from it different ways of building institutional, architectural and social structures.

The etymology of *archon* in Greek is a double bind of mastery and tradition. *Archon* means 'head', 'master': a single organising subjectivity. This claim to mastery is derived from the verb *archein* (meaning to be first, to begin from or with), of which *archon* is the present participle. The architect is therefore etymologically the master of building by way of planning and starting.

If we want to take away the *archon*, but still produce (support) structures (to *tecture*, to build), it seems to me that a helpful differentiation could be to understand if these structures are *unifying* or *diversifying* the gathering that they support. And equally important, are they being produced by a unifying or diversifying *process?* That is, are they being planned and executed through a single process or through an assemblage of (potentially conflicting) processes? (In Chantal Mouffe's words, are they making space *for* agonism and *through* an agonistic process?) It does not matter if the architect/organiser/teacher/designer/artists, etc. is a single person or a whole office or company, what matters in this particular analysis is whether there is *one plan* and whether the politics of the process are solely oriented towards designing that one plan. This one single plan is the bottleneck of spatial and organisational politics. We have accepted that there are politics before and after it, but that we still have to pass through the one plan stage.

In reality, both unifying and diversifying principles usually coexist and intertwine, so this dualism is purely analytical, used here to point to a forking of possibilities. For the sake of clarity, I will call the one plan principle *monotecture* and its other *polytecture.*[2] It is important to note that *tecture* is part of this etymology as an affirmation of the responsibilities of making and structuring. In spaces which are dominated by institutional design *-tecture* as the practice of *still building, still structuring* is an important tool of renegotiating the conditions of practice.

In my experience, processes of structure are pulled magnetically towards monotecture structuring, that is towards planning from a single consensual or hierarchically constructed subjectivity. If we come together as a group of artists in a space and we don't know what to do next, what is the first thing we do automatically? Yes, we sit down at a table, face each other in a circle and talk until a collective plan emerges. This is a crucial moment of the actualisation of the monotecture principle as a guiding paradigm

2 Compare the terminology to Anarchitecture, a movement around the artist and architect Gordon Matta-Clarke that also negates (An-) the supremacy of Archon in relation to tecture. The same core idea of disorganisation and collapse as opposition to architecture is taken here towards unbuilding: 'Completion through removal. Abstraction of surfaces. Not-building, not-to-rebuild, not-built-space. Creating spatial complexity reading new openings against old surfaces. [...]' Gordon Matta-Clark, Manifesto, 1978.

of togetherness and collaboration. Everything else, all diversity of process and purpose, happens as pockets within the general monotectural space, in relation and sometimes in opposition to it.

Most collective plannings are processes of monotecture. The real differences are the scale and aims but usually not the politics of making the structure. This persistent similarity between collective planning in my professional life as an artist and a major building operation, is why I felt it was important to introduce the monotecture's actual other into my discourse and imagination. To understand how pervasive monotecture is, we need to look at the very few instances in our practices where we can actually diverge from the rhythm of consensus, hierarchy, majority planning, individual execution and *still be supported.*

Architects use another disambiguation and usually refer to top-down or bottom-up organisation, which I find a helpful distinction, but which is nevertheless grounded in the dividing of the building process along the question of mastery, education and professionalism (the *archon*, again). There are many examples (particularly in the global south and indigenous practices) where the bottom-up processes proceed as polytecture. At the same time, there is a particular subset of bottom-up organisation, often referred to as participatory design, which in its actual process is similarly structured to top-down planning: its aim is to approach a structured consensual plan of action. The differences in process between participatory design and top-down planning are more often along the lines of self-authorisation than between different *kinds* of planning and (dis)organisation. The relationship between monotecture and politecture is by no means mutually exclusive or divided among simplistic lines of good or bad political spatial practice. What I mean to point out is rather that polytecture and monotecture coexist in a productive rhythm with each other, but that this rhythm is out of balance and often needs some adjustment. Monotecture tends to proliferate and produce monotecture. That is particularly true for institutional environments and the way in which they welcome and support practices of gathering and collaborative work.

Polytecture is the ever-present but radically different process of organising. *It radically disassociates the commonality of use and design rights from an organisational and political consensus and plan.* A politectural commons proposes that we will use this resource together, but we will use it differently, sometimes together, sometimes conflictual, mostly in shifting alliances. This 'we' is not constituted around regulations of use (meaning around negotiations of distribution of 'who gets what'), but around primary cohabitation, or co-ownership (which is the same as collective non-ownership) of the resource. The 'we' is not those who *plan* the use/design together, it is those who use/design. A prominent example of such an agreement will be familiar to most readers, it is the politectural use and care structure of PAF, which maintains only four clear commoning rules as its core regulation: the doer decides, make it possible for others, don't leave traces and mind asymmetries. All of its organisational super structures come out of and come back to maintaining this core of decision making by use/design. This structure avoids voting and democratic decision making, ensuring that potentially anyone who enters PAF is immediately enabled to use and transform it, establish their own structures, invite others, etc. Here a monotecture of the minimal contract of four rules produces a polytectural commons.

To come back to our example of what-to-do-now?-artists: arriving in a space, having that space together is already enough organisation. In fact, quite a lot of organising has been done in order for a group to go through that door together. Now is the time to undo some of these structures again, to fall apart together, to disorganise the imminent circle of consensus-making before it takes over as the only legitimate way of altering and using the space. It is a transitional moment where the mode or organisation no longer has to be determined by the structuring necessities of resource acquisition (which is what the process of making an application for a space essentially is), and where the collective space and the time together can now be recognised as common resources. The step to polytecture would be to actively disorganise: to keep all planning to an extreme minimum and *doing* to a maximum. Let everyone use the space first of all in a way in which they imagine this space should be used. This way, through different coexisting imaginations of this space, parallel spaces will start to emerge: for one artist this is a space of reading, for another it is one of sculptural practice, for a third one it is a space of dancing. To make these spaces happen, the artists will produce them through the necessities of their practice, by arranging some elements to make this particular version of the space a reality. Someone rolls out a dance floor, someone invites friends for lunch and builds a table, someone arranges their books into a shared library. What happens when the negotiations and structuring happen from a meeting of these speculative, partially realised spaces, instead of from a general project plan? There is no process of collectively deciding 'we need a library and a cooking place', and then distributing the necessary labour. Not that this is not a good process, but this process produces unnecessary structures and negotiations: Who or which constellation of persons has the power to compel the others to labour? What kind of democracy or hierarchy is this particular gathering? etc. All of these shadow negotiations are why, at some moment, monotecture has to come in. We are afraid to leave them in the shadows. At the same time monotecture will never be able to address them, because it turns to previous monotectures for legitimation.

If we start building from polytecture, we are already in the space of agency, practice and self-support before we meet each other in conflict or collaboration. When we enter a space of monotecture, we are either assimilated into its structure, or willingly submit to it by thinking of our practice and imagination as secondary to the communal, which seems like the right thing to do, either because we are paid, are already in some structure, or because we are good communists. The wrong assumption about the communal is that one has to submit to it. But a radical community can be a responsible and responsive co-presence without interference or mediated pressure ('you cannot do that, we have to discuss it with others').

In polytecture, use/design of space *is* power, in monotecture we are led to believe that space, attention, materials, other people, collaborative joy are scarce resources which we can only get hold of if we submit to a (however benevolent) master plan. That this power is apriori does not mean that it is evenly distributed or cannot be abused. It only means that it is not distributed centrally. When this centrality falls away, what kind of legitimations of power and self empowerment do we produce and affirm in a common space? Far from being able to solve this central question of commoning and self organisation, polytecture first of all makes space for this negotiation to occur. It is a practice of responsible and responsive self-empowerment, a re-rehearsal of politics by means of looking into the void of democratic reasoning proposed by post-foundational political thought of Chantal Mouffe, Ernesto Laclau and others.[3]

In polytecture, we come together as (...)[4] of whatever space we occupy, in monotecture we have to acquire attention, materials and purpose through redistribution at the central table while essentially playing State. It may sound like my argument is a libertarian one, but it is the opposite of that: I believe that to truly come together, we have to take a conscious step out of a space where we are 'not-together', but that space *has to be there*, we cannot skip it and just arrive in commoning. A coming together is magical and special but it turns dark and oppressive if there is no alternative to it. Monotecture in the guise of commoning would like us to believe there is no alternative.

---

3 For a comprehensive account of the necessity of this void (the question of the foundational reasoning for democracy that must remain unanswered in order for democracy [and in fact all politics] to occur) see Oliver Marchart, *Post-Foundational Political Thought*, Edinburgh 2000.

4 A project that remains unfinished for now is to answer the question: What kind of subjectivities and subjects in relation to their structure are the producers of polytecture? Possible inserts: stakeholders, producers, agents, commoners...

LESS ORGANISATION, MORE SUPPORT: SOME ATTEMPTS TO POLISET

The reflections I outlined above always accompanied the practice that emerged from Settlement and which I now call *poliset*. While polytecture is a structuring principle and mode of analysis of architecture, a poliset is a concrete practice of temporary communal inhabitation aimed at producing self-organised research[5] environments. In the following section, I will describe the attempts to initiate a poliset – a process I have engaged in on a number of occasions within different institutions, including among others an art academy, an artist residency, a museum and a performance festival.

As a condensed description, a poliset is a support practice:[6] a proposal for a collective space and time that has the conditions – material, organisational and modes of access – to host a multitude of other practices, many of which are 'host-practices' as well. These practices are, in the specific case of a.pass, the research set-ups (e.g. the material, conceptual, organisational and affective spaces that the researchers require in order to do their research) of participating artist-researchers, but that is entirely dependent on the group of people who decide to initiate this type of gathering. Overall, this proposal can be seen as a temporary communal renegotiation, restructuring, recombination, re-building of the institutional conditions for self-organised work. Its aim is to radically lower the threshold for 'getting into practice' and for what Moten and Harney call *study*:[7] the convivial state of the classroom before the teacher comes in.

As poliset happens in institutional spaces where virtually all resources are either institutional *or* private, this commoning practice pays particular attention to the shifting relationships between property and production within collaborative

---

5 ' [...] a generalised capacity to make disciplined inquiries into those things we need to know, but do not know yet', Arjun Appadurai, 'The Right to Research' quoted in Carolina Rito 'What is the Curatorial Doing?' in *Institution as Praxis,* Sternberg, 2020, p. 54.

6 The discourse on support structures is greatly informed here by Céline Condorelli, (Céline Condorelli, *Support Structures*, Sternberg Press, 2009).

7 'I've been thinking more and more of study as something not where everybody dissolves into the student, but where people sort of take turns doing things for each other or for the others, and where you allow yourself to be possessed by others as they do something. That also is a kind of dispossession of what you might otherwise have been holding onto, and that possession is released in a certain way voluntarily, and then some other possession occurs by others'. Stefano Harney and Fred Moten, *The Undercommons,* Minor Compositions, 2013 pp. 109-110.

environments. Its other aim is to understand research practice as emergent within the material and design negotiations of its support structures. This later focus can only be accomplished if the design of these structures is not pre-conditioned by the institution, but formed by the necessities of the researchers' doing and making. While these considerations are important within the actual process of a poliset (and particularly so at a.pass) this section will concentrate on the moment and politics of a poliset initiation.

A poliset is necessarily a temporary condition for several reasons: first of all, within the capitalist structures it is framed as wasteful. The institution gives away its resources with an explicit agreement to not receive anything in return. There is a limit to how far this can be taken. Second, the intrinsic reason is maybe even more important: a poliset should not become an institution in itself, it should neither aim at functionality, nor consolidate, nor establish habitual structures, nor solidify. The best way to accomplish that seems to me to limit its life cycle: to dissolve the poliset before it establishes itself and try another one sometime later and somewhere else. The third reason, as I will discuss a bit later, is that poliset is proposed as a melting phase in an institutional cycle of solidification: a necessary (and necessarily temporary) dissolution of structures, in order for them to grow organically from commoning and for the transformed institution to resume its supportive and productive functioning.

The themes, politics, collaborations and discussions of a poliset emerge from the work of the users and their collaborative engagements. It's main quality is ambiguity, it cannot be described in project terms, or in terms of its aims, as any of these descriptions would centralise an essentially decentralised and disorganised practice. Poliset therefore holds the space for all possible formats and aims and invites the [researcher/artist/worker] to formulate the necessary processes of collaboration and engagement from within their process. The space is neither fully organised around a form of consensus (majority rule, curatorial hierarchy, etc.), nor is it fully individualised in the sense of separated cohabitation of the collective atelier model.

During a.pass poliset 2020W38-40 in Brussels, these were the practices I could observe happening in the same space within a timeframe of three weeks:

> planning+building, building-out-loud, unbuilding, care (washing, cleaning), care (emotional support, help with apartment search), cooking, lunch together, reading, writing, note-taking, reading theory together, discussing in group and one to one, critique, feedback, collaborating (helping, sharing a practice, inventing practices), teaching, development of theory in situ, offering workshops, hesitating, waiting, doubting, dancing, performing, singing in a band, music improvisation,

> film set building, filming, directing, book publishing (corrections and proofreading), painting, sketching, video analysis, scenography, research development, mentoring, individual administration (applications, budgets, emails etc.), collective schedule organisation (proposals for showings and shared research), a.pass organisational meetings, tech support, body practice (warm-up, yoga, etc).

All of this was embedded in a general framework of low-level self-organised activity, hangout and smalltalk.

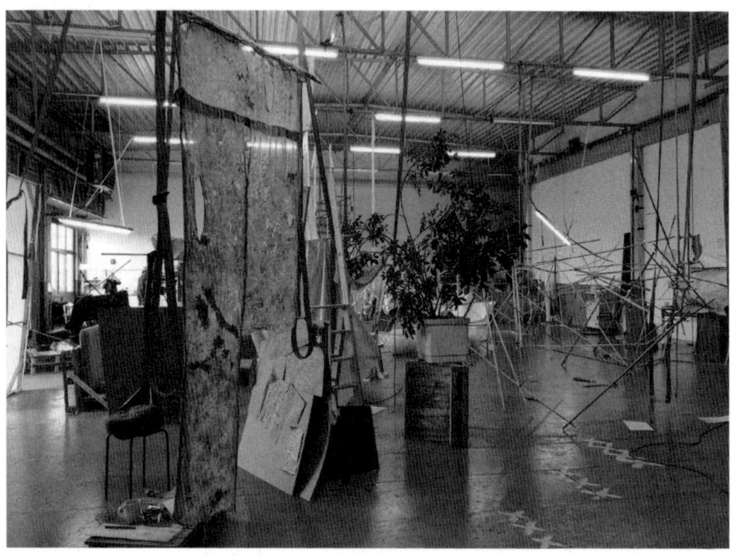

To initiate a poliset, I engage in several intertwined attempts. I call them attempts because they never fully materialise as they encounter institutional and individual limits. They are crucial as shared inquiries into the institutional space and together formulate a militant way of studying institutions by the way of engaging in them. The complication which I can never fully resolve is that in order to make these inquiries a however common concern, I have to operate exactly on the border between monotecture and polytecture. My work as an initiator of a poliset, with an experience of – and responsibility to it as a practice – is to create moments of transmission of these concerns to the larger group. The choice is how to go about it: whether to use the power to call for attention passed on to me by the inviting institution and paradoxically actualise monotecture in a supposedly politectural space, or to fragment these concerns and spread them over time, while already being in the process of disorganising and reorganising as a group (whereby dealing with the inevitable 'danger' that this re-organisation will follow habitual group politics). I have tried many different ways to work within this double bind, and while no transition from mono- to polytecture is smooth, I have found that it has to be a *transition*: a gradual collapse and disorganisation. Ideally at some point within this transition, the commoners of a poliset will find a way to be invested in keeping it fluid and unset, and the initiator will transition to be one of these stakeholders.

A poliset starts from working towards an indeterminate but not empty communal space. The group and institution which initiates it establishes a space that is full of materials, resources, and other kinds of support, for example, a common budget for invitations and contributions. The ingredients vary from institution to institution and from group to group. The important aspects are: the materials and structures are not only curated towards specific individual practices, but are a collection of indeterminate materials which can be used in multiple ways. The materials should be recycled, I usually find most of what a poliset might need in cellars and storage spaces of the hosting institution.

The first attempt is to bring all stakeholders of this practice together in one space. At a.pass and other institutions, that means that this practice ideally involves everyone or most of the people who are immediately connected to 'making this project happen'. This, for example, includes not only artists and researchers of a.pass, but also the administration and production coordinators, mentors, artistic coordinator(s), curators of a particular block, technical support, etc. The institution moves into its own spaces together with the artists and becomes unsettled on its own ground, opening its inside and outside doors.

Unsettling means quite literally, the process of leaving one's established workspace and joining the communal one. This brings all stakeholders into the same condition; having to re-imagine their work process and space in the presence of others, and also of becoming available and present to join processes they have no control over.

In an idealised version, which I have not been able to fully manifest, everyone involved in the making and maintenance of a particular institution would come to the shared poliset space. It is a utopia of creating new proximities and connections and a softening of the architecturally supported institutional structures so that they can be reshaped into a new support system. This, like many utopias, is also a dystopia which I shy away from due to the level of organisational power this attempt would require in order to succeed. To really make this happen on an institutional level, people with the power to compel others to join would have to use that power, which would be contrary to the politics of a voluntary gathering. So, I leave it at the *attempt* to involve all of the stakeholders of the institution and it's ok if this attempt reaches its natural limit and thus does not shift its politics in the process.

But what this attempt points to as its horizon is that an institution is a temporal structure that should embrace a rhythm of softening and collapsing, so that its 'soft body' – the common goals, relations, politics – can have the opportunity to shape its hard shell – its regulations, contracts, its material and immaterial borders.

The second attempt is to challenge the modes of access to the space. By access I mean simultaneously, who is able to come through the door and who is able to physically change the space. Poliset attempts to create a space within the institution that is radically open to use *and* redesign. Every institution handles this attempt differently. During a poliset at a.pass, every visitor is welcome to use the space according to their practice, thus becoming a user/designer. Moreover, every user is welcome to invite (and responsibly introduce to the space) any number of people who might be important for a particular practice. If this practice requires an audience, that user will invite (and take care) of an audience, if a practice requires specific expertise, the user can invite an expert, and so on and so on. The aim is to give over the power of hosting (and therefore of selecting and excluding) to the practitioners themselves. Oftentimes, in the context of a large institution like a festival, this networked openness is complicated to negotiate, because the festival would prefer to issue a general invitation to the space, and possibly charge for admission. But who is inviting in this case? If it is not the artists themselves, the very question of when to open the space would urge the poliset to consolidate and come up with a general plan of opening times, performative situations, 'something to see' etc., forcing it to organise as a monotecture. The marketing team would then write a text, which would be sent to me for approval, and just like that, all traditional power structures are re-installed. Therefore, a poliset does not have a concept of 'audience' in its language, but is open and welcoming at the same time.

The third attempt is to question and eventually disorganise whatever has already been spatially organised by the institution in its particular understanding of 'shared research practice'. That usually involves some kind of supportive arrangement of tables and chairs as well as a set of written or unwritten rules in terms of how, when, and by whom the space is used. To give one extreme example, I have recently taken part in a collective moving-in to a space that was given by an educational institution to a group of PhD in the Arts candidates. The collective research space consisted of 12 incredibly heavy, practically unmovable tables with 12 individual PC workstations on top of them. For two days, we had invested a lot of work in order to unbuild this set-up, so that we could come up with our own design for what we understood as research practice. This might be an extreme example, but some version of this idea about artistic practice exists in most institutional spaces that I have encountered. Artists residencies consider a space equipped if there is a table and a chair in it. Artists then sit around that table and show each other work that has been and can only be done elsewhere.

So, what is an institutional space which is void of its organisation? As there is no empty space in general – meaning no unmarked, unregulated space inside of an institution – the very notion of 'empty' has to be negotiated. Usually, I resort to imposing the absence of tables and chairs, and any other supposedly useful office furniture. To replace the institutional furniture, the group goes scavenging in the cellars in the beginning of poliset, has a budget to procure materials and donates materials from their practice to the common space.

This process is directly related to another attempt that always fails from the start: the attempt to start together. I propose a collective gathering of materials and a moving-in on the first day that ends with a potluck dinner. This is problematic in the same way as the organised transmission of the stakes of this project is problematic. All of these initial agreements and proposals have, of course, been pre-negotiated with a certain group of people: I have already been invited and given the power and means to clear the space, negotiate the timeframe and to negotiate all the conditions for the project to happen. So I am in a sense ahead, I have already engaged in being *archon* and now have to work backwards and dismantle that role as the poliset progresses and the group takes over.

These attempts can be summarised as one: Poliset tries to de-condition the conditions of practice in an institution, so that practice can happen *on its own terms.* This requires a dis-assembling of some standard institutional structures like spatial elements (a table, or a circle where the whole group meets), or temporal elements (a single schedule that segments everyone's time into private and collective), institutional representation (like organised hosting, or a designation of the whole space as an exhibition) and discursive organisation (what has value and meaning in the space). Some structures are either kept out of the space (like tables and chairs), some are introduced critically and sparingly based on need (like group circles) and some are kept decidedly polyphonic (like the question of what this space is for, or what are we doing here).

By removing some of the conditions,[8] I rely on (and therefore reinforce) the presence of other conditions, like the inherent separation between me as organiser and the organised participants. The only way out of this is through an attempt to decentre myself after creating the conditions for the gathering. I try to do this without being irresponsible to the needs of the gathering, or to the needs of the institutional support system.

The last attempt is to provide and discuss structures which would allow for both consensual and non-consensual modes of being together. It is important for poliset that the 'we' is not one group, but a fluctuating arrangement of ad-hoc groupings with different aims, stakes and politics. Participation must include modes of non-participation and refusal without excluding them from cohabitation or support.

All of these attempts are simple, even simplistic, but the complications arise from making these simple refusal counter-gestures a manifested practice in a space that habitually follows other protocols. The deeper practice, or the political conundrum, lies exactly in the moment of using dominant structures, powers and hierarchies to establish counter-proposals within them, in the moment of entering an institution in an organised manner in order to disorganise and establish commoning structures. As Audre Lorde rightfully teaches us: *The master's tools will never dismantle the master's house,*[9]... and yet they also must. Poliset is one practice among many which proposes that we can use and redesign institutions and that institutions can initiate and support processes of self-transformation while we are looking for new tools. While there might be a way to abandon altogether the infinitely nested support structure of institutions-within-institutions, there is still a parallel work of transformation that can happen from within it. A step towards this work is the *still building* of spaces within institutions in order for the institutions to be transformed by the practices which they set out to support.

8 This process is discussed at greater length in this book in my conversation with the artist Krõõt Juurak, 'A Good Workshop'.

9 Audre Lorde, 'The Master's Tools Will Never Dismantle The Master's House', Berkeley, 2007, as quoted by Nora Sternfeld in 'Give Her The Tools, She Will Know What To Do With Them' in *The Constituent Museum*, Valiz, 2018, p. 160.

Samah Hijawi

The Dove that Looks like a Frog

The Dove that Looks Like a Frog was born in 2011 to parents from Palestine – both artists, who have dedicated their whole lives and their artistic careers to the liberation of the Palestinian people from colonial rule. For its parents, *The Dove that Looks Like a Frog* is a symbol of the continuous fight of the Palestinians, and their demands for restitution and freedom. This history was quite a heavy and loaded history to carry.

Moreover, it was born in 2011(!!), the monumental year when people across Arab countries rose in protest for dignity and freedom. It was a time when the whole world held its breath with great hopes – because if the Arab people could gain their freedom, everyone could.

But hope fell into despair, and then darkness.

The Dove that Looks Like a Frog needed some distance from the whole mess...distance to bring a clearer view upon itself, and its place in the worlds it inhabits. So in 2014, it migrated to Belgium to join the a.pass programme.

It was a cold, dark, wet January in Brussels when it arrived.

Being the first of its kind to join a.pass from any Arab country, it was made to feel like a bit of an anomaly. It was confronted with wide eyes, questioning faces: slightly apologetic, sympathetic. Eyes caught up in centuries of navel gazing that obscure other expressions of lives outside the fortress of their worlds. This frustrated *The Dove that Looks Like a Frog* and it struggled and pushed back against this othering.

But the fact was, it was living in the heart of empire.

There were indications of wealth everywhere, gained on the backs of, and from the lands of other people. On top of it all, this violence was celebrated...monuments erected in cities of men astride horses, who in their time killed thousands. And in the complicit hush of museums, paintings marking Europe as the beacon of civilisation and knowledge, a civilisation for which many others have – and continue to be – destroyed by.

One day, as *The Dove that Looks Like a Frog* was meandering the streets of Brussels, it met the man who is apparently synonymous with the formation of the Belgian State:

Godefroid de Bouillon The First King of Jerusalem Born in Brabant Died in Palestine in 1100

Ah Bon? And what is the king of Palestine doing here?...in the middle of Brussels, high on the hill, overlooking the Grand Place...astride his fine, angry-looking stallion (no great man rides a mare, of course).

It was the last place *The Dove that Looks Like A Frog* expected to find a king of Palestine. And then the question presented itself: Does that in fact mean that *The Dove That Looks Like a Frog* is actually Belgian?

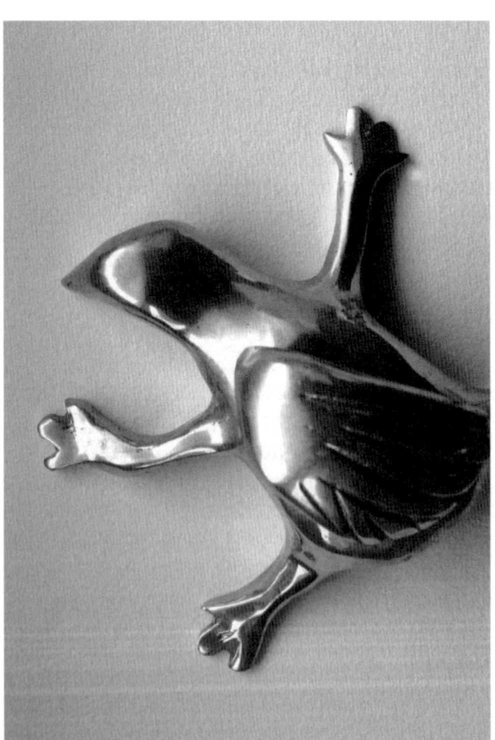

Images next pages in sequence:

The Dove that Looks Like a Frog, 2013
bronze, nickel mixture
15cm x 12cm

The Dove of Peace, 2021
photograph
42cm x 59cm

Godefroid De Bouillon, The King of Jerusalem, 2018
collage
59cm x 42cm

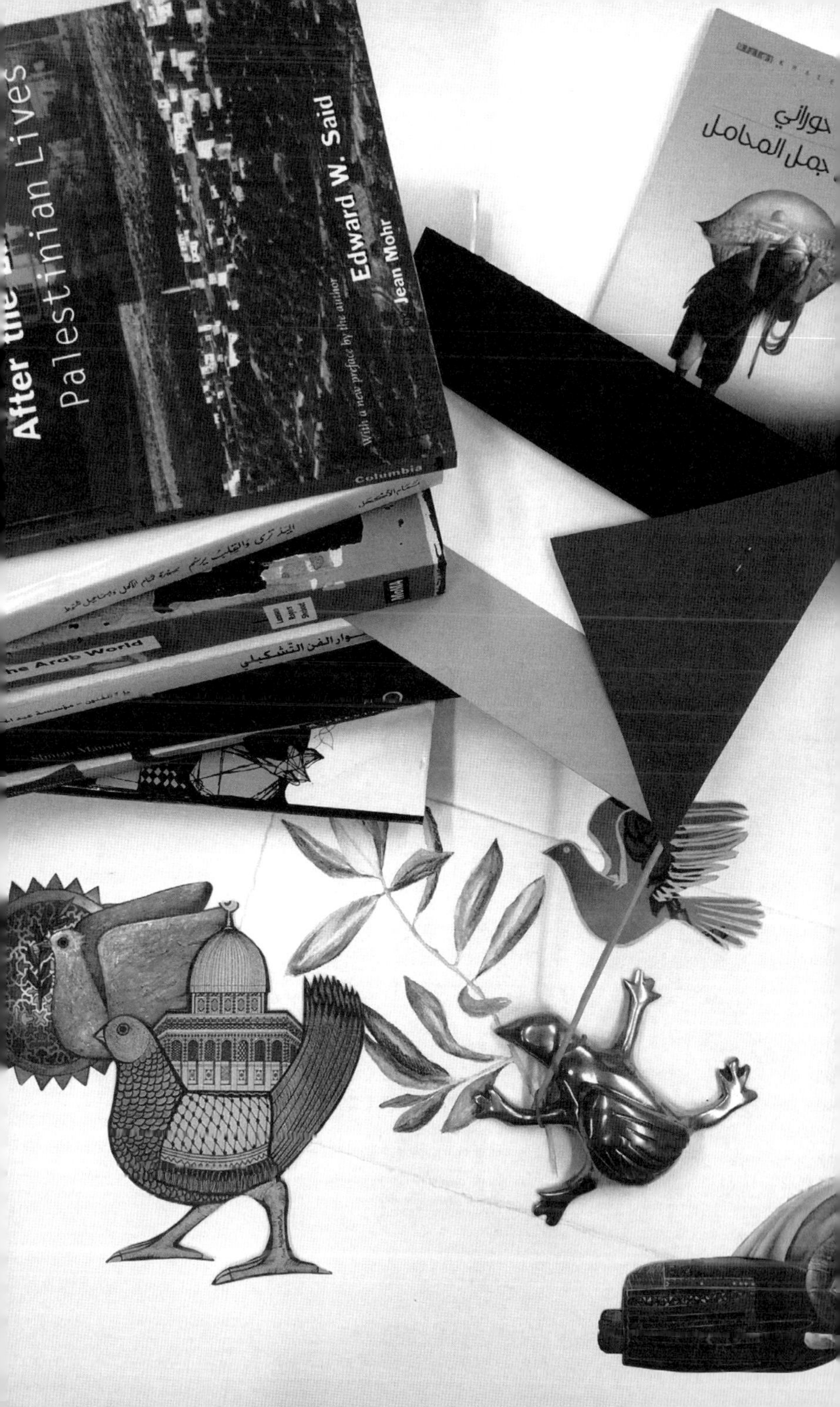

Palestinian Lives
Edward W. Said
Jean Mohr
With a new preface by the author
Columbia
حوراني
جمل المحامل

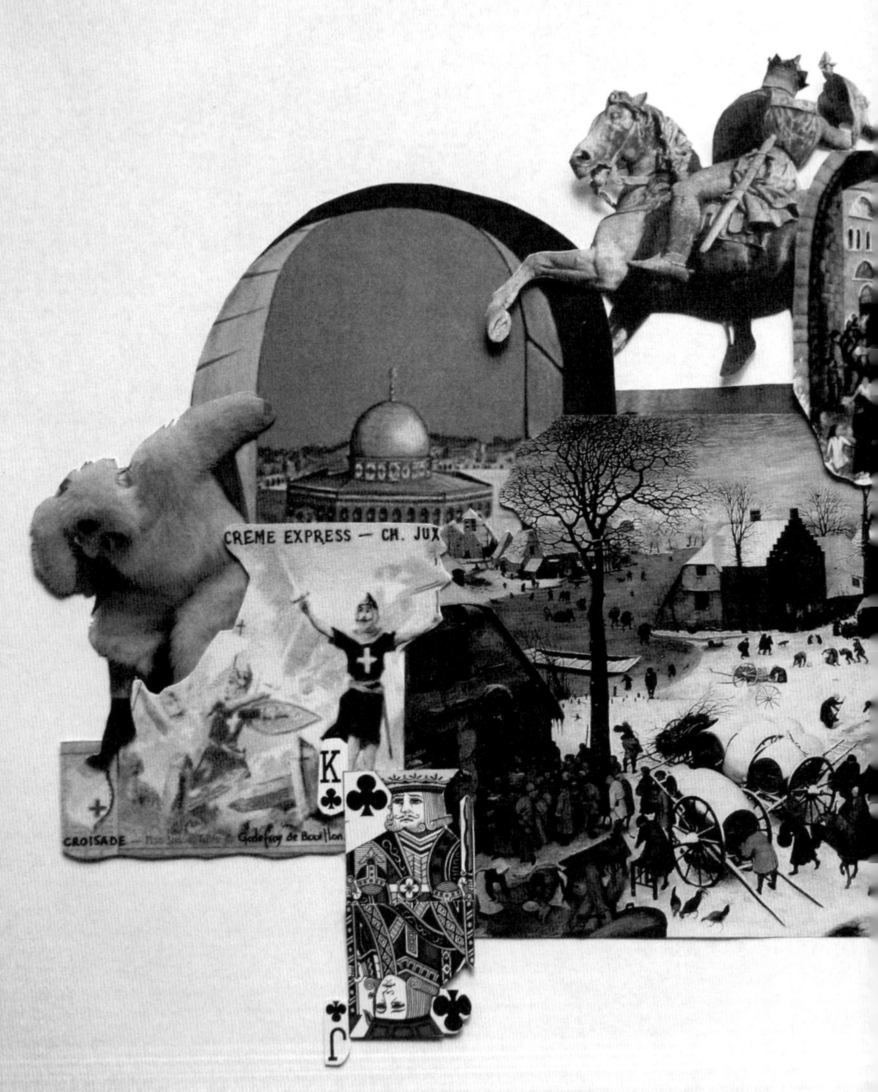
CREME EXPRESS — CH. JUX
CROISADE

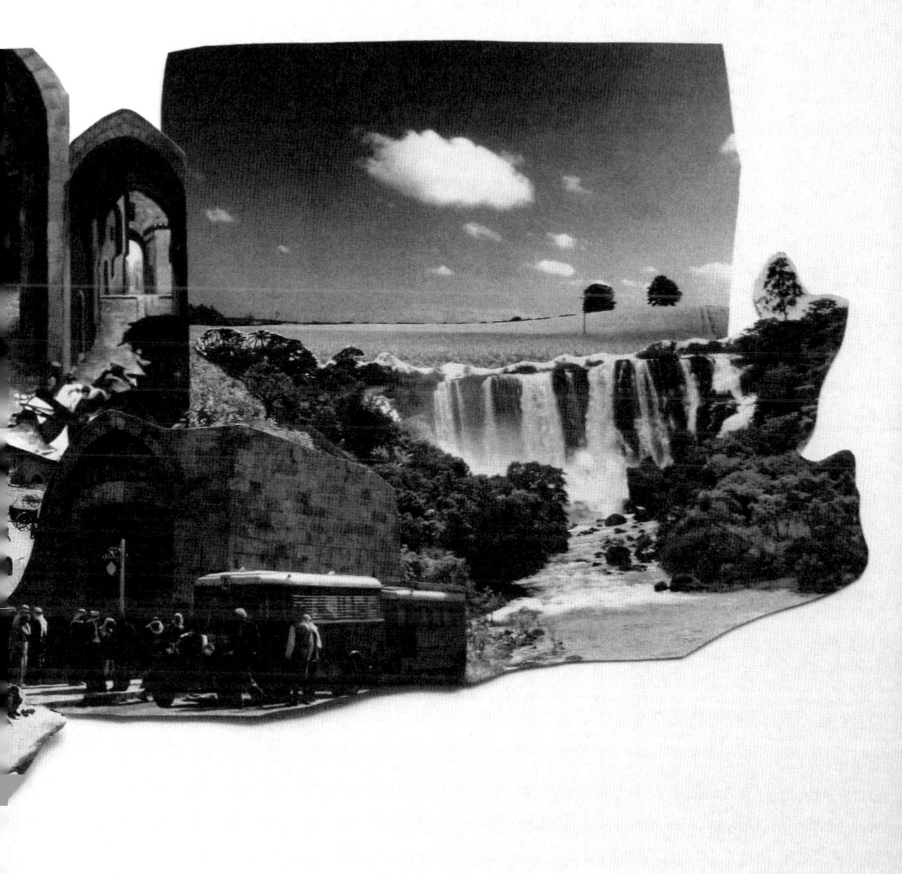

Amy Pickles
Chloë Janssens
Túlio Rosa

Notes after On Coloniality

PLAY

A year prior to the event On Coloniality, the three of us – participants of the postgraduate programme at a.pass and authors of this text – formed a working group to deepen our researches. We sought to speak together, and with others, about themes related to memory and contemporary dimensions of coloniality – a subject that connected our three research practices. Throughout this year, we shared mentoring sessions with different artists, and organised two events. The first, Cracks & Containers, May 2021, was held at a.pass, and hosted conversations with artists: Saddie Choua, Sofie Deckers, Sami Hammana, Quinsy Gario and a.pass block curator Kristien Van den Brande. The second, On Coloniality, November 2021, was hosted in KBK Brussels and PianoFabriek.[1] The programme included workshops, talks, screenings and performances to expand our conversations through (and into) coloniality with artists and thinkers working in this realm. In taking the event outside the walls of a.pass, we hoped to form a porous programme for people from within the institution and those outside to learn about the manifold dimensions of coloniality together.

These events became possible in 2020 due to the internal structure of a.pass opening space for curatorial inputs through the Participants' Assembly (PA). The initial intentions of the PA were to create a space where participants could talk amongst themselves and address issues related to the institution. Generally, what happens in the PA is decided by those from within, and it radiates outwards in different forms. A budget was added later to its toolbox, creating conditions for participants to self-initiate-and-co-organise content within the educational programme, up to €2,000 per block.

We were invited to share our reflections on On Coloniality and the activities organised through the Participants' Assembly, and as such posed questions to each other to elaborate on what happened in the process of preparing and accomplishing this event together. The following words are not a linear read, but a fractured cut of our ongoing conversations.

AMY TO TÚLIO

You work with references collected from archives on opposite sides of the Atlantic Ocean. These varied institutional, cultural and personal archives contain accounts of colonial processes that took place – and continue to take place – in these (socio)geographies that are connected, and distanced by, a body of water. When you bring these materials together, I begin to sense how we can displace

1 The full programme of On Coloniality is available on the a.pass website: apass.be

dominant, colonial narratives with stories that tell us otherwise. I feel my inherently British colonial mode of perception displaced amid other modes of being, and feel a multiplicity of sensing is at the forefront of your attention. When we went to see the *Tupinambá* mantle in the Art & History Museum in Brussels, you read *'Curar o Mundo'* [To heal the world] by/with indigenous leader Glicéria Tupinambá, and I learn again that I can comprehend certain things while not knowing them. Glicéria's text 'describes her encounter with the mantle [a type of cloak], and her process in the restoration of this tradition after centuries of latency'.[2]

My life is far away from the feathered mantle, but also very close. I imagine smashing the glass vitrine that displays the mantle to touch and feel for myself how the museum sewed two cloaks together to make a tall, imposing figure. The seam joining them lets me sense a fictional narrative sewn by the museum collectors, and while I place my fingers into a weave holding red feathers, I sense Glicéria's act of remembering. Through interweaving our differences, we can comprehend coloniality. We can make tangible its ubiquitous form. How do we make a space that allows these differences to come together, without perpetuating colonial structures of value and knowledge sharing? What modes of interaction can let us sense all the connections (across time, place, economy, narrative...) that compose what coloniality is?

TÚLIO TO AMY

I think that in order to allow these different stories and places come together, we might need to do a double movement. On the one hand, we need to acknowledge the differences that reside within the spaces and contexts we inhabit, while there is an urgency to develop a kind of sensibility and form of attention to the way in which locations, histories, knowledges and memories are fully entangled.

There is something the artist Kader Attia said[3] that stayed in my mind, and I come back to very often. He proposes that to remember is to restore the membership of something, to pair together what was artificially broken apart. For me, this way of thinking gives notions of memory and repair a whole different meaning. When addressing the legacies of colonialism, we often have the impulse to think about practices of reparation that demand the restitution of something (an object, resources, etc.). But the first

---

2 Glicéria Tupinambá, '*Curar o Mundo*' [To heal the world], n-1 edições, 2021. Available in Portuguese.

3 Kader Attia, 'Remembering the Future' in *Deserting from the Culture Wars*, Cambridge: MIT Press, 2020 p. 201.

step might be to understand how these two universes, that seem to be separated, are fully entangled. When Satch Hoyt shared his practice during our event, I wrote: If repair can happen, through objects or sonic materials, this is only possible because there is a connection between what was taken and what remained, a connection that never really disappeared. In the ongoing project, 'Afro-Sonic Mapping: Tracing aural histories via sonic transmigrations', Satch is returning sound recordings of music and culture made in the African continent, back to the communities where they were recorded. In the conversation we had, he mentioned that musicians in Angola, by listening to the materials, said they could finally 'play together' with their ancestors. What might allow this dialogue? It is not only the materials themselves, but sensibilities that musicians of the past and those in the present share. Repair happens not by re-placing the 'object', but through the restoration of this connection across temporalities, geographies and ancestral paths.

Our collaboration with Glicéria Tupinambá, which you mention in your question, was exactly about re-pairing, making her words encounter the mantle made by her kin so long ago. At the same time, it was about bringing something to the spaces we inhabit (a.pass, art institutions, etc.) that can challenge our perceptions and understandings – in this case the words of Glicéria in the form of a written and spoken text. The presence of the mantle in Brussels suggests a connection, but it is through the words and perception of Glicéria that we can really grasp what this might mean. The physical proximity or the possibility of smashing the glass and touching the mantle emerges when we create a space to look at the mantle through a different perspective. Our attention is then able to shift from the spectacular visuals to its history and materiality.

Going back to your question, I think space can be created by insisting on 're-pairing' things, putting materials together, re-establishing connections. When we invited Helena Vieira, a transfeminist writer and thinker from Brazil, our interest was to reconnect a concept that we have been using here, coloniality, with the urgency and the thoughts emerging in the context in which it was first elaborated (Abya Yala/Latin America). When Peruvian sociologist Aníbal Quijano started to work on this term (coloniality), he was looking for something that could account for the ways in which power and the regulation of life in Abya Yala were still dependent on the colonial rationale. By inviting Helena to trace the trajectory of this concept and its contemporary implications, we proposed to honour a specific tradition of thought that is grounded in Abya Yala, while reconnecting certain ideas with the experiences they enable/refer to. We repaired these two universes in order to be able to expand and move further with the concept that connects them.

AMY TO CHLOË

When discussing what to write in this text, you proposed to reflect on the budget as a preparation for writing, and as a document of our preparations for On Coloniality.

Working alongside you, I admire your attitude towards preparing. Your methods feel systematic, whether working with assembled materials or with people while another attention to arranging and ordering comes in through your practice as a graphic designer.

Inside KBK Brussels, you built an installation for On Coloniality. You built it in character as Chelsea, your alter ego. Chelsea is busy preparing for ecological collapse from our escalating climate breakdown. Tinned food, candles, books about plants, assembled debris was collected from the flooded areas of Wallonia, Chelsea is getting ready like *you* are getting ready.

Ahead of our event, you shared the publication 'Who's still doing minimal design? A conversation on DESIGN AND COLONIALITY between Nontsikelelo Mutiti and Chloë Janssens'.[4] This conversation was initiated through the format of a.pass personal mentoring,[5] but opened out into publishing. You developed the internal mode of a.pass mentoring – usually one on one interaction – by extending it out into print and paper to other readers.

When I consider these acts alongside your role as a facilitator – something you are learning in climate activism – it feels like you build into the future in a very considerate mode. To organise means to look ahead and it feels like you are planning your work – be it printed materials, facilitation, installation – to interact with others.

But I think you build for yourself too. Collecting, arranging and organising as a way to understand. Is that what also drew you to the budget, a system that tries to understand, to make sense? How does organising help you comprehend On Coloniality now?

---

4 Nontsikelelo Mutiti and Chloë Janssens, 'Who's still doing minimal design? A conversation on DESIGN AND COLONIALITY between Nontsikeleo Mutiti and Chloë Janssens', Self-Published for On Coloniality, 2021.

5 *a.pass* has a system of mentoring consisting of three structures: the dedicated mentors' sessions, the coordinator mentor sessions and the personal mentors' sessions. The dedicated mentors are proposed by *a.pass* each block. Participants can choose two out of the three proposed mentors for personal or collective sessions. Each block, the participants have a mentoring session with the artistic coordinator to discuss their a.pass trajectory, projects and mentoring plans. The personal mentors are invited by the participants in relation to their personal research. Each participant has access to a personal budget to deepen and enrich their research. This budget can also be used collectively, as in some of the cases we mention in this text.

CHLOË TO AMY

The a.pass budget was a key element that made it possible to organise On Coloniality. a.pass making this money available to us was already a gesture of building, or at least preparation for building the fundament from which we were invited to take further. Also, outside On Coloniality, the way a.pass makes a budget available for participants is a very strong tool for each participant to build, strengthen or expand their personal research. Building, thinking and preparing for the event, we had five budgets we could draw from: the a.pass budget that was made available solely for this event, the budget of the Participants' Assembly and our own personal budgets. The personal budget is a wallet each participant of a.pass has access to at the start of their a.pass trajectory from which they can invite mentors outside the institution for mentoring sessions. Because of the structure of the personal budget, it made sense to me to reach out to artists that I felt a connection with. It seems as if we used the different budgets for different purposes: personal budget for artists linked to our individual practices, participants' budget for artists related to communal interests (such as the workshop on nonviolent communication by Jeyanthy Siva), and the a.pass budget as a tool for bringing these different practices together. I don't think we ever defined the budget like this during the process, but in the aftermath, it seems that's more or less what happened.

Organising always asks for compromise. There were certain limitations, such as a set budget and changing COVID-19 restrictions. Questions arose, like whether to invite big names, which would lead to renting a big venue to invite a large amount of people. Small would mean less people and probably also a different, more intimate approach. Having a limited budget is like having a strict design brief – it puts boundaries from which particular questions emerge. Talking through the budget in our many meetings made our desires for the event much clearer than when we were imagining the event 'freely'.

CHLOË TO TÚLIO

I'm thinking of remnants. You joked with me after On Coloniality that we're a band that goes solo after their success. I feel that from now on, there will be no solo anymore. The entanglement continues in the after work. I feel like we created a soup of remnants. I feel an urge to draw lines between theory, artistic practices and different artists. I want to stick my fingers inside those practices and feel them! Now the event has ended, it seems easier to engage with the many artistic practices we encountered during, and in preparation of, On Coloniality. How are you processing the event and what are we in fact processing? Our own, individual experiences?

TÚLIO TO CHLOË

I'm thinking about how temporality is key to the way we make sense of things, and how it operates differently in each case. The encounter with the Zapatistas, for example, was the result of six weeks of engagement with RAZB [Réseau d'accueil des Zapatistes en Belgique] and the other activities of La Gira Por La Vida in Belgium.[6] For me, it was through the work of preparation, that included not only attendance to other events organised by RAZB, but also taking part in the logistics of their journey in Belgium (organising transport, food, facilitating translations), that the most important/revealing questions and experiences took place. It was through these practicalities and daily activities that a deep understanding of our differences, of our connections, of the meaning and the impact of their journey and their words could happen. With this example, what I might be trying to say is that we process these interactions in many different ways, within and beyond the borders of the encounter, be it a 'before' or an 'after' or any other moment in the spiral of time. I wonder if this is also the case of the public gathering we organised. It might be that we made sense of it already, while preparing, projecting, imagining?

CHLOË TO AMY

I think we both see facilitation as a way to build collectivity. In the frame of On Coloniality, I'm wondering: are we really facilitating for the group or just for ourselves? In other contexts, I often feel I'm facilitating my surroundings to fit myself inside it. That's kind of a strange trick. Facilitation is a very mindful exercise, because you really need to be in the moment to be a good facilitator for the group. You need a suitcase full of methods/

---

6 Between June and November 2021, several delegations of the Zapatista National Liberation Army (EZLN) travelled to Europe to have meetings, dialogue and exchanges with groups committed, from different perspectives, to dismantling capitalism, racism, imperialism, colonialism and other violent systems that destroy life. This movement was called 'Gira Por La Vida' [A journey for life].

actions/games from which you can effortlessly pick the right element for the right moment. However, it seems that we were always organising this 'momentous' magic up front (yes, from behind our computers!). I noticed for myself that I was in such an organising mode during the event that I had difficulties being present. How was this for you?

AMY TO CHLOË

This contradiction – of facilitating for yourself – sparks a resurfacing anxiety in me. In one sense, we did facilitate for ourselves. We invited guests we were curious to learn with and become closer to. We planned modes of interaction that we would 'benefit' from, and we were each working to present a particular focus on coloniality from our overlapping, but singular, research. We are now writing this text, and we are aware of all these actions gathering our 'cultural capital'. I don't think we moved away from the a.pass tradition of personal budget for individual development, but we did shift our motivations towards collective aims.

Our work together felt volatile. At times nearly impossible, then generous, and there were even creative revelations. Working collectively allowed us to sustain a determination to keep thinking, arranging, reconsidering and challenging the programme we were making. Our collective forced all of us to compromise. Collective exhausts us while at the same time feeds us. Collective makes me know it can be different. I would never have organised nor facilitated our programme if I had worked alone.

Would you say there is a hierarchy between facilitation and participation? In the tension between these roles, I am learning that to develop participant-led content within the structure of a.pass, there has to be a lot of listening.

We needed to attune our ears in many directions and now, in this 'after' of On Coloniality, I think we lacked an attention towards the practices of our fellow a.pass participants. We concentrated on a public programme that could open up the dense and immense topic of coloniality. With that in mind, we gave ourselves over to deep consideration of content and we felt an urgency to host a multitude of voices. But we could have been more thoughtful towards the ears that the voices were reaching.

During the afternoon of the first public moment of On Coloniality, we hosted a collective reading of 'Decolonial Listening: an interview with Rolando Vázquez', by Zoë Dankert.[7]

7 Rolando Vazquez in an interview by Zoë Dankert, 'Decolonial Listening', for soapboxjournal.net

This conversation had been shared with us and a.pass participants by artists WORKNOT! X Sarmad in their work 'correspondence bike messenger round bxl' where the three of us cycled around the city delivering packages of curated printed materials and caring matter on the topic of coloniality. WORKNOT! X Sarmad visited us on our final day of the programme, and when I read their proposition again, I find their intentions for their in-person visit: 'we see this session as a collective learning moment of sharpening our ears, and sharing our thoughts with one another'.[8]

Their words remind me that listening is a way of sharing. Listening is a mode to really notice and spend time with a position different from your own. I hope that by practicing listening we can learn to facilitate as a collective, to learn how to learn together.

For On Coloniality we learnt from and with: Jeyanthy Siva, EZLN Delegation (Gira por la Vida,) WORKNOT! X Sarmad (Alireza Abbasy, Golnar Abbasi, Arvand Pourabbasi) Daniela Ortiz, Saddie Choua, Satch Hoyt, Sami Hammana, Glicéria Tupinambá, Vermeir & Heiremans, Line Algoed, Juan Pablo Pacheco Bejarano, Elodie Mugrefya, Nontsikelelo Mutiti, Helena Vieira and the Institute of Colonial Culture (initiated by Philippe Mikobi and Maarten Vanden Eynde).

8 The following text was shared in the On Coloniality programme: WORKNOT! X Sarmad, workshop 'correspondence bike messenger round bxl' 'In this session, we will discuss decoloniality by thinking through issues such as institutions, listening, whiteness, and displacement. Specifically, we will think about the role of logistics that (re)distribute access and resources in order to facilitate flows of thought and strategy. This session is considered the last delivery round of 'correspondence bike messenger round bxl', which started a few weeks in advance of this event as creating a network to share and receive thoughts, notes, gifts, etc., from a distance. The bike messengers, the participants and the dispatchers will all be present. We see this session as a collective learning moment of sharpening our ears, and sharing our thoughts with one another. The starting point of our discussion will be based on the already-distributed packages; the excerpts of texts, care packages and objects. We will share some of the contents from these packages'.

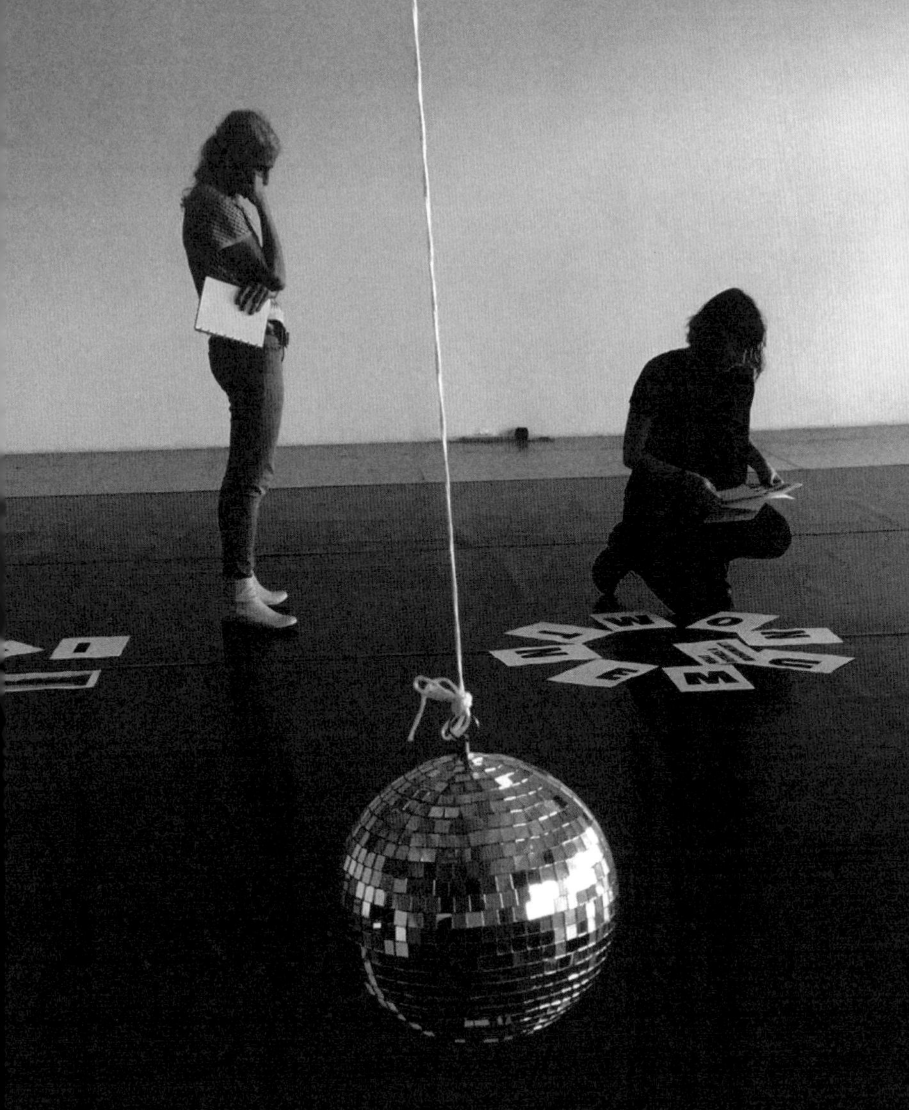
R
HOW IS A
BORDER
MADE?

Part IV

Looking outside-in and inside-out

Lilia Mestre
Philippine Hoegen

The Hyper-attentive School

A Conversation with Guy Gypens and Mathilde Villeneuve

PH: There are two subjects I'd like us to discuss together. One concerns a.pass specifically: I'm curious what you see coming out of a.pass, from your perspectives, your positions. Guy, you are Head of Performing Arts at KANAL – Centre Pompidou here in Brussels, and you Mathilde are the Artistic Director of Buda in Kortrijk. How do you perceive the role of a.pass, let's say, in the artistic field? As programmers and directors of institutions that present art, you both have experience working with people who did a.pass. Do you see something particular that is produced or that's specific about the practices of these people? And then more generally, I would love to know what your thoughts are, from the positions that you have, on the state of the field now and in relation to that – what do you think is important or urgent in art education on this level? But perhaps we should just start with: How do you know a.pass?

MV: I had met Lilia several times, she talked to me about a.pass and I was invited to join the End Presentations at a.pass as a visitor in January 2020. I was very curious about this education that sounded original and specific, it resonates with issues about research in art I am interested in and that have occupied me. For example: when I worked at Les Laboratoires d'Aubervilliers – a transdisciplinary space for research and experimentation in art that I co-directed in France for six years, before coming to Buda – I collaborated with the artist and pedagogue Adva Zakai, who developed a project during one year with the graphic designer Maki Suzuki. In Les Laboratoires, we usually started from the beginning of the research of an artist and supported it all the way until forms happened. In this case, it became publications performed in private apartments in the city of Aubervillers. The way Adva works is in a very, how to say, 'unbuilding' way – something I associate with a.pass. This impression was confirmed when I found out more about the way you work, which seems to be an organic way that unfolds according to encounters, collective exchanges of knowledge, and where research and practice are completely linked.

It reminded me also of the problems that I encountered when I was working at the art school of Cergy (ensapc), close to Paris. There we experienced the European reform which required art schools to attach themselves to universities, to be able to create equivalences between them. And one of the requirements was that students make a short thesis at the end of their five years of studying. We had a lot of debates about the place of this thesis in the trajectory of the students, how it should relate to the practice, or not. Should it be a kind of theory of the practice? Or could it also take on the form of a performance performed in front of the jury? What is the relation between art forms and writing? Can writing be considered as a practice in itself and evaluated as such? etc. I felt that all these questions were already much more developed in a.pass because this was actually the core of the whole project, this strong link, and how theory can bring forth practice and practice can bear theory. And what I felt also was the importance they – you – give to extending... how to say? Looking at a practice as always intertwined with research. Yes, trying to extend what we usually conceive of as the way we produce a piece or the way artists produce performances, with a product you could call research, and with creation, diffusion. These instances are questioned also economically in a.pass, as the methodology is understood as non-linear and as an intertwining of forms and research, and ways of sharing with a public.

PH: So you mean the research continues throughout all the different phases of the project and the project is not conceived of as having one goal or result or product, but much more as a continuum of forms of research?

MV: Yes.

PH: Is that something you recognise, Guy?

GG: Certainly, but I got to know a.pass in an earlier constellation, when the scenography training was still a decisive component and the institute was housed in deSingel in Antwerp. In my mind, there are two versions of a.pass: the one before and the one after 2007. Elke Van Campenhout laid the foundations for the current a.pass from 2007 onwards, with artistic research as the guiding principle and the reason to move to Brussels. It was in that same period that I was appointed artistic co-director of the Kaaitheater. Before that, I had been working as the general manager of Rosas for 17 years, and in that capacity I was also involved in the start-up of PARTS. PARTS and a.pass were very different programmes in terms of content, but they were both subsidised from the same budget line by the Ministry of Education. Both operated outside the classical university structures. I think that my view of a.pass, or the Posthogeschool Podiumkunsten as it was then called, was mainly one from a more classical functional angle.

When Elke introduced her 'systemic change', I didn't really understand the essence of it at first. It was only when Maria Lucia Cruz Correia asked me to be an 'outside eye' for one of her projects within a.pass that I began to better understand the complex weaving between research and artistic creation practice within a.pass.

As a producer and programmer in the 80s and 90s I had witnessed from close by (and contributed to) the developments of and the growing commodification on the performing arts market. The 'what' the 'product' was ruling. The 'how' was less important. They were frivolous, deregulating times. In the first years of the new century, experimental arts organisations started to challenge that. In Brussels they were called Bains Connective, FoAm, Nadine, a.o. By 2007-2008, we were experiencing a global economic and financial crisis and the ecological crisis became painfully apparent. Business as usual became an impossibility. In that sense, a.pass' switch to research practices was exemplary for the rise of the 'how' in the arts world. At the Kaaitheater, we responded to that with formats like Burning Ice. And a.pass became an important inspiration and contributor. What was produced by the students in a.pass rarely ended up in our classical programme. But in a format like Burning Ice, built around the urgent socio-ecological transition, we created a space for artists who shared that sense of urgency and whose focus on how to live and act differently was at the core of their artistic practice.

It was precisely this research into 'standing differently in artistic practice' and 'standing differently in the world' that a.pass offered its participants. The 'how' became the essence and to some extent the 'what'. What you eventually get to see during presentations became less and less a finished product and more and more a practice in which the process was central. This was not obvious to programmers, nor to an audience. 'Witnessing' the practice as such requires a different way of looking at and meeting with the artist and a different way of showing the work. a.pass thus became a place where my own practice as a programmer was challenged and where things became clearer in my mind. It became a place where I, as an outsider, could look for 'allies' and where I could engage in a kind of research of my own as a programmer. This work as a 'programme maker' was very new to me at that time.

In the 1990s, I had programmed two editions of the Springdance festival in Utrecht, but otherwise my career had mainly been within cultural management.

This process was intensified by projects such as Pharmakon.[1]

MV: Can you explain what these projects that you're talking about were?

GG: Pharmakon was a three-day programme in the Kaaistudios around the concept of 'pharmakon' by the French philosopher Bernard Stiegler.[2] It was a collaboration between a.pass, Bains Connective[3] and Kaaitheater.

LM: A seminar involving guests and the participants of a.pass with performances, practices, talks and experiments.

GG: It was a challenging project, certainly for the audience. It was a mix of a thematic programme and a thematic research environment. Opening something like that to the Kaaitheater audience was anything but obvious. In the Kaaitheater, some of the audience always turn up simply because it's in the Kaaitheater.

MV: Which is a good thing!

GG: Certainly. The reactions of the audience put things on edge. If we, as an art institute, not only wanted to show finished art products but also confront our audience with the 'how' and all the uncertainty that comes with it, this required a different kind of guidance and care for that audience, as well as for the artists. In many ways, a.pass was for me a partner in that process. After Pharmakon, similar projects followed with a.pass on other themes such as 'The Artist Commoner, (self) education of new subjectivities'.

---

1 Pharmakon: Whitch Culture? was a three-day 'performative conference' at Kaaitheater that examined artistic and theoretical strategies to counteract the pollution of our society's culture. This conference was a collaboration with a.pass, part of the residency Thematics, a programme for artists and theorists run by Bains Connective. October - December 2014 and part of the transnational Pharmakon project organised by the Institut Nomade.

2 Bernard Stiegler, French philosopher (1952-2020), gave a lecture during the Pharmakon conference on November 28, 2014.

3 Bains Connective was an art laboratory with a multidisciplinary residency programme. In 1997, a group of artists from different backgrounds invested in the renovation of the former swimming pool of Vorst/Forest in Brussels, to create a space for experimentation. The project was mainly driven by the desire to share, exchange and sustain alternative artistic practices in an autonomous environment. http://bains.be/mission-statement/

PH: And how is that now? Because you speak in the past tense, I'm very curious: Where are you now? What went on in the meantime?

GG: Well, two years ago I left Kaaitheater and a while later I started working at KANAL, the museum for contemporary art under construction. The interesting thing about KANAL is that it is an institute that is being built from scratch. That process of 'institution building' interested me. And a.pass was a source of inspiration in this respect, too, from the very beginning. One of the first people I talked to after I started at KANAL was Vladimir Miller. The reason for that conversation was our collaboration in 2019 around his a.pass project 'Settlement'.

LM: That was a big experiment for a.pass actually. The 'Settlement' is a practice that was developed by Vladimir – now it's actually called 'Poliset',[4] because of what the word settlement actually brings about – so it's a practice of space. Of starting with a bare space and building the space up according to the material or spatial necessities of each participants' research, to get in touch with materialities and to see how that reflects in space and creates a certain sociability. On this occasion, the practice was transposed to KANAL and developed there, raising the question: What is this movement of transposition and what is the place of the visitor within this environment? Because again, it's a place where you need to spend time... I think it went quite well, actually.

MV: And you stayed for how long?

GG: Kaaitheater presented the project in KANAL as part of the Performatik[5] festival. So I followed the process as a privileged spectator, not only the presentation but also the construction and the preparation: the moving in and the 'settling'. From that experience, Vladimir and I started our conversation: What would it mean to do such a settlement, not only 'in' KANAL, but 'with' KANAL.

---

4 See 'From Settlement to Poliset' by Vladimir Miller on pages 192-208 of this book.

5 A yearly festival by Kaaitheater in association with a.pass, Argos, Beursschouwburg, Bozar, CC Strombeek, Centrale For Contemporary Art, KANAL–Centre Pompidou, TOPAZ/IN/FINITY, Wiels, workspacebrussels and ZSenne ArtLab. Every other year, Performatik showcases contemporary performance art or 'live art', together with a great many Brussels partners. For 11 days, artists enter a twilight zone in which they tinker with the codes of both the performing arts and the visual arts.

PH: This is something I'm very curious about: in these 'process based', or 'constant research' types of practice, or even situations, there's always the big question of: and what about the audience, what about the visitor? And you both being heads of institutions, this is what you are also preoccupied with. How much room do we give ourselves for things to be difficult for a public? And what role does artistic research education have in that? What relationship do you think we should be building with a potential audience or visitor?

GG: My only concrete artistic experience so far in KANAL was the exhibition *It Never Ends* around the Swiss artist John Armleder.[6] It was my first experience of an exhibition anyway. It struck me that the attitude towards 'time' with which an exhibition visitor starts his tour is very different from that of a spectator in a theatre. For a museum visitor, the 'experience of time' seems more 'open'. He hangs around in the museum, spends the time he wants. In a theatre, this is much more compelling. You know that you have to be in the theatre at 20:30 and that, say, an hour and a half later you are outside again. If you leave earlier, that is a problem. In an exhibition, the spectator is freer. The other side of the coin is of course the 'span of attention' that an exhibition visitor can muster for a work of art. But the fact that visitors 'hang around in the space' offers interesting possibilities. In the Armleder exhibition, we created a specific space for performances within the exhibition route, which extended over four floors. Armleder himself had very much insisted on this. He wanted the visitor to pass through this performance space in any case and for an intensive programme of performances to take place. COVID-19, of course, put a lot of stumbling blocks in the way, but it was a positive experience nonetheless. The visitors looked at the performances in a different way. They were confronted with them anyway and they had to pass by them a second time when they went outside. There seemed to be more peace and openness to the often very slow and contemplative performance work. I think this spatial setting, with different and perhaps fewer codes, offers also a potential for work that is more 'process-based'. But what I said before, it also requires a different way of 'caring for' an audience.

PH: Mathilde, I saw you writing, did this trigger something?

---

6 *It Never Ends – John M. Armleder & Guests*, exhibition at KANAL – Centre Pompidou, September 24, 2020 to April 25, 2021.

MV: There's a difficult question there which we should ask ourselves all the time. Because we shouldn't presume to know the taste of viewers, nor their capacity of receiving, of living an experience or a situation. It's always very important for me to keep bringing that up because it's crazy how we as institutions tend to forget this.

The question is always: Is it accessible? But accessibility is often treated in a very simple way – too simple! The question is more than that. Of course, there are discriminations in society and differences in access to certain experiences or certain educational environments and I don't want to put that under the carpet. But it's important to try to re-complexify the question of accessibility. So that is one point. Then the second point is: sometimes people think that because a performance or experience might be deemed 'difficult', they would rather not do/show it. I would never choose this position. The third point would be that the way I'm navigating this is through multiplicity, through different kinds of experiences proposed to the public and different types of 'access' (meta, affective, sensitive, more directly political...), in the same way that different art forms coexist today.

It's a bit what you said actually, to work with different kinds of attention spans. Hoping that you can move from being a viewer in front of a performance, to a participant, maybe doing workshops, being in a garden, etc. That's why I want to develop this programme Learning Together[7] in Buda, which actually Agnes[8] initiated with two sessions, and that I really want to give a place to, in between the strong public moments of festivals.

PH: Can you explain what Learning Together is?

MV: I think in Buda, Learning Together is the programme most connected to a.pass. It shares some questions, like the doubly critical space of how we do art: How we produce art and what it means to teach it – what kind of pedagogy can we invent? Or, what kind of space can we create to share knowledge and practice? This is really an attempt to try to use art institutions to open up or create conditions

7 Learning Together is a pedagogical platform implemented in BUDA, a collective space for critical reflection, forging links both within and outside the artistic community. The aim is to equip each other, to inform each other's practices and to cross-fertilise the production of sensitive and theoretical knowledge.

8 Agnes Quackels was the artistic director of Buda, Kortrijk from 2011 to 2019.

– meaning space and time – to imagine other ways of sharing research, knowledge and practice. That can be initiated by artists or by curators, it can be initiated by me in dialogue with you. And with no predetermined frames. It can be one week of workshops, like the week-long cycle about death that I'm doing with Fabrizio Terranova for example, through writing workshops, programing films... At the same time, he will be an artist in residency at Buda, coming a few days regularly throughout the year, working in his own field, and he will also take a moment to share his own research. It is important for me to keep opening different possibilities of sharing art.

PH: And now there is an active collaboration planned between a.pass and Buda, right?

MV: The first plan is to host a second iteration of the conference Research Futures[9] in Buda and see how it can be shared with the public. As you know, the public in Buda is quite a challenging question in general, mostly because of its location and its nature, which is in between being a working place for artists and a public one.

LM: I think the notion of time is very interesting actually. How much time is needed for one to actually get acquainted or invested, or dedicated to something? There is something to be said for staying, hanging out informally. Which is also something that comes from the society we are living in: there is maybe a lack of these intertwinings between products and life, or work and life. These are ways to create philosophy again, I would say: How we think about life and what are ways to get in touch with materials and experiences, thoughts... how do you linger there, so that something can bounce off it, a need to live, to continue.

MV: But it's challenging. You have to fight to open time! It is not easy to slow down and trust that things will happen, that connections will be made in time. We are so used (and asked) to look for and get an 'immediate' result, it is a big and collective task to unbuild our relation to productivity.

---

9 The Research Futures conference took place in 2020. As a publicly funded educational platform, a.pass is reviewed by the Ministry of Education in regular five-year intervals. Within this context, a.pass took the opportunity to propose a collaborative process of self-evaluation to four other educational institutions in the field of artistic research: DAI – Dutch Art Institute, NL; Jan Van Eyck Academy, NL; Royal Academy of Fine Arts Antwerp, BE and Uniarts Helsinki, FI. https://apass.be/researchfutures/

GG: I totally agree. In Dutch there is an expression: 'letting time do its work'. In reality, of course, it is rather 'the work that defines time'. Simply creating a space that offers the potential for a different experience of time is not enough. Our affective relationship with time is one of efficiency and intensity. Changing this is not easy. It is also very subjective. Every spectator is different. A project like 'Settlement' was interesting because it worked in different registers. There were different ways to 'make contact', to 'linger'. Pharmakon was a very different situation. Visitors found themselves in an 'environment' with which they felt a kinship or not. Some visitors felt very uncomfortable, others were completely absorbed. It was a bit all or nothing.

LM: But there were also second chances. If you came to listen to Bernard Stiegler, you came with a specific intention, but then you would fall into something else, and you could connect or not with the other propositions. So there were also multiple entries. There were also presentations by the a.pass participants which complexified things and opened questions actually about the environment that was created. The audience could look at many things and see what happened at the interstices of those things.

MV: Actually, I was thinking maybe it's important to say that art doesn't have to be all-inclusive, because it's not a compromise. An art form is not a compromise in itself, so it will not please everyone. It doesn't have to please everyone. It's okay if some people don't feel like entering. They don't have to.

LM: It might be that feeling good is not necessarily the only way to find your way in. You can also enter by resistance.

GG: I agree. But in this case with a.pass, the problem is not that we are too all-inclusive.

LM: No, no. For a.pass it's a real challenge, also because participants are always 'in'. So how do you open up to the outside – what is the invitation?

GG: As a spectator, you not only see a presentation of art works, but you enter a community of makers. You're entering a kind of bubble. And that can provoke different reactions. It's not the same as in a 'normal' curated programme of performances in an institution where the institution stands between the artist and the audience. In a.pass presentations and projects, the institution and the artists are one, even if you bring them to another theatre or space. For me, that was exactly one of the reasons to bring the projects to Kaaitheater. It was somewhat risky and speculative, but it challenged the position of the institution. But for some visitors, it could no doubt be a bit of a daunting situation.

LM: It's a double bind because this place is focusing on the work of people, and not so much how to be open immediately to the general audience. We are not thinking like an exhibition or presentation space opening up to the public. I mean, yes, in some ways, there is the gesture, the invitation, and the question of the politics of the invitation to the other. But it's always a bit of a difficult place because we want to protect that space of questioning, right? To not go too fast into finding solutions for inclusion, for example. They have to come but maybe they have to come a bit later. But I think it's great to raise these questions together with presentation places such as theatres, galleries or art centres...

GG: a.pass functions as a kind of inclusive enclave where artists feel safe. Opening it up is important because it can work as a stepping stone for both artists and audience. But a stepping stone shouldn't be too slippery, or you should provide something to hold on to. And it's not really a problem that you decide for whom it opens itself. The collaborations with other institutions can maybe be a bit more focused on that very question: open for whom and how many?

PH: But maybe then the question is also the when and the why. These collaborative moments between presentational institutions – or houses as they're called here in Belgium – and an educational institution like a.pass, why would you do that? Why would you make those connections and crossovers? I would say it's to learn from each other and for the participants in the programme to sort of flirt with the publicness of that house, to find their position there. But always within a process of learning. And then, what comes after that? I was struck by the fact that you, Guy, said that in the past the people coming out of a.pass – or maybe still in a.pass – fit very well in Burning Ice, but not in the classical programming. I'm quite curious how you see that now because I have a feeling that quite a few people who were in a.pass do find their way into classical programming. So perhaps it is, again, a question of time?

GG: Over the last ten years, things have changed for the better. The 'how' really became important in certain arts institutions. I hope that was the case for Kaaitheater. We could have taken it further of course, but the new artistic coordinators certainly have that ambition. So, indeed you could see an evolution in programming artists whose work was more process and research based. But this was due not only to the openness of the institutions but also to the artists themselves. They too evolved in their capacity to make their work accessible to an audience.

MV: And maybe also there is a difference between when artists are still students/participants at a.pass and enveloped in that community, and when they leave a.pass. The way they present their work will be quite different.

PH: I was just thinking of the term 'performing education'. Is it possible to say that when the whole a.pass team comes to Kaai or Buda and engages in a project which is public, where an audience is welcome, but which is very much also about the thing itself, that actually what you're doing is performing education. You're not performing an artwork, you're not making a symposium necessarily, but you're showing and doing – which is performing – education, or pedagogy.

GG: The cooperation with John Armleder was interesting to me in that context. Like many of his fellow Fluxus artists, Armleder developed a pedagogical and educational practice in the 60s and 70s. The influence of the art scene on pedagogy was very strong in that period. I have the impression that we are in a similar situation today. There is again a mutual influence between art institutions and educational institutions through experimental pedagogy. Not just the a.pass excursions to other institutions but also projects like Learning Together, which Mathilde mentioned, and the Free School of the Kunstenfestivaldesarts are examples of this. Of course, there are big differences with what happened in the 70s. For Fluxus, the element of 'play' was crucial. Today there are other things at stake.

PH: Right, it's about survival now.

MV: Yes, there's another level of urgency.

LM: By the way, we will meet a group of Zapatistas[10] this week. They will come to a.pass. I'm curious to see what we will learn. In relation to what you said – the level of urgency – it's all about how we escape the big neoliberalist situation we're living in? And how not to be paralysed, 'over-thinking' everything we do? The resistance they practice is very simple in a way.

GG: More and more artists step away from their art in favour of activism.

LM: Very much. I was talking with Anna Rispoli about being a mentor in the next block and she was worried about this question. She was telling me: 'I don't know if I'm an artist anymore. I'm getting more and more involved with activism'. And I feel it also within the participants, there's a big question about current practices: 'can we still call it art?'

PH: And can we afford the luxury of calling it art?

GG: It reminds me of the text that Christoph Meierhans wrote about his engagement with Extinction Rebellion. He says that the practices he developed as an artist are actually not changing in the context of Extinction Rebellion, but it's not art anymore.

LM: But then there is the fear that it all becomes very pragmatic. Personally, I like to touch on fictions and monsters, ways of looking that actually go beyond certain fixed pragmatic realities, more like inventing somehow. Things might stop being art because they become pragmatic, like a tool or a form of sharing. Whilst I think the motor is also this other side of inventing: thinking of a society that is not yet there, or that could become...

GG: Art, imagination, stories, ...in the gap between past and future. Yes, it's what we humans can do. But if we consider the state of the world and the role our imagination has played in that, we should maybe also be a bit wary of it.

MV: How do we reinvent the present?

---

10 A delegation of the Zapatista Army of National Liberation (Ejército Zapatista de Liberación Nacional, EZLN) was on tour in Europe in the Fall of 2021. On their journey, they visited different groups and communities that resist territorial dispossession and the destruction of nature. The Zapatistas' intention was to strengthen ties of international solidarity that allow us to imagine other possible worlds. They came to a.pass following the invitation of the postgraduate participants organising the seminar On Coloniality in November 2021.

GG: It makes me think of a beautiful a.pass moment in the permaculture garden in Anderlecht.[11] Being there with the a.pass group who had worked and 'lived' in the garden for weeks created a moment of hyperpresence that was quite unique.

PH: 'Hyperpresence' – can you explain?

GG: Well, being there in a hypersensitive way to try and grasp the complexity of the place and the moment. I remember thinking that if that is what a.pass provokes, it is more than worthwhile.

MV: You became a hyperattentive school. This is very nice!

LM: Thank you!

---

11 The Zenne garden is an association of people who experiment with practices of agroecology and permaculture gardening. Since 2007, the association has been practicing gardening on a precarious urban interstice piece of land along the banks of the Zenne river in the industrial zone of Anderlecht in the city of Brussels.

Vladimir Miller

State Artists without a State: Artistic Research in the Knowledge Economy

A Conversation with Ana Hoffner

Ana Hoffner ex-Prvulovic* is an artist, researcher and writer. She* and Vladimir Miller were colleagues for a brief moment at the PhD in Practice at the Academy of Fine Arts in Vienna. After completing her PhD in Practice, Ana Hoffner went on to receive a Doctorate in Philosophy from the Academy of Fine Arts Vienna and the New School in New York. This conversation took place at the end of 2020, shortly after Ana Hoffner was appointed Professor for Artistic Research and was tasked to establish a PhD in the Arts programme at the Mozarteum University in Salzburg. The moment of establishing a new programme more or less 10 years after artistic research became ubiquitous in academia raises questions and calls for a review of the current politics of academisation of artistic research. These questions are the subject of this conversation.

VM: For me, artistic research is linked to a desire for working through processual knowledge, or through a process of re-knowing by immersing oneself into a practice. You brought this example from your practice of redrawing certain works from female artists who took part in the very first exhibitions of the Non-Aligned Movement in post-war Eastern Europe. Immersing oneself in the same process, as if the sedimented object can be stirred up and one can re-experience the knowledge of its process.

AH: The process of redrawing was a constant confrontation between my artistic education and the school of drawing that these women represented.[1] It started as a tribute to their work and their position as female artists, but subsequently became a process of historical comparison by means of practice. I could tell, for example, that these women were from the Ljubljana Graphic School. Both their work and education questioned how to create space on the two-dimensional surface of the paper. There was a lot of thought put into questions about how to put space onto a structure, how to stack geometric forms, and how to structure one's thoughts within that.

I did not have the same questions in my own artistic education and so I came very quickly to my limits: my work was about finding those limits. I have a more punk rock approach to technology, and probably, the practice of redrawing was not about being able to do it as a goal, but embracing the not-being-able-to as a research practice.

---

1 Духовна Деколонизација (Spiritual Decolonisation) – Part I (2021) is an homage to the few women from Yugoslavia who took part in the Non-Aligned exhibitions and, at the same time, a more general reflection on the position of women artists in utopian artistic or political movements of the twentieth century. In the Non-Aligned Movement, culture and art played a great role, as the acknowledgment of cultural equality, the struggle against cultural imperialism, and the claim of a cultural heritage different from the classic Western modernity were strong principles from the beginning. Still, the invisibility of women artists in the archive shows how gender equality was still looked down on, albeit the importance of women in the independence struggles was encouraged by the Non-Aligned Movement. Only seven women from Yugoslavia took part in the exhibitions of the Non-Aligned organised during the whole period of activity of the movement.
The drawings of Духовна Деколонизација (Spiritual Decolonisation) – Part I are made after the works of three of them: Ankica Oprešnik (1919–2005), Zdenka Golob (1928– 2019) and Tinca Stegovec (1927–2019). The artist* found archival material depicting the works and made copies in her* studio, without trying to reproduce, exactly, the original technique, style, or format but rather putting herself in the situation of exercising or of learning from another tradition than the one she* had been learning in and from in her* own art education. Text: Anne Faucheret.

This practice of drawing with a different ability creates those moments of experiencing this difference in history and education. The outcome – the drawing – can be attributed to exactly this encounter of the positions between post-war and now.

VM: This encounter creates the seed for a historical and social contextualisation, in the way you just mentioned. I appreciate how in this process the complexity of research unfolds from a transtemporal(?) meeting of practices.

AH: I was interested in the process of canonisation and the difference between the practices of pre-war avant garde artists and post-war artists; the former, from a certain perspective, took more artistic risks. Their practice went from the complexities of the body, dimensions, space and politics 'back' to more abstract problems of drawing itself.

And still, I appreciate their biographies and I appreciate this post-war context. They were state artists but they were state artists for a different state. To become a state artist in a socialist state meant to agree to a certain conceptual space and to a certain idea of social change. The state and its economic system were one, therefore the problem was of a different kind. For a very short moment, during socialism between 1945 and 1989, there was a different concept of the state in this triangular relationship between the artist, the state and ideology. That was maybe my motivation for this work of re-drawing: I wanted to know how it was to be a state artist in a non-capitalist state.

VM: This reminds me of Tom Hollert discussing his new book *Knowledge Besides Itself*. What I remember from the (podcast) interview was that the book sketches out the role which artistic research played in the larger transformations of what has become known as the knowledge economy. It integrates artistic research critically into the knowledge economy while looking for what kind of critical impulses can come from adopting this integrated perspective. It also describes the power of the larger system to recuperate artistic research in this process. In this discussion he traces some notions of artistic production back to a time when artistic production was not an autonomous field, but a highly integrated part of the state's ideological, economical and cultural apparatus. In this interview, I was surprised to hear him describe artistic research almost exclusively in terms of engagement with the archive and engagements with documentation. It was a very clear and engaging perspective on artistic research. I understood it as a limitation that was proposed in order to be contradicted and at the same time to clarify the complicated relations between art and artistic research. I think it is a limitation that welcomes whatever is developed in the process of overcoming it. But, I think I am likely misrepresenting the book, as I only listened to this (one) interview about it. Let's not discuss the book, but just this speculation on the limitation itself.

AH: I would disagree with this limitation as it would mean that artistic research is always research into the past. But if artistic research is supposed to also question the notion of research itself, then its larger intervention must be into the questions: 'What is the experiment? What is the laboratory? What is experience in research?'. Artistic research is showing that something is beyond 'research-able', the '*Unerforschbare'* (unknowable, unresearchable, *ger.*). One of the most interesting moments in artistic research is the point where something cannot be researched anymore at all. The moment when one has to take up other means. This contradicts the work of the historian in the archive and the process of documentation. This idea of un-researchability is not compatible with their practices.

I think as practitioners of artistic research, we cannot restrict ourselves only to the factual and the production of the document because we would be constantly caught up in referentiality. When we look at a photograph, for example, it is not only because it is a historical reference, but we include everything else in our gaze as well, for example its very ideology. While I don't know [Tom Hollert's] book yet, that would be what I would imagine 'knowledge beside itself' means: something beside the fact and beside the document.

VM: On another occasion, we were talking about two movements that are happening within artistic research in the present moment: an unruly negotiation of its self-conception and (at the same time) a process of its integration into academia. Both are processes of definition, one coming from the inside and the other coming from a process of trespassing. Questions are emerging at the borders of the academy as a negotiation of what can and what cannot count as artistic research on academic grounds.

With respect to these two movements, you are at an interesting moment as you are establishing a new programme for an artistic research Phd at the Mozarteum, a well-established institution. Considering that artistic research's academicisation has been going on for some time now, there is the capacity to re-evaluate this process. Maybe my first question is just bluntly asking: What do you think this large institution wants from this new programme? You mentioned that there are certain desires associated with this new programme already in place: knowledge production, creative industries, business – but also European applications, money and funding.

AH: That's pretty clear: they want to be fancy [laughing], to be the coolest University on Earth. This fanciness makes itself apparent in the Performance Contract (*Leistungsvereinbarung*) that lists how many research projects they have, how successful they are, etc. How many *Drittmittel* ('third funds' *ger*, funding from outside contributors, for example EU) the university can acquire. There is a fear of intellectual competition and the division of funding between Universities is tied to this competition. So now I'm a player for one of them. As much as I think that I want to support this and that project, in the end, this effort is going to be put in a framework which determines that this university, with me in it, is doing better than this and this other institution.

VM: This is the very essence of neoliberalism: public institutions competing against each other for funding.

AH: Yes, competing for funds, but competing entirely on the symbolical level – which is not to be underestimated. They want to be the next Vera List Centre, to be the coolest, because there is seemingly no contradiction between being the coolest and having the best applications and having the best funding. That is the whole ambivalence, that is how they get us, artistic researchers. That is how people with strong desires to do something or to change something get implicated in it, because I also want the programme to be fancy, but for different reasons. When speaking about the programme with the management, the research management, the rectorate, the professors and the students, one can speak the same language and mean completely different things. It is very tricky. I signed the contract for building a PhD programme and applying for its funding, but the way I think about what I am going to do with it is another thing. Maybe luckily, the negotiating partners don't always go into detail and this ambiguity can be a common ground.

VM: I find it interesting that the ambiguity within the language that an institution uses to describe itself can be the space within which one can change its structure; its directions and desires. It is the space inbetween the existing structures where one can situate oneself and produce something other: the soft spaces, one could say.

AH: Maybe it's not by chance that I developed this longing to be a state artist. I imagine that it would be satisfying to have the liberty of working for one cause: for the project of state socialism. And the other freedom: to not have to take part in the art market. The idea was about having the freedom to practice what you want to practice, without the craziness of selling your practice and yourself constantly. I think this kind of position is now so completely gone for so many decades that it's beyond anachronistic to discuss it. But it's strange that the longing for it doesn't go away.

VM: The idea of the state artist helps me to understand what artistic research desires in terms of support. As artistic research turns away from the market, what does it turn towards, if both the market and the state are capitalist in the European context? Educational policy now has been going towards supporting artistic research as a new modality of knowledge production. For the artists, there is pressure to go in that direction that also comes from a lack of sustainable alternatives, which would be neither market, nor state funded. State funded academic education is used by artists as a way to turn away from the market. Are we becoming state artists again, except that the state is neoliberal now? I argue this with a grain of salt, as a caricature.

AH: Yes, being a state artist for a capitalist state is a nightmare, and not the original intent. But you are right, that was the reason for me to go into a PhD programme. Over the last two or three years, after I finished my PhD, I went through a process of a different political radicalisation. I went back to Marxism and to questioning production conditions. I have become an old-new-fan of Hans Haacke for instance.

His work for me marks institutional critique before the performativity of institutional critique. I am looking again at his research on the slumlord Shapolski[2] and his work on housing conditions and gentrification in the early 70s, as well as his Guggenheim work which is about the board members who were contributing to the state coups in South

2 Shapolsky et al. Manhattan Real Estate Holdings, a Real-Time Social System, as of May 1, 1971.

America. I started my own series on the interconnections between the weapons industry and the art market. Right now I think it's worth considering again, that maybe one can imagine an art world that is not in proximity to neoliberal exploitation, money laundering, weapons industry and all kinds of other dubious businesses. In my old fashioned Marxist stance it is again getting out of hand.

I am not sure that the capitalist state, or specifically the European Union, is less problematic as a support structure for the arts and artistic research, it just operates on a different plane. When I look at legislation coming from the EU, you can see the effects of the opening up of markets, like for example in Bulgaria, Romania and other countries which joined in 2004. They were forced to open their markets and not allowed to restrict any land trading. A lot of land was sold very cheaply in Romania and people were forced to leave their homes because they could not afford to live on their own land anymore. There are really devastating effects of neoliberal policies around the corner, coming in with these new income generating norms. The EU expanded its market to generate these new sources of income.

VM: While we know that, we don't really make a conscious decision to go into research that is supported by the European states. I am just stating the fact that these implications are usually not the ones we are considering when applying for funding or joining public programmes.

AH: I think the choice to go into research has a lot to do with the intellectual space, as it is not possible (at least for me) to find that intellectual space in the structures provided by the private art market. Universities provide that space, and that informed my choice to go into academia. The available models of supporting artistic research at the university are: being funded by an external research fund, being funded by the university itself, being partly funded by teaching and combining teaching and researching. I find the last model very good.

VM: One of the most productive modalities of researching for me is teaching what you don't know. At a.pass there is a strong encouragement to teach the thing that you are looking for, to formulate it and to externalise its methodologies. Methodological questions become very apparent when I try to teach something I am myself researching at that moment. But I am also trying to survive as an artist, to smuggle artistic process into teaching. For example, my biggest problem with my PhD was that I could not envision how to present a final stage of my work, because it is so much about a process and a practice that is continuously researching itself. It cannot really be exhibited, only participated in.

AH: One of the major problems in the academisation process of artistic research is that it is not accompanied by a shift from exhibition of research to participation in the event of research as the mode of its communication and critique.

VM: Yes. Research is almost always mediated through its representations.

AH: Probably the most challenging part of artistic research is what you would call, in classical terms, the traceability of research. Within artistic research, traceability does not happen as a re-reading or in other objective terms. In artistic research one has to go through a process of experiencing, participating and so on, because the research does not show itself to you otherwise. Isn't that the main challenge?

VM: Absolutely. In my conception, artistic research as a material process is inconsumable, it cannot pass through the membrane of the hosting institutions and its publication modalities. This is its resistance to recuperation within the knowledge production economies. There is no straight traceable line between the process of research and its publishing compositions which enter these knowledge markets. Conventionally, the representation of research within documents tends to replace the research process, we then refer to the document often as 'the research'. In my experience, it is very hard to convince institutions to support access to the research process instead of supporting access to its compositions and documents.

AH: The problem starts when it goes beyond the individual. Institutional artistic research has embraced the process but it has embraced it in a 19th century, individual, romantic way. As long as the researcher stays the solo artist and within the realm of sensual experience, process is embraced. This is a Kantian aesthetic experience, where it just matters how one perceives things, and not so much whether there is anything outside of that experience. One development of this deeply Kantian stance is that suddenly subversive and challenging proposals like queerness and decoloniality have to be shown to make sense, by that I mean that there is a shift in understanding queerness as something that is reasonable or can be rationally justified. Suddenly queerness has to make sense, and decoloniality has to make sense, as if rationality were the only ground of understanding experience. But what about experiences that don't make any sense in the language available to us? By integrating these concepts, these very experiences into the reasonable, we completely lose ground of their potential to challenge the reasonable itself.

VM: It is troubling that this reasoning, reasonable-making, is happening now from the inside of these discourses, while it was always a given that they were met with not-understanding and pressure to make sense from the outside. I often perceive this development as a reification of, for example queerness, as a stable ontology. It is a tough discussion to have, because of course it is clear that marginalised positions should strive for stabilisation – it is part of the political process of shifting these positions and decentralising other established ones. It makes it hard to find positions from which to critique the realist reification of these fundamentally unstable challenges as new ontologies, without challenging them in the same defensive way in which the established discourses challenge them.

AH: The realist reification and the new sense-making of queerness and decoloniality bring both discourses into dialogue with the natural sciences. Queerness and decoloniality are becoming realist methodologies. They now have a common realist way with natural sciences in which they deal with phenomena: the moment the phenomenon appears, it has to be taken for real. How can we get out of this again?

VM: One way would be to destabilise the category of 'scientific' itself. One of the books I am reading right now (*New Materialism*), shows how unstable and destabilising scientific research is to science itself right now (and maybe has always been).

AH: I come from a psychoanalytical practice and for me, this practice is also a helpful approach to this problem. It is a practice which happens in the space between two people, meaning it happens for and because of the other, and there are all kinds of transferences going on all the time, where the practitioners know that their projections are not to be taken for real. They are there to be looked at. I have been practicing psychoanalysis for seven years and I know from that experience that anyone's interpretation of themselves is, to put it simply: a version. But it opens up a space that is very productive and interesting to work with.

For me, it would be interesting to look for proximities between this kind of practice and other non-normative forms of research, like for example, artistic research.

The contribution of artistic research might be its focus on relationality and not on objectivity and to develop an ethics of participation; participation in each other's process.

VM: If science is already weird, full of gaps and precarious bridges within itself, then is it also not the task of artistic research to bring that 'artistic' element to the supposedly ordered and stable environment of science? Being weird is not artistic research's contribution. I often find artist researchers to be quite rigorous with the way they use archives, social situations, ethics of research, etc. I say this to counteract a strange separation that is proliferating in the language of the knowledge economy: it separates science and art research into two different categories of research in order to argue for them to come together. Can we just admit that everybody is doing weird research?

AH: If you look at the EU funding for Horizon 2021, there are many examples of technological research that is supported exactly because of its weirdness and is encouraged to try and fail. What is officially regarded as sensible research by the funding bodies is so often the opposite. And the same people would say that anything that comes from the arts makes no sense to them.

VM: Yes, we have already talked about this, I think in response to there being funds for research which are separated into technological, scientific and artistic, institutions produce membranes which are able to interact with this funding structure while at the same time maintaining and protecting the artistic process on the inside. On an administrative level, a.pass operates a lot like this. The institution itself is under pressure to maintain this membrane but also to ensure that enough 'results' and sensible formulations travel through it towards the funding bodies. This tension is mostly felt on the administrative side of a.pass: to become attached and supported and at the same time maintain an autonomous space on the inside. The educational framework is possibly best suited to maintain this kind of tension. I think it is one of the reasons for the academisation of artistic research: the educational institution can help to 'pass' it in the queer sense, 'pass' the research within the normative funding environment.

AH: Somehow I always have a good feeling about a.pass, one that I don't have with large educational institutions. Maybe because a.pass comes from self-organisation and has found a small loophole where it can exist.

VM: Maybe we are lucky that we are not big or important enough and can be left alone to a certain extent. Although, also for a.pass there are of course evaluations and applications, funding and policy negotiations, reports, etc.

AH: I am not sure in how many other countries that could still work, because so many independent institutes had to close down under the European pressure of integration into universities. Now it seems like we have only universities and nothing else in that landscape.

VM: I'm excited to see how your ideas can be negotiated in the new space you are entering now. I think there is emancipatory power in your knowledge of the politics of structures you lay out here.

AH: It is a big question of how much is possible in the end? Where do you really reach the limits? There are several things I will try to do. One of my main interests is to work from radical transnationality, to include as many precarious regions of the world as possible, so that we can bring together topics which are hidden from our viewpoint. Another challenge is going to be to work across research fields and not to separate into research in fine arts and research in music as it was initially proposed by the structure of this position. Maybe there is some kind of potential in embracing everything. Not to focus on visual culture, or performance or music but to follow this wish to do it all. Maybe that can produce something that is besides research.

VM: I am very drawn to the way you would like to work across the established disciplinary divisions of the university. A PhD programme seems like a perfect place to try that.

At the same time, I want to describe another observation I have been thinking about recently. Somehow it is the other side of transdisciplinary practice which has now been commonly accepted in many master studies. What I see happening in the concept of transdisciplinarity is that by going into transdisciplinary work these environments tend to abandon the processes and discourses of the contributing disciplines, the disciplines which establish the 'trans' space between them. If we take the premise of artistic research that 'art knows', then exactly this knowledge is situated in discourses and processes of a discipline. I am asking myself if there is not a development at hand where this knowledge is being abandoned as too 'disciplined', and therefore old fashioned in the practice of transdisciplinarity. If this is the case, this new space between the disciplines fills this discursive gap with a common discourse, which is actually a meta discourse: that of cultural studies. To put it polemically, I ask myself when was the last time when I was mentoring a master student, that we were still speaking from disciplinary knowledge? Do we still use performance theory, art theory, etc., etc.? Who is the art theorist we admire? There is a bigger and bigger gap between the cultural theory we use when coming together to share our work and the 'work on the ground' when we go back to our ateliers. Do you see this as well?

AH: Yes, but what you are describing is not transdisciplinarity as I understand it, it is the abolition of material conditions of practice in a misunderstanding of transdisciplinarity. No matter if one is drawing or composing, we all come from practice, there is always a past in this, a history. What are the tools we make for ourselves in these practices? We cannot easily get rid of these questions. It is really problematic to give up disciplinary questions because they are deemed 'normative': What are we giving them up for and what is their replacement?

Andre Lepecki addresses something similar in the beginning of 'Exhausting Dance', where he writes about an audience member suing a dance company because he did not see dance on stage, but something else. The discussion of means is really substantial in the arts. In his example, the discourse about seeing or not seeing dance on stage becomes immediately ontological: What is dance? I think this is the connection I can make to your question of disciplinary knowledge.

VM: (dance is hard to see)

In artistic research, this is one of the most important internal negotiations for me: What is the material condition for research? To put it differently: it cannot be just a de-substantiated field where other practices come to play… how does research create its own material conditions, and how does it recondition the practices which it involves?

But this is material for another conversation, dear Ana, thank you so much for this one!

Loes Jacobs & Lilia Mestre

Knowledge Production and Epistemology in Artistic Research

The Responsibility of the Institution, and its Blindspots

The 'Ideal' Artistic Learning Environment

Support Group conversations

INTRODUCTION

At the beginning of 2020, a.pass began a structural shift: the Participants' Assembly and the Support Group were set up as two means to reflect and encompass the current vision of the organisation.

The idea of a Support Group comes from the desire to keep the institution linked to more than one 'thinking head' and to question what kind of permeability can be of support for an artistic research institution. This move also corresponds with a fundamental interest that has been present since the beginning of a.pass which finds a response in the Participants' Assembly: *How can the a.pass participants engage in the making of the a.pass programme?*

For the first Support Group meeting, a.pass invited a mix of people from the artistic and educational field, as well as alumni. Through a number of video calls and collective writing pads, we tested the idea of the Support Group as a dialogue module for the institution. The main question is: Could it be sustainable to constitute a group that could vary in size and function depending on the needs of the institution and in relation to the needs of the field of education, culture and art making? As well as understanding how and if members of this group can become mentors, curators, workshop facilitators, project collaborators and critical partners of a.pass.

The focus of the first meetings revolved around the function of the Support Group itself, the making public of artistic research and the role of the Research Center as a construction between a.pass and the artistic research field.

The outcome of these meetings were put together in a website developed together with Sina Seifee (sg.apass.be). It marked the beginning of a desire to tackle more questions on the topics of educational environments, institutional critique, artistic research, etc.

The following texts are the result of a collective writing experience on pads between various members of the Support Group: Kristien Van den Brande, Lilia Mestre, Livia Andrea Piazza, Loes Jacobs, Nicolas Y. Galeazzi, Philippine Hoegen, Sara Manente, Sina Seifee and Vladimir Miller. Three main themes were decided upon with the aim of contributing to this publication: knowledge production and epistemology in artistic research; the responsibility of the institution and its blindspots, and the 'ideal' artistic learning environment. The texts were edited by Loes Jacobs and Lilia Mestre. Most of the texts are de-authorised, as the Support Group functions as one polyphonic voice, but some quotes in which one person expands upon their own field of expertise are marked in a different font. All questions are in italics.

It is important to note that these texts are immediate, spontaneous responses to the themes and questions set beforehand. The discussions arose as people were writing in the pads collectively. The members of the Support Group were invited to engage with their own expertise, knowledge and experience.

Links to the original pads:

pads.domainepublic.net/p/lvlcn2dftgdtltlm
pads.domainepublic.net/p/cndbxgy39g7zl6ul
pads.domainepublic.net/p/2eff5yji4al79bzc

KNOWLEDGE PRODUCTION AND EPISTEMOLOGY IN ARTISTIC RESEARCH

[https://lexico.com/definition/epistemology: 'The theory of knowledge, especially with regard to its methods, validity, and scope, and the distinction between justified belief and opinion'.]

What kind of knowledge does art produce? Why is that important as public capital? Does the institution need to set conditions for this production? And if yes, what are the 'bestest' conditions (assuming that the best conditions don't exist)?

KNOWLEDGE PRODUCTION

What can learning be without knowledge production?

'Knowledge production' in the last few years has developed into a kind of leash that the neoliberal funding system is using to tie artistic research to the academy (in which it is already seemingly incorporated). The persistent question of knowledge production towards artists feels more and more abusive in the current politics of funding. It feels like being asked to create the leash by which artists and researchers will be tied (or less contentiously, 'connected').

What is learning without knowledge production? One distinction that can be made is to understand knowledge production as 'outside of research'. Co-researching and communal publicness of processes has not so much to do with results, but with the sharing of experimental methods and practices. *Isn't knowledge production something bigger than publishing articles and books, aka 'products'?* It would be helpful here to elaborate more on the subject and to attempt a provisional definition of knowledge to work with.

Knowledge production, in the academic field, is something that comes at the very end of artistic research, as one of the evaluation criterias for looking back. *What did this research produce in terms of knowledge?* If it is set as a goal from the start – and the problem with the academisation of artistic research is that it is the sole criteria – it feels quite stifling, and not tuned in with the non-linearity (method, validity, scope) of how artistic research happens.

Should we attempt to define knowledge production specifically for the field of art? Or, are we then falling into the exact trap we are trying to climb out of, namely making claims on the authority to determine what knowledge is?

It is a process that brings militant research – originating from the workers movements of the Italian resistance in the 60s. This was a mode of research of the workers: a research on their own conditions, a mode of self-understanding of communities commoning together in a form of struggle. It has since been adopted by activist propositions, for example by Occupy, but also by anthropologists, who do not distinguish between political cause and research questions or perspectives, and experimental entanglements with complex systems in methodological proximity. In the framework of militant research one could argue that the publishing of research is happening 'outside' [the academic context]. The very question 'but what will you publish?' – which creates authored, distanced complications to the communal exchange and learning process – is in this case avoided. In order to claim knowledge production for ourselves (and not on a leash) we have to re-define its production context and the processes it is associated with like 'public' and 'publishing'. If 'epistemology in artistic research' means '*what and how can we know?*', the answer can be 'through communal entanglements, sharing processes and [conditions]'. It does not exclude presentation and/or conventional publication, but for the sake of balancing it out, we have to claim that area.

To talk about the validity of methods of knowledge production can be tricky because sometimes we have confirmation of that validity a posteriori. Other times it is the appropriation by others that shows the full scope of one's own methodology. *Is validity an appropriate marker in the arts? Do practices relate to each other in relationships of validity? Whose question is this really?*

The words 'ontology', and maybe 'experimental ontology' are more useful in relation to artistic research. *What if 'we' look at this thing/concept differently? Could we say that 'experimental ontology' is the epistemology for artistic research?*

Karen Barad speaks of onto-epistemology: a fancy way of saying, 'you find what you are looking for'. Or ethico-onto-epistemology as a fancy way of saying 'you are responsible for what you are looking for'.

Elizabeth Povinelli makes a difference between: art, which offers affects, science, which offers propositions, and philosophy, which offers concepts.[1]

Where do we situate artistic research here? Rather than adhere to these disciplinary borders, how can the shared presuppositions (e.g. its racial underpinnings) of these distinct disciplines be questioned? Artistic research plays an exemplary role in this line of questioning because it doesn't belong to 'either/or' of these disciplines (the not belonging might be a key for other narratives). It uses all of them: affects, propositions, concepts, and experimental set-ups. It is not a theory of knowledge that can be defined a priori, or as a uniting field. It can only be defined in retrospect, looking back at what is produced, one can try to define what its method, scope, validity (theory) was.

We talk about 'external' knowledge production of artistic research, in the sense of what it contributes to society, to arts, to other fields of knowledge. At the same time, we don't really know how to teach it to ourselves. Current modes of learning and teaching are based on jumping into the cold waters of doing, without much guidance. Mastery in arts education has undergone a process of critique that has led us close to a didactics of supported and critiqued self-education. But it has a problem: it is somewhat Darwinist and in a paradoxical way, it relies on the very thing it tried to abolish, namely innate mastery. Instead of transmitting the knowledge of how to compose pieces, how to direct, of showing by example and discussing difficulties, students are supposed to find it out by themselves, through failure. It is as if these didactics rely on the idea of a 'sudden, intuitive genius'. The strong intuitive makers will emerge from the process of trial and error. But this approach can reproduce the very master in the student which it tries to abolish in the teacher.

---

1 Based on: G. Deleuze & F. Guattari, *What is Philosophy?*, Columbia University Press, 1994.

Are we not somehow doing the same at a.pass in relation to artistic research? By refusing to teach it, by refusing to consolidate artistic research into a set of possibly contradictory didactics, are we maybe overly reliant on the 'innate' abilities of the researcher? Where is the space to understand artistic research as a discipline with teachable practices, problems, politics, and conflicted discussions of what is a good or helpful practice? Should this not be the first – or the other – question of knowledge production of artistic research?

How do we teach what we don't and cannot know?

What is radically different at a.pass is that the researchers and participants have already developed practices and/or substantial academic and artistic experience. So it's not a question of learning what artistic research is, but of the desire to engage in other ways of researching while studying the conditions of research. Not only with the tools and experiences that one has, but with a group of peers, mentors, and curators. The desire for the collective as a way to practice and share ways to experience, read and write the world.

MAKING PUBLIC

> Note from the editors: Making public is an ongoing challenge when we speak about sharing processes and not products, and when we speak about relating to the public as co-researchers. For example, why is it important to share this text or even any publications with the public? Or, why is it important to try to come to a readable text that encourages thinking together on the questions that come up while practicing, making assumptions, doubting, articulating, disagreeing, loving it, etc. Potentially, making public allows for an articulation with others. Editing allows one to reformulate and arrange so that it becomes possible to offer a potential contribution, and also for it to be received. Maybe it is about contributing with indeterminate certainty in order to think together.

When should research become public and how does this change the research process? How early do you start thinking about the 'public'?

Sharing one's research is sometimes stepping outside of it (disclosure), sometimes it is staying in oblique zones that are not transparent. The figure of the trickster comes in, the one that shares in different shades of disguise. A theory of knowledge implies an impetus towards full disclosure, self-transparency... *What does self-transparency really mean?* A certain degree of tolerance for the absence of full disclosure and self-transparency is one of the aspects that characterises artistic research in comparison to other forms of research. We have to keep in mind the always shifting relation between knowing and not knowing in knowledge.

Imagine a DARK ROOM... How do you explore it? Do you take a torch and shine it into this or that corner, always getting over-exposed, partial glimpses of walls and pillars, disorienting and blinding yourself while trying to build a system or map out of these partial views? Or, do you touch the walls, touch the partitions, listen to the space, keep in touch with it as you wander around, slowly getting to know it by other means while you accept the darkness as its being rather than a hindrance? What would 'knowledge' be in this room, if we don't separate it from what and how the room is? How would you 'show' something, guide someone to a place you have become close to?

Or:

A researcher is drawing *A CIRCLE IN THE SAND* around themselves. The researcher says: 'this is what I know'. Then the researcher draws a larger circle, still with themselves in the centre. 'When my knowledge grows, so does its perimeter. The more I know, the more I am exposed to what I don't know'. This parable is deeply nested in our (Western) imagination of science and research. There is an unknown, unexplained world out there around us, we are its undeclared, naturalised centre. And by knowing we heroically transform the unknown into known. It is a parable of conquest, territory and othering.

Artistic research **cherishes the unknown** in a different way from other knowledge production processes. Cultivating the unknown could be one way of saying, as it's written, to gather around it. Once we gather around it, one of the good effects is probably getting more comfortable with the unknown and avoiding wanting to make it immediately known ('conquering it'). Another good effect of cherishing the unknown, or staying with uncertainty, is that we get to know more about the reasons why we think what we think. It would be interesting to cherish the unknown in all the knowledge it builds and in all the knowledge it unbuilds and in this way, get out of the dichotomy known-unknown, on which so many neoliberal dynamics of value production are based, not to mention the colonial approach of conquering. **Paranoid reading** may be a useful way to get into processes that instigate the desire for knowledge. *Is there anything that is 'unknown'?* This relates to the question of transparency. *Can we really see the unknown? What would be the conditions for such a quest?* Maybe new narratives are helpful as forms of telling what is there. **Desire** as a practice of connecting and disconnecting... *How can we think about knowledge in terms of this practice?* Not a knowledge 'of', but 'as' distributed engagements.

An institution and the people involved have knowledge – they are an intellect. *How can they speak and engage from that knowledge? How to foster sets of conditions for knowledge production and the new practices that enter?* Knowledge is produced in the entanglements in (between) practices, projects, obsessions, methods. The question might not be how to produce knowledge as external to practice, but should be: *How to take the practice as a particular kind of intelligence, and to ask what can this intelligence engage with in a meaningful and transformative way? What are we not seeing? Where are our blindspots?*

THE RESPONSIBILITY OF THE INSTITUTION AND ITS BLINDSPOTS

a.pass works with a horizontal structure. By creating the Participants' Assembly and the Support Group, a.pass delegates content and modes of doing to its 'users' and network. *What is the responsibility of the institution in doing so? What is the responsibility and accountability of 'users' in horizontal structures?*

'We do not have "perfect" politics. We do not believe in factionalism or rigid ideology. We can die having had the "correct" positions but having accomplished nothing and freed no-one. The desire to be "right" or "perfect" is the highest form of cynicism.'[2]

The responsibility of a.pass as an institution is to take care of the complexities that emerge, to support complex objects that provoke further questioning, and to take care of that space of agency, i.e. maintenance, facilitation, documentation (as well as taking care that its consequences are 'carried').

Is the institution a content-provider, or a content-delegator, appointed to represent particular content?

2 The Red Nation, *The Red Deal: Indigenous Action To Save Our Earth*, Common Notions, 2021.

The responsibility of a.pass might be to choose what is and isn't delegated, moreover, to provide a frame (like the Participants' Assembly and the Support Group) to discuss and change what is delegated and what is not, and somehow accept that any decision taken will necessarily be partial, situated and provisional, but sometimes irreversible. This marks the limitation of responsibility and might create blindspots, which are inherent risks in any form of organisation. There is the wish to think about an exemplary process which enables risk, error and fragility as factors that we will never be able to escape, and to create a safe environment for them.

Another way for the institution to take responsibility is through horizontality, to care for the voices that are not heard or don't make themselves heard.

a.pass is not really horizontal in the common use of the word, e.g. that there are no differences in power, no hierarchies. Since we know this is not the case, but we do insist on using the word to describe a.pass, should we look at the desire that is implied in its use? The desire might come from not trusting or not believing in hierarchies. Should we then not rather redefine hierarchy and articulate an attitude towards it, or even a protocol for power? Or maybe redefine horizontality? Can we replace hierarchy with responsibility and accountability?

Hierarchy shouldn't be pitted against horizontality. And horizontality doesn't necessarily mean that everyone has equal power within a particular structure. There are different responsibilities in the different parts of the institution (modules) and they imply different accountabilities, but each of them has their own value and is essential to democratic institutional frameworks. Horizontal means working in a way that the main module engages with all other modules that have different responsibilities (keeping the overview of the drives and hopes, and thus keeping the horizontality going). *Of course, we can think about radical horizontal structures with a common accountability but is this realistic for a funded institution?* On the artistic-curatorial level, there is the use of T(~~A~~)Z [Temporary (~~Autonomous~~) Zones] with specific hierarchies that have a contract at the beginning and dissolve after a set time. On the organisation-institutional level, calling oneself 'horizontal' comes with the responsibility to set up feedback-systems that check whether or not horizontality (and of what kind) is taking place. Without these feedback structures, the discourse of 'horizontality' is empty and might end up becoming its opposite: it takes away people's agency to problematise hierarchies.

How to enable responsiveness with each other within particular relations that occur in a.pass?

We need skilled listening (which is not to be in your own thoughts and concerns all the time, but actually try to really get what the other is saying). This is very important, and sometimes very difficult in the field of art where people are always so busy performing themselves. Places that are supposed to enable listening and producing knowledge together, are among the worst in terms of developing listening skills. What is done is exactly the opposite. We need to find ways to establish listening. Listening exercises during but also after encounters. *What mediation processes could facilitate listening? Maybe this writing practice is one?*

I see a certain rejection of institutional frameworks. I wish that instead of rejection there would be a way to think together. I guess I'm looking for protocols that support the difficulties that emerge within these frameworks. *How to get away from finger pointing, from fear, from distrust?*

a.pass tries to get away from a position of self-centred institutional power and to work in a participatory way with participants, curators, guests, administration, board, etc. Through this participatory infrastructure, the institution tries to bring to the fore the concerns and ways of doing the practices developed at a.pass, as well as thinking about decision making processes and the distribution of labour.

By creating the Participants' Assembly and the Support Group, a.pass delegates content and modes of doing to its 'users' and network.

'Delegating' and 'users' is a discourse by which we might dig our own grave. The kind of relation it defines is one of service providers versus users/consumers, where each has rights that can be claimed. *What terminology could replace this one?*
Both Sara Ahmed and Paolo Virno wrote about use and using.[3] They both bring up the fact that by using, or queer using, one might corroborate or change an established path or way of doing things. The responsibility and accountability of the users cannot be imposed. *What kind of invitation can be made?*

It's interesting to think about institutions which are funded by public money and the idea of 'service' and 'user' relationships.

---

3 Sara Ahmed, *What's the Use?: On the Uses of Use*, Duke University Press, 2019.

Paolo Virno, *L'idea di mondo: Intelletto pubblico e uso della vita*, Quodlibet, 2015.

How can this relationship be sustained not as a system based on profit but as a way of working together? What is user-friendly in this case? Maybe institutions should try to escape the frame of the service provider and self-define in other terms? Institutions are, in general, contexts for encounters; their spatial dimensions serve as a place where people (and their histories, bodies and concerns) encounter each other and the institution (made of people and their histories, bodies and concerns) can help. Encounters might result in something or they might not. They might affect people in a good or in a bad way. But the implication would be that each 'encounter-maker' has some responsibility for the encounter. Of course, then the institution is made by all these encounters together with its uncontrollable complexity.

There is a tension between the quick ability to respond – which is more difficult for a stable, bigger institution to do and sometimes can only happen with a radical cut – and the opposite risk of the instability created by an institution that is constantly shifting, changing and adjusting to any minimal seismic movement.

The more we unfold these issues, the more we become conscious of the layers within an institution. There can be tensions between these different layers that are not (made) visible to all (full transparency is impossible and also not always good). And there are different responsibilities and capacities to respond to every layer of an institution. *Should everyone be capable of jumping from one layer to another?*

Participation includes everyone related to a.pass' structure. The institution is the host, the organ that invites, and the caretaker of the structure. It's also the role of the institute to ask questions or formulate a framework of dialogue in relation to what's happening. All participants need to be aware that whatever they discuss happens in that framework. The institution becomes the facilitator of discussions about modes of working, of collaboration: what are the expectations and engagements, how are they equal, what's in the code of conduct, etc. It is important to acknowledge that participation is a public discussion and an essential contribution to a healthy institution. That doesn't seem like a responsibility, but it is.

When we talk about responsibility we have to talk about irresponsibility as well. *How do we recognise interesting modes of irresponsibility? Maybe the idea of queer use that Sara Ahmed proposes can inspire us?* The queer use in that context means the improper use of something, so to use something irresponsibly. *Who's accountable then?*

Blindspots, there are always some.

The whole point of blindspots is that we don't see them. The best we can do is keep enough critical distance between the different parts of the institution that they might catch sight of each other's blindspots. Blindspots are not static and they can become visible. One shouldn't be scared that they will always appear where one least expects. They are cathartic and painful, and they always appear from unseen cracks.

Blindspots become visible when things go wrong. When people don't feel they are entitled to join the institute, when people don't have access, when there is a miscommunication of the expectations on how to be a participant – or any other actor – in a horizontal structure.

The good news is that when you spot them, things can change a lot. A 'blindspot spotting' practice can be a great thing for an institution. The Support Group is doing this too: Blindspot Seeker. A text by Eve Kosofsky Sedgwick[4] on paranoid and reparative reading is key in relation to blindspots and the mode of critique it produces or requires. To always be wary of blindspots or to insistently point at blindspots produces a paranoid subjectivity, paranoid engagements, or paranoid discourse. *Perhaps we could rather accept blindspots for what they are and engage in strategies of 'repair'?*

The very discourse of horizontality produces a major blindspot, namely that one cannot point at or play with hierarchies, which are inevitably present.

How to look for blindspots?

Is there something that I consider a driving force of the group or the institution or the work that is not allowing me to see the other forces at play?

What is the perimeter of what I consider as my responsibility or object of inquiry? Is there something that is out of it but is actually affecting/being affected directly by my work or the institution?

4 Eve Kosofsky Sedgwick, 'Paranoid Reading and Reparative Reading; or, You're So Paranoid, You Probably Think This Introduction is About You', *Touching Feeling*, Duke University Press, 1997 pp. 123-151.

THE 'IDEAL' ARTISTIC LEARNING ENVIRONMENT

What would the 'ideal' artistic learning environment look like? Can an institution, especially one that thinks of itself as a learning environment, be an 'ideal'? Is an 'ideal' a category that an institution can or should think in? Can an 'ideal' be a model for an institution? Can we use the 'ideal' to check the actual models, their premises and their influences?

'Ideally', an institution is able to put itself at stake as a learning subject – a subject that learns – and a learning object – an object, infrastructure, discourse, etc., at stake for the learning of others. 'Ideally', the learning is mutual. Whomever comes in learns as much as the institution itself. In this way everybody brings in knowledge. This presumes relationality and interdependence.

When are we really comfortable to learn? How much uncomfortableness is needed to be able to learn? What is the definition of learning? Where and how does it happen? When can you say you learned something? What are we learning? What are the tools and methods that shape that learning? What are the procedures to discuss and change them?

An 'ideal artistic learning environment' needs openness, freedom to explore, experiment, and gather different meanings and opinions. It needs a good host, somewhere, someone, something where people are comfortable with the uncomfortable, so they feel an urge or a wish to create, react and/or disturb. It is a place where people feel their agency or are able to develop their own (sense of) agency. Learning happens when one feels safe enough to show the fragility of not-knowing and wanting to get to know, to share, to exchange. Being comfortable with communication is important. This requires people giving and receiving knowledge (in whatever form it takes). Everyone is considered a specialist, a 'knower' of some-thing(s), and everyone is approached as such. Yet the opposite is necessary as well: everyone is considered to be learning, a non-specialised, questioning, wondering subject.

Whether it is a physical space, a digital environment, whether it is inside or outside, this environment is always dedicated. It is a space that gives room for different ways of sharing and exchanging. From intimate to group sharing, from the very comfortable to the uncomfortable 'pushing oneself out of the comfortable' but still wanting to learn. This requires an environment where there is access to different kinds of languages that trigger exchange or facilitate processing.

It is a space that can be used in different ways by different people who have clear roles: the participants, the mentors, the administrators, the coordinators, etc. Institutions can (un)learn through people shifting roles within them.

'Ideally', an institution is a learning environment, an unfinished place. A place that remains a potential and a problem at the same time. 'Ideally' it has a strong awareness of this paradox of aspiring and searching for a 'bestest' state, providing at the same time a nourishing ground for this 'bestest' to be searched.

'Ideally', change happens all the time within the institution. This process of mutual influence between the people composing the institution and the institution itself is always going on. Possibly, the institution itself is the container of change with new knowledge coming in, or new associations being made.

Which kind of 'parts' does it have? Does an artistic learning environment need a structure? A structure is what makes things possible, allows things to move, be passed on, etc. Something to hold onto, to react to, to interact with.

An institution is somehow a framework that is constituted by different 'parts'. *Is this framework there to contain things, or is the framework an intrinsic part of the content of the institution?* In the first case, you might create sections, departments, divisions that structure and constitute the institution. Prioritisation and hierarchies might be hard to avoid. In the second case the structure appears in the coming together of all 'parts' or elements. This intrinsic awareness that everything together creates the institution might make an interdependent structure with distributed capacities and empowerments.

The 'parts' might want to be detached from the structuring of people. 'Parts' might be more overlapping fields of needs and interests that are in communication with each other. Things like budget, events, questions, visions, community, are all fields where moving individuals are interacting with each other (cfr. shifting roles).

'Ideally' all these 'parts' communicate well and stay close to each other. They are aware of each other and the different languages they might speak (for example, artistic visual language versus financial figures). They all work together for the same goal, i.e. creating the 'bestest' conditions for learning.

Sina Seifee
Pierre Rubio

Dancing with Knowledge

Conversations on pre-modern bodies in a digital information era

PR: Sina, after our preliminary session where I proposed some thematics and general questions, you selected and chose some directions for this conversation. You wanted to talk first about technology and digitalisation. So, what are your politics of database and index making? Since the artistic and research projects you are invited to digitalise[1] are already technologies in themselves, do you 'technologise' them further through the sieve of the digitalisation process? When and how does this leap from one dimension to another occur? And one more related question: you are asked to design websites but you're not a designer. You resist being labelled a designer. So why do you think that people ask you to not-design-design their websites?

SS: Hahaha. I was put in a position to make digital interfaces in the last two years, with a.pass, around a.pass and with a.pass participants. I'm very curious about that understanding of my abilities as somebody who is interested in categorisations, sorting, listing and their histories and aspects and relationship with making something using a tool that is from now. It could be thought-provoking to talk about what Nora Campbell calls 'technological gaze'. When we make a website, we are producing a technological gaze. When visitors go to a website, they are looking through that gaze that we are producing. What is this gaze? What does it do? What kind of subject does it produce? For example, what was the gaze that we produced with RRadio Triton, the experimental radio project we developed in a.pass in 2017 and which we then transformed into a digital interface? This is something I have been thinking a lot about when it comes to interface design. Right now, whilst we are using Skype, I see a glitchy, affected version of you coming to me, but I'm also looking at a technique and I'm also constructed as a subject, in a flat monitor, with all sorts of things happening... so there is a technological gaze that constructs me as a new subject. I'm very used to Skype so this construction has already done its work on me... especially the very young generation, people who grew up with these things, totally different from us. For me, it still is very different from the biological, physico-virtual life because I grew up in a world that was not digital. So, the technological gaze for me is something I researched, I read about, I also made it myself, in my praxis. For example, the work I did about the German cartographer, Adam Olearius, cartographing in the 16th century, early modernism. Cartography was one of the very powerful emerging ways of constructing a subject that looks. But I don't have the skills to really analyse and to read different subject positions that are produced when I work with these interfaces. For example, when I google something in a list, or when I browse a website where everything is fluid, and you click on something and something else happens, and so on. But some of the problems that I developed a kind of sensibility to are, for example, when information becomes aesthetic, or when a network is presented visually. I've become very cautious of these kinds of techniques or strategies. For example, the websites of educational organisations that visualise their knowledge in terms of an impossible purview, meaning: a pictorial rhetoric of a connected web of mobile bodies – hosting swarms of items that resist fixed positions. This for me, is a kind of technological gaze that produces an impossible mobilised subject, who is floating in a world that is fluid. This is the image of how the organisation of a school produces 'me' as a particular looking subject.

PR: I believe it is an unwanted side effect. These educational organisations aim at the exact opposite when creating a digital representation of the complexity of their structures.

SS: Maybe. But I think the website in that sense, has joined a very ongoing and strong aestheticisation of information, and a hegemony of fluidity. I have been made suspicious of the fluid state. Capitalism is very much defined by the idea of fluidity. So we are totally dealing with a world that has to be fluid and liquid. When I design things, I ask myself: what kind of subject position is being produced. So, there are things that I try to avoid. For example, I try to avoid creating a free floating God that has access to all things. (I'm also not completely clean on these things). Much of it comes from the technological culture, but not from the technology itself. So how to negotiate with these things? For example, I've also been resisting mapping as one of the ways to create a sort of mastery over what we're doing. I have also been insisting – nobody listens to me in a.pass about that – for years now: we need more narrating and less mapping. Mapping is a supposedly non-subjective way of looking at where everybody is. It's a lie. It creates an illusion of what mastery is and also what the relationship between things is. But at the end of the day, we don't know where we stand in relation to each other, nor what our relationships are. So, mapping doesn't help with exactly what it is supposed to do: describing our relations. And yet, it's a strong image that we have to create, because we are also asked to make abstractions of what we are doing. Narration is very difficult, and also has its own problems, it has a big problem of perspective. You have to narrate from a perspective and the map gives you freedom from that perspective, so that finally, we can see everything. You are detached from a subjective position. But, a narrative way of telling what you're doing would be like following a trail, for example. A narrative way, as an example, would be somebody writing or telling a story, rather fabulously. It is still a lie, but a better one. What he or she felt, saw and thought through the process that they were engaged with. It allows us to go to the details of what was happening and we can respond to that with anger or with resentment or suspicion. I'm joking when I say nobody listens to me in a.pass, I'm the one who cannot do storytelling... and most of the time I still make maps myself, and I make cartographic images all the time. So, I'm totally part of both of these phenomena. But I do try my best not to give maps or mapping a special status.

PR: What you're saying is very valid. It's a critical take but also a generative invitation because what you propose to your 'clients' when you are invited to design a digital interface, is a crisis. You refuse to simply map but at the same time, you emphasise the necessity to categorise. But we, the digitally illiterate, associate mapping with categorisation. You invite us to dissociate them. So you can provoke a nervous breakdown in every 'client' of yours... hahaha...

(...)

PR: Today you used for the first time the term information when you pointed at the problem of its aestheticisation. But don't you think there is an issue with the notion of information itself?

SS: In the beginning of the last century, coinciding with the emergence of global consumption culture, information was the name of the entire world. Everything became information. The human body, the world, then the Internet, then the revolution of informational technologies and all of these things. But when things become informational, what happens to our imagination, to our knowledge? In an institution like a.pass, which is pedagogical in nature but also a place where artists test, try out, and become, here, I think, we are dealing much more with knowledge, knowledges, modes of knowing and styles of knowing rather

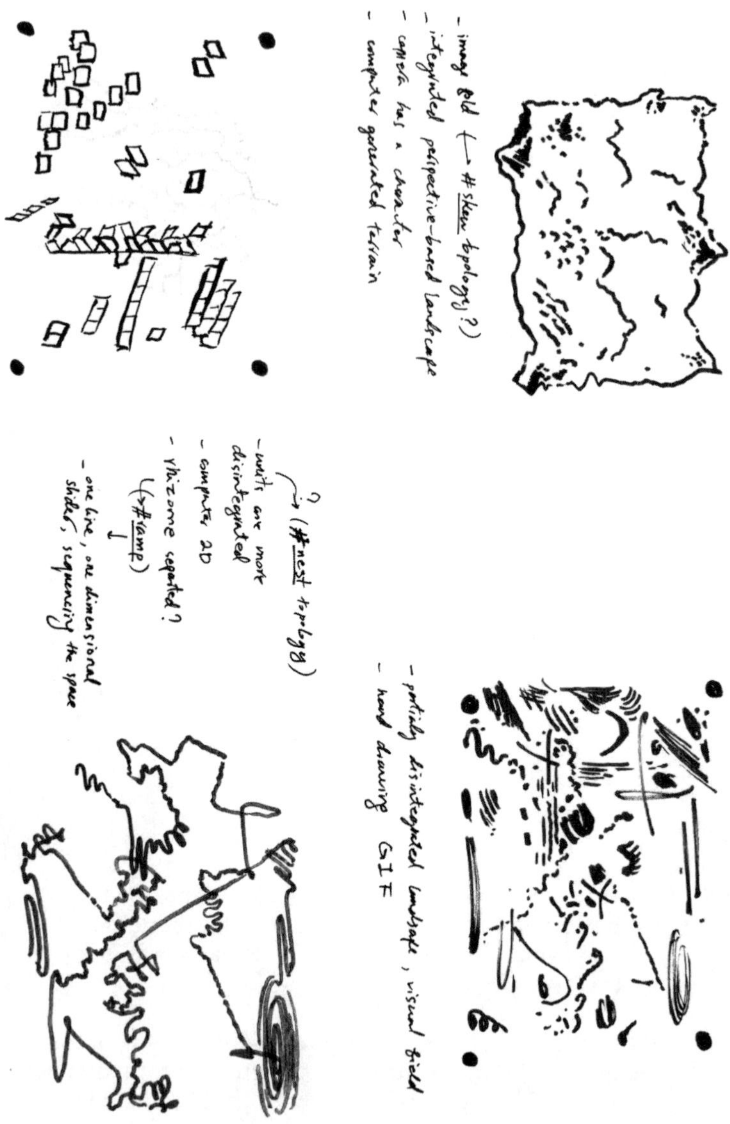

Skewed hand-drawn ideas for RRadio Triton interface. Applying three types of topologies (skew, nest and ramp) to our objects (timeline and files). Negotiation between synthesis and disintegration, towards a visual field with the touch of hand. The aim was to weaken the status of the map by strengthening the status of landscape, or interface as a pathway through an unmistakably specific landscape of sounds.

To see the implementation visit: rradiotriton.apass.be

than information. For an institution like a.pass, turning everything into information would actually deprive people and ourselves from seeing what kind of knowledge is generated. Because, for example, if you go to a museum here in Belgium and people say that this view of Africa is our knowledge, that means they take responsibility for a perspective. You can understand its situatedness, its ideology. It's a game you're invited to play. But if you 'inform' your audience, then you deprive yourself of all of that reflection.

PR: I understand your resistance to some aspects of the meaning of 'information' and when you oppose it to knowledge it becomes interestingly problematic. But another side of the notion of information is to envisage it as a singularity that can achieve the co-individuation of the receiver and the sender. It's a structural analysis of the dynamics of information. What are the functions of information-as-singularity? What does it do? You are pointing at a cultural definition of information when you oppose it to knowledge. But let's not throw information into the bin too fast because of the current cultural understanding of it and because we are inhabiting and inhabited by the information society. You analyse the term information through a tension with accountability that you associate with knowledge, but we could also say that knowledge has nothing to do with accountability? Information can also be analysed differently. For instance, if you study Simondon, but also other systems like the ones of Bateson or Whitehead, information carries very different meanings. For me, its most interesting sense is to be found in the etymology of the word which links in- and -form. So, the ability of any kind of element to be created by or to create a – constant or momentary – form. This is why I introduced the notion of information and its problems at a.pass. There, people are often struggling to try to give a form to impossibilities, for instance.

SS: I agree with you that there is much more to the notion of information. Perhaps what I'm pointing at is a culture generated by the informational era. I don't want to be too fast to jump or endorse the culture or conduct which looks at communication as a transmission of information. I'm trying not to jump in, especially when I'm asked to design websites. It is also related to a larger reflection on modernism, consumption and the theory and histories of knowledge for me. And it's related to the work I'm doing.

PR: And maybe as well to a reflection on what I call 'systems of control'. You mentioned earlier that you want to use 'a tool that is from now'. But what is a 'tool from now'? What is the relation between this technological tool and the old cybernetic project of human engineering? Today, 'apparently', cybernetics has totally disappeared. But don't you think that it is everywhere controlling our lives?

SS: Your reference to cybernetics is very relevant in this context, but it's not controlling, it is defining what we are, what we desire, what we think, what we dream... And I think we are in a negotiating relationship with technology that is becoming more and more like the air that is everywhere. I don't think we are in a master-slave relationship, we are defining each other. It has its problems. Absolutely.

(...)

PR: Just for the sake of an anecdote, I still don't have a smartphone. It's more and more difficult to resist the injunction to get one...

SS: Hahaha... You know what is my practice of resistance against technology? Learning to write. The relationship I have with the English language has a lot of things in it that I'm starting to really think about. Why am I really going for this and emphasising writing? I can't write yet. My writing is bad. I want to learn it and the lectures I wrote and performed were also ways of starting on that path. I see this relation with language as a mode of resistance to technology, because I think digital technologies are illiteracies or modes of illiteracy. I mean, when I code for instance, I enter an unknown linguistic realm. Many parts of it, I've absolutely no idea what I am writing. I write a code but underneath it, there's another writing mechanism that I don't have access to. Literacy has exploded, we are in an era of illiteracy in relation to digital technologies. We are partially literate. When I code I am partially literate. I think writing has a very old, pre-digital way of expression in sign language that is extremely important for me.

PR: But you're also an artist and, besides drawing, there are plenty of other forms of writing, no? Why do you focus on writing with words and in English... Why English? You never write in Farsi?

SS: Unfortunately not. English was the world that occurred in Europe for me because it was the language that a foreigner, a universal subject, speaks... Of course, you can attack me and say that the English language is just another technology. But I would say it's an older one, a few thousand years older. Illiteracy for me is a very important keyword. Illiteracy and literacy, both of them. A lot of people are recognising that literacy is changing constantly and we are dealing with new forms of literacy based on the media cultures we are in. For example, there have been studies about the new generation that show it is actually the most literate generation ever, at least in certain countries. But there's something else for me, which is the way we, as cognitive humans, as cognitive creatures are relating to our surroundings. It is an important part of being together, you know?... When and how is knowledge undermined, questioned or put aside or highlighted? And also, what are the consequences? What are the costs of it? What happens... for example, when reading becomes non-reading? When does reading become a ritual? Or when does the meaning of words become irrelevant in a conversation? For me, there are moments when I notice that this is not a time of transcendence of the community to a state that is beyond language, but in fact to a state of illiteracy. I mean it now in a negative sense. That means people have to attune or find themselves in relation to an underlying authority or affective state, which is not always good for the community. So these are the questions I had and still have. Illiteracy also helps me to understand the larger ways that we understand each other or refuse to understand. It's interesting and in the a.pass environment, there's also a double edge all of the time because you can never force people to speak in a certain way or read in a certain way... also, people come with different habits of reading, different relations to the texts. We are in a time that we want to be rather inclusive, right? So it's not really a category for me to put others into, but a kind of a measuring device to understand what is the climate of quality of writing and speaking in an environment. I think I'm also at a stage of my life where I care about writing and reading abilities. I think for me, democracy is strictly bound to abilities to write and read and talk, but in a way that is informed by humanities, by sciences, by the division of knowledge that we are dealing with, and not going to a place where charismatic speech acts or emotional warning becomes the way that we make each other care. For me, that would be a sign that there is something wrong with the discussion, with the level of discussion. But this is a hard topic, I don't think everybody would care for it. I started caring for it when I was a curator in a.pass. I was positioned to listen really carefully to what is being said and discussed and how. And when I, myself, am unable to listen or unable to talk or I lack the words or a particular way of relating to... I think that there are a lot of people working and writing on topics that we are also interested and busy with. Why should we refuse that, and say: 'Hey, I want to discover this all by myself, and through my body'. Also, I see a recurring and constant criticism on the level of THE enemy, against academia, in artistic research environments. Academia has become a caricature of target practice. These are the things that make me think about literacy and illiteracy. I'm of course aware that literacy has a history in imperialism and colonialism, people have been violently forced into particular kinds of literacies... For some Christian priests, for instance, who went to educate the indigenous people, literacy was a sort of colonising weapon. These are the things we should also know about… But this has less to do with the time that we are living in... It is a highly literate culture we are living in. A multidimensional one. You're asked to read pop-culture, to read social media comments, to read political statements, to read books, to read philosophy... These are complex modes of literacy.

(...)

PR: Going back to the paradox of non-design-design, when you develop an index or a website, which kind of agency do your literate critical views on modern thought produce? Are you informed by them (and how) when you digitalise artistic and research projects? Where is it articulated?

SS: Yes, this is something I am kind of extracting or learning from pre-modern bestiaries, as I call this research. When people composed those kinds of books – that are to some extent an equivalent to our natural sciences encyclopedia or to the ordered knowledges that we have now – it was a very strange time: information didn't exist. The stories of the phenomenal world that people composed: the perspective, the body and the cognitive skills of the writer were not yet fully separated. This was the thing that I was touched by, in my research. It is one of the things that I embody and bring with me when I do other things. That kind of relationship with the moment of communication as translator or as designer or in 'non-designer designing'. This is perhaps where my research is applied if I try to look at my own practice… Of course, when I use the word bestiary, it's a sort of safety net. The audience identifies it with an ongoing conversation with an object that is not yet fully known. I'm also cheating a little bit when I say 'I work on bestiaries'. This means 'let's postpone the conversation to an unknown future when I know more about this subject'.

PR: But in relation to your previous remarks on information, these bestiaries are also vehicles or vessels for information, no?

SS: I think information is a very new concept. It happened very recently. It is a kind of modulation and codification of the facts of the world that we are experiencing. Because, for example, if you go back to the 18th century and look at the art and the literature, the way people started a narrative or organised something, you can see that the idea of information is the way that we look at knowledge now. We could say that the idea of information was always there but there's something very new about the age of information.

PR: I understand. But I resist... The Chimera, for instance, present in one of your bestiaries, a monster made of heterogeneous parts, questioning the structure of what a human being or an animal can be, is a very operative piece of information. The Chimera is not something only to gaze at but also something that generates forms, trans-forms, in-forms and ultimately changes our form whenever and however we are in contact with it. The Chimera is operative as a factor of transformation, and is this not what information does too? – and maybe I could also change the Chimera into a sort of informational feedback loop? – Don't you think the problem is more that our contemporary world instrumentalises information for control purposes?

SS: Totally. Perhaps the pre-modern styles of knowledge are as bullshit and problematic. But what makes it a place to dream and to think is that it has lost its effectiveness. Nevertheless, I see old techniques of organising knowledge showing up in contemporary assemblages of media and corporations. You can see in big entertainment phenomena that cosmology-building and encyclopedic-building are manufactured in the old style, and it is not so much informational. It is interesting to play with the tensions between these things, and going back to the pre-modern, helps you understand the set of problems that come with modernism. It also helps you understand problems that modernism saw in the pre-modern and the reason why it actually happened.

(...)

PR: I think it's time we talk about knowledge.

SS: Hahaha maybe.

PR: At a.pass this term is everywhere. We produce knowledge, we 'don't-know-ledge', we process knowledge that we have to be accountable for, and so on and so forth... In a.pass the question of knowledge is a framework and specifically for artist-researchers like yourself who address and test the capacity of art to make knowledge its proper topic and to act epistemically. In order to qualify different types of methodologies of research and artistic practices, you introduced the term 'modes of knowing' in a.pass, but what about now? Where are you at with your reflections about what I could name for now, the epistemising potential of art?

SS: For a.pass, I have been using two terms recently in my own notes. First was the 'styles of knowing'. I think we are doing this a lot. A 'style of knowing' is very difficult to attack because this is 'my' way of knowing. Knowledge, on the other hand, could have some sort of authority and if it's presented well other people might accept it. In a.pass, I have seen two sources of knowledge. One of them is when we find the etymology of words, somebody says that this is the Greek origin and everybody accepts it as a way of rooting concepts. This is an instance of validation of a form of knowledge. The other one is when we give a reference to a book or to an author. These are the two moments that actually, we dance with knowledge. But most of the time, we are dealing with 'styles of knowing' and many times, we don't mean the same words people are using, especially in an environment like a.pass where people come from really totally different worlds and have very different relationships with the English language. But recently, I got excited about another idea which better describes my own relationship with knowledge, which is the notion of simulation or the 'simulacra of knowledge'. I realised that, for example, in my re-construction of the medieval world, I'm so far from knowing systematically whether I would have done a PhD on medieval bestiaries, for instance. What I'm doing is really not systematic, not based on sequential thinking processes and is so wide open that when I look at it, it produces a simulacra, an illusion, a fantasy that presents itself AS knowledge to me and to an audience – if they love me enough and don't want to question me on that. When I read very interesting or well written literature that is coming from universities, where people are much more limited and have to construct a position to say something about their subject, I think there are less possibilities to create a simulacra of knowledge. Simulacra is measured by its pure effectibility. One of my problems with the simulacra is that it has the problem of any simulacra: it's performative, it's interesting and it's exciting, but nobody else can use it.

PR: I think simulacra is not as bad as you say. People could use your simulacra, but maybe only some parts of them, or some structures... They can also be useful as ideas. Maybe you think people can't apply this specific form of knowledge because it's a singular arrangement of things? Is it not universal enough for you maybe?

SS: It's fine because it makes me more an artist and less a philosopher. It's inspiring. I use the word inspiration in the sense that it is not controllable. That means, you don't know what is the responsible consequence of an inspiration. Perhaps what I'm lacking or asking for, is a different kind of consequence which comes from having the concept that describes or responds to a part of the world that is also somebody else's problem. When you have before you a genuinely interesting concept, for example when you Pierre, read Simondon, he conceptualises a world that is also your problem. He gives you a different way of comprehending, problematising, analysing or just generalising that world that you also have stakes in.

PR: Paraphrasing Deleuze and Guattari, the difference between philosophy and art is that philosophy is busy with generalities and art is busy with details. Do you situate yourself in between? Are you the type of artist of now, especially in artistic research, who combines art and science?

SS: I'm entertaining the idea that it is possible to create a hybrid zone from a scientific discipline or from multiple disciplines – from the humanities most of the time – with artistic practice. In my case, animal studies, or some parts of anthropology AND art. But what I'm dreaming of is to know what would be the relation or the responsiveness of that academic field that I'm feeding from? This is what I'm suspecting and investigating with my own hybrid trajectory. But the simulacra of knowledge that I have recognised and named as such is not a generalisation that can be applied onto the whole of art...

PR: For you the problem is the possibility of a non-readability of your work by the authors of the very resources feeding your work. You fear that your work might only be decipherable by artists. But, when you introduce yourself you almost always start with 'animal studies', and then you talk about your art. You position yourself as a scientist at first but there are different chronologies as well. Some artists will make art first and then study something and become scientists eventually.

SS: This is perhaps why in our previous conversation, I proposed the term parody. Perhaps this is also another style of talking about our relationship with the knowledge that is produced outside of art and dancing with the knowledge and styles of the sciences... I see my practice as a parody, myself as a parody-scientist, producing a parody of knowledge. When I do my lecture-performances, it's coming from a moment of discovery, and rigorous speculation, like somebody who has just come from an experimental laboratory. I'm thinking about parody a lot. I realised that a lot of us, myself and other people that I've worked with at a.pass, are working with intellectual parody. In parody, the expressive powers of a style is used without real emotional commitment to it. Through parody you end up as if you have mastered the knowledge about something but you don't have the proper location of it. But yet, you tease. Think about the past in a.pass, Laura Pante makes parodies, Elen Braga parodies, Vanja Smiljanić parodies, Gosie Vervloessem parodies... To name a few, but there are many many of us who are dealing with the parody of knowledge as a mode of knowing... And we shouldn't mistake parody with the genre of comedy when it's used to talk about something without talking about it because it's annoying or too powerful. The parody that I am talking about is one of the heritage of deconstruction and is a specific mode of, yes... knowing.

PR: Assuming that you manage to convince the scientists whose work inspires you to attend your performances, you have to explain to them that you are not going to parody knowledge for the sake of humour but that parody is your condition, that you have a condition, it is parody, and that you are doomed to it in some way. Hahaha. You can't behave otherwise because you are a product of the fringes of art and science, of unexplored grey areas that mix with very identified knowledge.

SS: If you say it is a parody, it is not a parody anymore! Hahaha. It is perhaps related to the general concern or problem I'm thinking about: Can we prove to artists that they are wrong? Is the artist wrongable?

PR: Artists can be wrong! It depends on the taxonomy that you put their work in relation to... history of art, aesthetic relevance, political relevance, engagement... Artists are judged. So you can declare that some are wrong. Artists are the most judged.

SS: Artists are the most judged?

PR: Yes! Good, bad, good, bad...Thumbs-up, thumbs-down, it's like the circus games in the Roman Empire...

SS-PR: Hahaha! (laughing)

(...)

---

1 A handful of these project can be listed as such:

ajayeb.net hypertext for research notes, a word scrambler and a site for writing about bestiaries 2016-ongoing;
archivingartisticanxieties.me online publication and collaborative writing tool for Adrijana Gvozdenović's research project 'Archiving Artistic Anxieties' 2020;
parallelparasite.apass.be video archive and commentary system for 'Parallel Parasite: Timeline Repository' curated by Lilia Mestre 2018;
rradiotriton.apass.be interface and data model design for experimental radio project 'RRadio Triton Data Retrieval Interface' curated by Pierre Rubio 2017;
filters.apass.be workshop on the problem of building abstractions with data 2018.

Nicolas Y. Galeazzi

Case's Studies

A Documentary Play in Three Acts

PERSONA

THE CASE: represents an institutional framework – including the framework for this play. It has no body and speaks seemingly from many different places on, behind and from above the stage.
In this particular case, the institutional framework is a certain artistic research platform. It is curated by multiple perspectives and therefore under constant debate and transformation.

3 VOICES: it is said that initially, the playwright wanted to describe only this one CASE. But too many contradictory perspectives within himself have been pouring over the case and picking it apart. So, the playwright decided for the time being to let only three of these VOICES argue the CASE in depth. The three VOICES represent three different perspectives on artistic research and the creation of good conditions for its development. Looking from afar, the positions of the three VOICES may not seem so different, but to themselves, their differences sometimes feel like unbridgeable abysses.
THE CASE looks at the debate amongst these VOICES with a mixture of skepticism, frustration and fascination from a pragmatic, but nonetheless poetic perspective.

ARTIST: an artist whose artistic practice is research. This VOICE stands for playfulness in art, performativity of research and a commitment to artistic research beyond academic demands.

RESEARCHER: a researcher whose methodology is based in art. This VOICE represents critical thinking and performance as critical practice. It approaches art as the 'research & development department' of society.

CURATOR: an artist working at an artistic research institution. This VOICE stands for an artistic approach to institutions, as well as instituting as an artistic practice to transform society from within.

SET

An almost empty storage space in an educational institution for artistic research. There is only a white plastic crate in the middle of an empty stage. Spot on, in the spotlight. Sometimes it sounds as if the voice of THE CASE is speaking out of that crate. The crate is filled with paper: large sheets, small pieces, index cards, many post-its, some A4 stacks, loose pieces of paper, all in different colours – a mess. It is labelled 'COLLECTED CASES 2010-20'.

When the VOICES appear, it seems they are busy in a room next door and have only come here to quickly search for something, to catch inspiration, or to simply take a short break.

To avoid distraction while reading, it helps to imagine this set in a classic blackbox theatre.

PROLOGUE

THE CASE: Hello. I am – THE CASE.

(Pause.)

You might think I am only that little crate you see on stage, but I'm also the stage itself and all that frames and holds it together.
I'm the kind of case that only provides the shell for content around which everything revolves. Yet, everything depends upon the fact that I decide upon the boundaries for whatever evolves here.
In this particular case, I am the institutional face of an artistic research place – and therefore, understandably, I store, amongst other things, in such 'crates' the leftover traces of its lost and found research cases. Forgotten and outcast, these traces echo the pulse of collective thinking processes, and voice from the institutional peripheries the sound of fragile unfinished knowledges.

(While the audience listens to the prologue of THE CASE, ARTIST appears on stage, and approaches the illuminated crate. ARTIST searches for something and understands that the crate must first be brought to order. ARTIST takes some bundles of paper and starts to spread and sort them on the floor. ARTIST stops abruptly, puts some papers to the side, and leaves.)

THE CASE: I am – just – THE CASE:
Don't get me wrong, my duty is simple, I only provide a form. Of course, I know the form shapes the content. But the content shakes the form, not that I want it to, but such traces of collective consciousness, which I collect in such crates for future processes, will shape the faces from inside out of such institutional places.

(RESEARCHER appears and sees the mess. RESEARCHER puts everything back into the crate. At a certain point, RESEARCHER chooses a note and reads. RESEARCHER leaves with the note.)

THE CASE: I do not understate: this crate is great. Filled with scribbles, sketches and mappings.

Drawn up on scrap paper, notepads and wrappings, posters, postcards, charts, and post-its. In there, there are collective search in processes, experiments' loose-ends of collected approaches. An archive of artistic left-behinds, garbage, out-cast, things left the minds. Stored there, to be seen through new lenses; for saving them from becoming wasted thoughts.

(After a moment, CURATOR appears and sits next to the box, watches it for a while, then closes the eyes and digs with the hand into the heap of paper to a bundle – enjoyment. At this moment, the prologue is over and CURATOR leaves the stage, seemingly without having read anything.)

THE CASE: The following play, the play you read here, is based on these traces, paving a trail into your ear.
While writing, the playwright was playing a game: letting his eyes stray through the crate, randomly picking up concepts to his plate. Just following his faith, they were forming new sentences; content that is talking about researching me – THE CASE.
Walking through these notes and his thoughts in his way, three VOICES appeared to resonate in his head. One echoes an artist who doesn't want to fear failure; the other one roams as a researcher, a critical nature; the third is the curator that claims not to curate here.
The playwright tried to process all these VOICES. Letting them speak and act his internal contradicting forces. He wants us to read and continue the game, giving shape to me – remaining the same old – CASE.

ACT I – ARTISTIC RESEARCH AND ITS CURATION

The first Act, where three VOICES discuss the best conditions for their relationship. The furniture of two exemplary Curatorial Models, together with collective notes dug out from an old crate, both help and confuse their discussion.

(The three VOICES appear on stage carrying 'Curatorial Models I'. It is a sculpture that looks like an empty bookshelf built-up in several directions with different levels, boards and materials. The VOICES place the shelf at a certain distance from the crate. The ARTIST looks for that bundle placed next to the crate during the prologue, but cannot find it. RESEARCHER holds the piece of paper he took earlier next to his face and takes a selfie with a phone. They look at the picture. ARTIST recognises the note as one from the searched bundle and places it on the shelf. CURATOR turns to the audience and takes the floor.)

CURATOR: *(presenting the shelf)* 'Curatorial Model I! The Commons'. This shelf-like object represents an idea. It applies the idea of 'public book-shelves' for people to leave their books for others to read, in the context of artistic research as a method to share works. This shelf is an empty shell with an 'f' – free for everyone to place things on it – and forget about them. No longings, no belongings. On that shelf, everything is considered unfinished at any point in time, and at any time everyone is encouraged to finish it. A circular economy of 'half-finishedness', and an exercise in artistic commoning. Sharing, not owning; caring, not competing; entanglement, no specialisation. Simple things we surely all dream of.

RESEARCHER: *(makes a selfie with ARTIST, looks at the picture and speaks to the audience)* Actually, the Shell-f never came into action, nor existed in the spaces we worked in. It only existed in our thoughts!

CURATOR: ...and for preparation purposes. It was essential to conceive our proposal for Curatorial Model I. It was the concrete backbone of the ideal to build a commons economy.

RESEARCHER: What existed in the studio was time-based.

CURATOR: Yes. *(Takes a paper from the crate and gives it to ARTIST who meanwhile sits at the shelf.)*

ARTIST: *(reading aloud)* "Every Friday of this three-month programme, we open the space for a commoning session, dedicated to a practical inquiry into the question:

What do we create by being together?

This Open Space practice requires us to pursue three things at the same time: first, to follow the individual research interests. Second, to focus on connections and correlations amongst the different researches. And third, to observe the emergence of communality".

(ARTIST looks around; looks at CURATOR; CURATOR looks at RESEARCHER and RESEARCHER looks at ARTIST.)

RESEARCHER: *(after a short moment of watching ARTIST)* However, this model failed! The shell-f was not a shelf, and the Open Space was not open at all – just a bit loose.

CURATOR: It did not fail! *(Searching again for something in the crate.)*

RESEARCHER: It did!

ARTIST: ... It didn't work in terms of sharing, but it was fun to steal from each other without consequences.

RESEARCHER: Probably for some it was fun! (*Taking a selfie with CURATOR and the crate in the background. To the audience)* ... and so, it never grew beyond the tight grid of that Shell-f-idea. It never became that 'Commons' for the Arts we hoped it would become. This would have taken much longer. It was still us who controlled the processes, us, who curated the whole programme according to our idea of an 'artist's commons'. As hard as we tried, we could not get rid of our 'ownership'.

ARTIST: Forget about that one! The responsibility of these kinds of 'ownership' glue to you like an octopus kiss.

CURATOR: The students – sorry, the participants – didn't see us from a perspective of 'ownership'! They just didn't really want to latch onto the idea of the commons.

ARTIST: ... Probably not in the beginning. But did you forget the evaluation session at the end of three-months? The students – sorry, the participants – almost slaughtered us for not being more transparent, for guiding and designing too much, for not creating a real commons, for only doing it for ourselves, etc. *(Taking a paper roll from the crate, unfolding it and hanging it on the shelf.)* These notes are the proof!

RESEARCHER: And they were right! We even mentioned repeatedly that this set-up is rather to problematise the commons, in order to understand economies better in general. But they understood the 'economy' better than us, and found our problematisations cynical.

(RESEARCHER is taking a selfie with ARTIST and the poster in the background, examines the picture.)

CURATOR: Not at all! We transparently proposed an unfinished platform for unfinished practices, which reacts with unfinished proposals! This can be so motivating if one engages in the proposition:

(CURATOR starts to unpack the crate and put notes, piles of paper, paper rolls and some notebooks onto the shelf. By placing the unpacked objects, CURATOR explains and embodies with enthusiasm the ideal procedure of this imagined workflow.)

CURATOR: That's how it should work: let's say person A puts something onto the shel-f, and leaves. Person B takes it and transforms it, and person C sees that, and copies it – with some personal changes, etc.

ARTIST: It was an illusion: mimicking a commons almost did the opposite. The participants asked for either total participation or for more institution, more guidance, more clarity.

RESEARCHER: Sure, it was a proposition from an educational institution, so it remained an educational tool.

CURATOR: Why is this a problem for people who freely decide to take time off in an educational research institution. As a field of problems, it was a gift – they could have taken and distorted it in whatever direction they wanted.

RESEARCHER: No, they couldn't because in their minds we were holding the power and the model on tight leashes, while we pretended to be on the same level as them.

ARTIST: No, they couldn't because they were looking for something less patronising, less communal, more critical perhaps, and with clear positions! We can change authority at any time, but make it clear, please! Therefore, let us propose the second model!

(ARTIST and RESEARCHER get 'Curatorial Model II' while CURATOR continues to pin notes and papers, now all over the stage. Curatorial Model II is a table with five chairs, a big pot of soup on a hot plate, vegetables and some cooking tools on the table. RESEARCHER sits down. ARTIST turns to the audience and takes the floor.)

ARTIST: Such a table was at the centre of 'Curatorial Model II'. It is titled, 'making/conditions'. This time we didn't care so much about the facts and forces of curating. We rather embraced the standpoint of a host, and made clear decisions.

RESEARCHER: *(cutting vegetables for the soup)* ...and justified our power to ourselves with: 'to come without a clear proposal would be a loss of time for everyone', or, 'someone has to make a statement, to provoke the debate', or, 'making conditions has to be an experiment in curatorial meta structures itself', etc. I don't know whether that's better!

ARTIST: The participants were happy with that, and I had no need to justify myself! I had fun proposing this.

RESEARCHER: And what was your fun?

ARTIST: This time we met twice a week. Start and end times were not defined, only lunchtime at this table was set. A condition that respects personal needs and timing. For me, that was at the heart of the model. Simple, as such. I don't think you need anything more to curate an artistic research framework!

(RESEARCHER and CURATOR look at each other.)

CURATOR: But that was not everything, though.

(RESEARCHER takes a selfie with ARTIST in the background and examines the picture before continuing to prepare the soup.)

ARTIST: Probably, but for me, it was central! Look – there is that note on 'conditions': *(ARTIST is reading a note that CURATOR has pinned to the shelf.)* "Setting a condition is always a reaction to other conditions".

CURATOR: *(takes the note and pins it back to the shelf.)* Can I elaborate on that? Thanks. To me, everything is taking place in a kind of 'resonance room'. One set of conditions creates ten other sets, and those respond back again. It's a morphing body of relations. Resonance sets fundamentally different conditions than capitalism as it opposes its alienation. *(CURATOR becomes rapturous.)* I love the idea of resonance as curatorial principle. It's perceptive vibrancy. Economy is just receptive violence. Curating becomes an anti-capitalist practice if it sets vital and vibrating conditions for the space between people rather than for the unique, outstanding individual.

ARTIST: There was this 'Book of Questions' in the crate *(tries to find it),* I remember only one question: "How can we create conditions for artistic practices not based on economic, but ecological thinking?" 'Resonance', 'ecology', – for me, that's the same!

RESEARCHER: Hey guys, calm down! Making-conditions is always as much aggressive as it is creating relations. The model was actually about alternative entrepreneurship, no? *(Searches for another big hand-drawn-poster in the crate and attaches it to the shelf.)*

RESEARCHER: Or let's say, about setting things in motion, and that's needed. Let's adopt the economy as a subversive tool. It's time for shaking up, guys, not 'vibrating'!

CURATOR: Why do you think you know what to 'shake up'!?

RESEARCHER: I call it 'speculative practice', you might call it 'abuse of power!'

ARTIST: Ha! Where is the difference?

RESEARCHER: *(putting more salt in the soup)* Guys, we need more urgency! If we have the capacity for 'making conditions', we should use it to invent a new system! I don't care if you call that teaching, coordinating, curating, organising, animation or what else.

(Pause. RESEARCHER is stirring the soup.)

RESEARCHER: Curating is stirring up these contexts and mashing them into a different perspective for the future. We need to take responsibility and see what our artistic tools are capable of. To me, that is urgent!

CURATOR: Who is the 'We' you are talking about? Without rethinking our positions of 'curator', 'artist', 'teacher', 'student', we are not creating new systems! It's a question of the distribution of responsibility, and this is not in the sense of claiming authority, or asking who does what, but it's about how to take the balls that someone provides. That's the same for students as for curators! How do we respond to what others do?

ARTIST: *(has found the 'Book of Questions' and shows it to the others)* Speaking of responsibility: "How can we think of institutions as 'critical' agents?" In capital letters: "SPEAKING ABOUT AN ORGANISATION, OR SPEAKING TO ORGANISE". In very small letters: "We are both acting subjects and subjects of our own action".

RESEARCHER: And here is the questions-book. It asks on the first page: "What is the agency of failure?" And later: "How can I change the world by failing to change the world?"

ARTIST: The answer is: "Keep asking questions".

RESEARCHER: Soup is ready.

(ARTIST, CURATOR and RESEARCHER spoon out the soup together.)

INTERLUDE

THE CASE: All these approaches, regimes, and provokers. Regimes of approaches, evokers of notions, perspectives of sceptics, practices of activists, urging the merge of everything into everything – artistic research is cruising through stages, crawling over these cases, crossing legs and laces, crossing swords with – borders.

'What bothers you about borders?' I ask the crate. 'My horizon is messy', it says, 'in that state, I need a frame to be safe and sane'. I say, 'it's the same, in the centre – I'm losing the end, there! There are clashes of concepts, crashes of contents. We are fed fat by seeking for searching – fed-up by lost-ness in knowing. Let's search for it! – By sharing!

'But take care in...' shouts the crate from afar, 'it is a search on the fringes of re-search – research quickly becomes an institution's urge – it will eat the pure search, will puke it back into that bucket where always already anything anyway is known. Production of knowledge, they call it, shall they swallow it, shall the swallows fly with it!'

Scissors are scissors, a coin is a coin, and a box, like me, is a box, like you. I represent what you do, represent what you don't. The traces are key: I eat what I see, if you want it or not, I'll set it free. Whatever I am, I'm carrying the treasure and caring for pressure. However, I'll decide whether something's art – or if it'll disappear.

(During the Interlude of THE CASE, the VOICES finish the soup. RESEARCHER empties the crate. CURATOR and ARTIST are shifting the shelf into the spotlight of the crate and place this onto the table. They carry the table onto the shelf and create a wacky installation, integrating all chairs, the pot of soup and vegetables. They work until the end of the Interlude.)

ACT II - ARTISTIC RESEARCH AND ITS INSTITUTIONS

The second Act, where the VOICES discuss the necessity, purpose and obsolescence of institutions for artistic research. The Curatorial Models will be reconfigured, and the resulting confusion leads into a party.

CURATOR: There was that note about the evolution of institutions. *(Goes to the crate and searches for a piece of paper.)*

CURATOR: Here, it says: "There are three I's. First, there is an 'I'dea. Then you go for the idea and make it public, so it becomes 'your' idea. It's identifiable and represents your 'I', even though the same idea can emerge wherever – that's the emergence of egos. And then you cast this 'I' into the form of an 'I'nstitution – and it becomes productive..."

RESEARCHER: ...dries out and becomes hard. No, that's not my style!

ARTIST: The 'I'dea, the 'I', and the 'I'nstitution. It's a triangle full of projections.

CURATOR: What is missing...?

RESEARCHER: The problem is, the story of institutions is a different one: there is an 'I' that dreams of something and needs a lens to see what it is. It calls the lens 'institution' and enjoys that lens to see clearly. But soon it starts to dream only through that lens; dreams, which the 'I' never would have had without it.

ARTIST: Actually, the real story is: there is the 'I'nstitution that imagines the ideal 'I' – and creates conditions for the ideal relations amongst multiple 'I's. All of which are supposed to realise their unique dreams – which the 'I'nstitution then sees as the fulfilment of its own most marvelous dreams.

RESEARCHER: ...and everyone imagines the idea would ultimately be their own.

(RESEARCHER takes an index card with hand notes that catches the interest of the three VOICES during the rearrangement of the furniture.)

RESEARCHER: Let's see what this one was writing: "DEINDIVIDUATION: every time you do something alone, add someone else..." *(To the CURATOR.)* Would that be a curatorial approach to you?

ARTIST: Oh my god, such a dictatorship of the commons. Doing things alone and following only your vision can be freeing and inspiring!

CURATOR: And then the pressure and responsibility increase – and the more complex the situation becomes. Doing things alone creates a surreal focus of ownership and belonging – with the consequential conflicts!

RESEARCHER: You create conflicts either way: by creating territories and freedoms, or by commoning a relation.

CURATOR: An institution is there to negotiate the exact relationship between the two perspectives.

RESEARCHER: Most institutions are there to avoid the real negotiation of these perspectives. The perspectives have to be negotiated face to face anyway.

(CURATOR goes to the wacky installation and chooses an index card from the same pile the previous came from. Unfortunately, part of the installation falls apart and has to be rebuilt in a provisory way.)

CURATOR: *(addresses the installation.)* Sorry. *(To the other VOICES.)* See this card, it says:

"INSTITUTION AS A TOOL". Then, someone else adds:

"Caution! Often the institutional framework overpowers the intent of the people. Then all of a sudden, the pure idea of the Institution carries the real power, rather than the people who run it".

(Fixes this note somewhere visible onto the shelf's frame. Unfortunately, the installation falls apart again, and needs to be rebuilt, but RESEARCHER takes the shelf and tries to turn it several times on its head and back in order to find a better position.)

RESEARCHER: I can imagine situations where that might be the better 'idea'.

CURATOR: Wow!? Is that a statement for more regulations?

RESEARCHER: I just think people are neither less nor more stupid than institutions.

ARTIST: So, you think of institutions as people, not as tools!

CURATOR: *(watches the current position of the shelf and continues to move it around in search of a good place.)* Call it 'resonance', 'ecology' or 'actor-network', 'new materialism', – or simply the relations between things... they are equal agents, dependent on, and conditioning each other. An impossible marriage – impossible to leave.

(RESEARCHER searches for another index card.)

RESEARCHER: The last note in this series is:

"CONTAMINATE: No compromises, nor consensus! The question is, how to create the best situations for individuals that arise from practising togetherness".

ARTIST: The backside of the note in my hand says: "About collectives: allowing individual lines in collective processes vs. overcoming the 'ego' of collective achievements".

CURATOR: ...and the last sentence on this note?

ARTIST: "Testing common sense through individual practices vs. reflecting individual practices through collective processing".

CURATOR: Does that mean governance would not be about making decisions, but about allowing togetherness?

RESEARCHER: That sounds so soft-power!!

(ARTIST tries to find a way to position the table in a way it would not look like a table anymore.)

ARTIST: I would love to sit at it up there.

(RESEARCHER pushes the shelf in ARTIST's direction.)

ARTIST: *(still reflecting about a solution for the table.)* Artistic research – let's get back there. It's just another market, isn't it? It's a concept that represents the rise of immaterial economies. *(Reading from a page that hangs on the shelf.)* "Artistic Research as it is practised today is capitalising through deconstruction, critical dissection, and problematisation of any practice. But for artists, research is at any moment a means of understanding and communicating the fragilities of life. The difference today is that it is precisely these fragilities that are exploited to produce structural capitalism." And later it says, "I better see artistic research as a way to make a living through poetic exploration and silly play".

RESEARCHER: *(standing at the shelf and chanting softly the following sentences.)*

"AR requires a specific context.
AR is a multidisciplinary practice.
AR is a never-ending story".

(Reading to the audience.) "Everything on this shelf is for everyone! Nothing is complete! Everyone is in demand to finish the works of others! Do not clean after the job, but work with the mess of others! An entrepreneurial gift economy – without the involvement of

money – showed to be a fantastic driver for an artist commons!" – I like it!

(ARTIST is beginning to decorate the place for a party with garlands, golden balloons, candles, neon glam and purple velvet all at once.)

CURATOR: *(dreamy)* Did you hear the crate speaking? Beautiful. It only does this when the barrel is about to overflow! Such a tension of powers, institution, art, economy. *(Copying RESEARCHER'S chanting.)*

"AR is the self-limiting perpetuation of critical thinking.
AR is the self-indulgent celebration of doubt.
AR is the imposition of values on non-valuables".

(All three VOICES sing the last sentences repetitively.)

ARTIST: I have one: *(holds a paper up)* "DOUBT AS DRAMATURGICAL PRACTICE?"

(ARTIST is asking the technicians backstage for some music, while RESEARCHER tries to become part of the shelf.)

RESEARCHER: Or as a research tool?

ARTIST: Or doubt as a principle of relationship?

CURATOR: No, as an institutional practice! Institution as a doubting agent.

(CURATOR starts dancing with the empty crate, the others follow.)

RESEARCHER: doubt as a lifestyle...

(RESEARCHER starts dancing with the shelf, and ARTIST is trying to secure the party decoration.)

CURATOR: Sure, doubt is an economy. It's a valid currency within the arts.

RESEARCHER: What a cruel, perfidious figure, that currency!

ARTIST: Not cruel! Just disturbing. It keeps things going, it's grist to the mill of any research, and fuel for the showdown of discourses. Doubt is what makes research dramatic!

CURATOR: I don't know. There is a lot of doubt around – it's very muddy – not enough to get into deeply. It seems like doubt is just growing in mass while everything around it stagnates. Doubting everything just accumulates to a kind of ideological paranoia.

(The CURATOR's dance gets wilder.)

ARTIST: Do you mean, doubt is opposite of love?

CURATOR: No, just f* institutional critique.

RESEARCHER: Do you mean critical thinking excludes love!?

(Meanwhile dancing together with ARTIST on the table amongst balloons, plates and vegetables.)

CURATOR: I don't care! I'm just fed-up with this constant stream of people, things, ideas, bacteria, forced to entangle, to mash-up, to make any random f* sense to someone and then disappear with the next trendy discourse. Transformation, transformation, transformation – and becoming, becoming, becoming. Get practical!! *(Shouting at the others.)* What a fucking stress!? *(Throwing the crate at the technician backstage and shouts.)* Shut off!! – *(No less aggressive, but silent.)* Unbearable noise!

(Silence.)

RESEARCHER: *(takes a secret selfie of the situation.)* And...?

CURATOR: Do you see any sense in what we are doing?

ARTIST: *(trying to get back into party mode by cutting funny figures out of paper for the garland.)* Imagine an institution that is just a door, an immensely open gate towards an enormous field of resources. The institute would not be a doorkeeper, it just places a frame in the middle of the landscape to mark the possibilities, and you can pass it from all sides.

RESEARCHER: What a sacred imagination! Do you remember the *Torii,* those spiritual Japanese gates? This institution would be seen as an oracle immediately. Full of abusive projections.

CURATOR: The field of resources is there anyway. Why do we need framing? The framing is such a tool of power, it will always be contested.

ARTIST: Let it go! The only thing needed there are places and moments to meet.

RESEARCHER: Some kind of address – different ones. Places you know you can meet others; in this jungle – or desert of resources.

(After a pause.)

CURATOR: If you ask me, we probably just need a bunch of different looking glasses, binoculars, lenses, zooms etc...

(ARTIST and RESEARCHER don't understand.)

CURATOR: ...randomly distributed over a huge field. No need to know where. There are no tags. Just stumble and wonder! And then, let's dance.

(Music. RESEARCHER, ARTIST and CURATOR start to dance again over that imaginative field, explorations of space, bodies and stuff...)

ACT III

Artistic research and its Outside

The third Act, where a third Curatorial Model let the VOICES dream about the ideal form of sharing their honourable thoughts with the world. But they end up dreaming the nightmare of unavoidably being part of the same society they would love to shout at.

(During the dance, the atmosphere changes. The light is turning greenish and opens to the walls of the theatre. The music is gradually changing towards sounds of natural landscape mixed with industry and traffic noise. ARTIST, RESEARCHER, and CURATOR make themselves comfortable on the floor. RESEARCHER takes charge to explain the third model.)

RESEARCHER: The third 'Curatorial Model' we present is not the paradise we just danced in. It is more of a wilderness. 'Curatorial Model III', suggests we hold all events of the programme out of the house. All gatherings with the researchers take place open air: we didn't place a foot inside spaces for the whole three-month programme. This model is called 'Troubled Gardens'.

(Reading.) "Where to investigate and experience behaviour as ecosystems better than in the outdoors – an outside that immediately takes us in, makes us a part of it! Therefore, this model IN-vites you OUT. 'Outdoor' – at places with-out-doors. Where weather and biosphere meet industrial (side-)performance, migrant activities, walls, traffic, sun, written and unwritten laws etc. interact with each other".

(To the audience.) As an example, imagine a campfire on muddy ground. A mix of pallet and other firewood is used to sit on, surrounded by green, loads of Japanese knotweed, nettles and mugwort, overarched by plum trees. A greenhouse and a vandalised shelter in the background. It's rainy and cold

that morning in spring. We are in a collective garden, experimenting with permaculture. It's an oasis in the urban setting, surrounded by industrial sites, train tracks, and street traffic. Homeless people are occupying any hiding place under bridges nearby, and piles of garbage line the path to the garden gate.

ARTIST: *(falls into RESEARCHERS word.)* A bunch of artistic researchers are hanging out in silence around the fireplace. Birds are chirping, worms peep out of their holes, someone adds more wood, and someone else writes impressions, thoughts, critiques into the 'ONE-BOOK'. This big-sized notebook was our daily ritual. For half an hour at the beginning of every work day, we shared our thoughts in silence. There was one book for everyone to take notes. It was our main tool for documentation.

RESEARCHER: Why did you cut my word? There were many other moments and other places – as much relevant to this model.

ARTIST: Wasn't it the best thing of the 'Troubled Gardens', that most of it remained undocumented!?

CURATOR: That was rather stupid! So many great experiences and thoughts got lost and are no longer available. Romantically submerging into the outside might have made you think – inner experience is enough, what?

ARTIST: I'm not against documentation. I often just don't know what to document for? With what device? One notebook for all was a brilliant filter. How much data that will never be used do you want to collect? In which way are devices and data disturbing the situation that should be documented?

RESEARCHER: No, it's the other way around: a critical way of documenting can create a powerful situation.

ARTIST: One shared notebook for all created such a situation. Written open-air in the communal garden in the midst of an industrial site hacks well into the bubbles of our individualised research. There is a note on that in the crate: *(is searching)* Here! “Interrupting a current flow: Is this closing down possibilities? Or opening to new grounds?”

CURATOR: A very interesting question! Interruption is very welcome, for sure! To me the question is, which part of the flow shall be interrupted and on which other part new grounds built upon. Exactly for sorting that out – what needs to be let go of, what needs to be rethought, what needs to be rebuilt, we need the traces of a process. Look at the crate!

ARTIST: Any means of documentation already proposes a pre-sorting of the questions you are asking. Look at that mess in this box! Wonderful! *(ARTIST is searching in the crate for the ONE-BOOK.)* Where is the ONE-BOOK?

RESEARCHER: *(lying and relaxing on the table to reflect upon the following.)* Actually, there were multiple outsides. The air, the non-humans around, the industrial reality, the communal garden etc. – and then, the potential reader of the documentation, the way we opened our research to each other, etc. All of that asked for an interruption to the proliferating production line of the knowledge market.

ARTIST: Every closure opens new possibilities. Wherever you are at, interruption, a change of protocol, a change of perspective and a change of practice is essential!

RESEARCHER: Not only essential, change is urgent if I’m looking at the word!!

CURATOR: A lot of disturbance can be created by precise documentation, and its dissemination! Research is a political tool, after all.

RESEARCHER: Wishful thinking!

ARTIST: To disturb someone else, you need to disturb yourself.

RESEARCHER: You probably mean, 'when disturbing someone else, you disturb yourself?'

CURATOR: I would say – *(pointing at ARTIST)* 'when you feel the need to disturb yourself, you first disturb someone else!'

RESEARCHER: G-r-e-a-t, 'disturb your neighbour as yourself'. Could we please leave the teabag-advice level?

CURATOR: ...and get back to the elitist one? The 'Troubled Garden' model was a confrontation with the outside, with the common, the 'normal'. How to break down the ivory tower of artistic research to a level that resonates beyond the artistic circuit? The model of the 'Troubled Gardens' should have challenged our responses to bigger environmental and social questions, much more than it did.

ARTIST: Challenge in what way? Some notes in the ONE-BOOK take that demand quite far – into the non-human world: *(searching for these notes on the ground)* You have just put them somewhere here... Here: *(reading aloud)* "Let's be taught, challenged and changed by the weather, by plants or animals in the same way as critical education can do." Or another one says: "Care for the snail you just crushed with your foot as much as for your research!" And think about that one: "You do research not for, but within, an environment".

CURATOR: That's not what I meant with the 'normal'! Still, too often artistic research pretends to be somewhere beyond its social context, being able to reflect upon it from the outside. But there is no outside of society! There is only an outside to this self-confinement of the artistic-research-bubble, and there is the question, what, and how much it is able to impact social change?

RESEARCHER: *(jumps up)* Disturbance! It's disturbance we give back from there. We need to create an outside for that. If we merge completely with what we think is our environment, if observation and questioning doesn't create an interruption of the 'normal', how should we come up with criteria to know if reality is what we think it is? How do we induce change, if not by looking for other versions and visions beyond what we see as 'normal'? That's why we went out!

CURATOR: You are always within the 'normal'. It's either your norm or another's! For change to occur, we need to embrace that fact. We need to play within them all, understand them. That's why we went 'out'!

ARTIST: I don't get you guys? We went out because it's nice there! And because interrupting the course of normal performatives on all sides. It pulls you out of the known context and hopefully pushes the context to somewhere you didn't expect before. The biggest challenge is, though, to choose your contexts to disturb and to be disturbed by. Because the context has to be disturbing to you, *and* should, at the same time, enable you to disturb the context. I need to cook disturbance and be cooked!

CURATOR: And who cares?

(Pause.)

RESEARCHER: What do you think about that note in the ONE-BOOK: "A caesura is always a crisis. A crisis is always breaking to something 'new'. Crisis is the nourishing ground of emergence..."

CURATOR: 'Crisis', 'emergence', 'going beyond the normal' – all part of a specific context. That doesn't go beyond! But people beyond our codex have a right to understand, and we need their critical gaze! We need to make concrete choices within the current of the world. We need to take a stand and to be understood if we want to change!

ARTIST: We-need-we-need-we-need! You are driving me crazy with your societal demands!

CURATOR: And you are driving me crazy with your ego-perspective, from your spherical arrogance somewhere outside and beyond everything!

RESEARCHER: Calm down, guys! We never know anyway if we are part of something, or whether we are actually excluded. How can you distinguish whether a context is influencing you, or you are influencing a context? You might be exploited at the same time as you are excluded.

CURATOR: That's why I was a fan of the principles of permaculture that we discussed in the 'Troubled Gardens'. First one is: observe from within! Give time, adjust your actions and observe again.

ARTIST: *(to itself)* The world's need for being in flow is so immense, it falls in a self-running mode, running open-eyed against the wall!

RESEARCHER: I think we need to develop another vocabulary of taking part in change in order to really make a difference.

CURATOR: You propose another vocabulary for critical thinking!? What do you think about those cards from the crate:

"Inhabiting or displacing systems.
Provoking the collective death.
Production-line of questions.
A revolution is needed in everyone's private garden"

ARTIST: Listen to these cards:

"Ask: What is not here?
What are you unable to find words for?

	Who is here but not included? Who feels responsible but can't help? Who can help but does not feel responsible? Where is the place of the individual?"
CURATOR:	*(getting mad again with the ARTIST.)* All this constant questioning! 'Where is the place of the individual?' So self-centred! 'Act here and now, and with the ones that are there!' would be my card to add. The point of leaving the institution's walls was to be confronted with other realities: to see the need for action! You remember that wasteland where Roma families and homeless people installed their living.
RESEARCHER:	...until the bulldozers of the police erased it!
ARTIST:	Why is that more real?
CURATOR:	Not more, but a reality that requires immediate attention.
ARTIST:	And that's our task? Why us?
CURATOR:	That's the best question of the evening! Just go and ask them!
RESEARCHER:	It's everyone's task to care about the world, why not start wherever we stumble?
CURATOR:	But please, don't create situations where you just stumble over your own feet into the fluffy arms of another institution.

(Light fades out. The VOICES continue their discussion, improvising.)

EPILOGUE

THE CASE: This was the great case of a CRATE that created a case on display in this play. You see it on stage. The stage in your gaze: wherever you look, there is a case. Without a frame that shifts your gaze, your gaze is a cage – but the stage is out there. Take me as a case; I crave to materialise the case of an institution's face that shifts your gaze to another phase. My duty is common, I provide the frame. You do what you want, but place me beyond your games.

Within that play, they who give their VOICE, could go on forever, never moving one step ahead there. Whether discussing nothing or everything; they're sliding on ice, very thin. Their cynical clinical criticality is killing me. Surfing in circles, their waves of struggling for their aim, they declare themselves as never being clear. And so never they dare ever to go for these aims for real.

Art seems to be such a strange case of reality.

Strange to me: first, that dream of being frameless free is projecting us into whatever the frame should be – for us. And then, the frame casts us into how it wants us to see. A projection in which we long for seeing us being free.

(Whispering) Create me, I'm there; feel me, I'm for you; fight me, I'm with you:

Archive, admin, workshop, packing, tool-set, booking, garbage, cooking. Noting, floating, framing, shaming, claiming, timing, taming, scripting, restricting, fitting in.... Everything you don't dare, everything you want to, everything that guides you to whatever you're obliged to. Form shall be content; content shall be free; free is my fee. Whatever you call it, whatever you call art, if ever you call it work, just do it together!

Your projections into my face makes me THE CASE I am for you. I am the mirror you created. I'm that meta-figure that figured out how to create you. I'll take off with you. If YOU don't take me as a tool, I'll form you to mine. My love is your most critical form: radically circling in one place; in your eyes, it might look like an ever-changing case. It seems such a pleasure to circle in illusion beyond any pressure.

I feel ashamed: in this arena, I was the one providing the horses. Was that all right? I know I can't know! How shall I get out of the *manège* myself? As projection, I'm part of its ejection.

I was holding it, assuming it's needed!

Without such islands – shelters or platforms, frameworks or field tracks – we would not survive the craziness of our times! But with them, we live in a labyrinthic vertigo! I'm not a carousel! I don't want to be ridden for nothing. Change is needed. They should know. Many things will come. Will they be ready? Will they take care? Will they take me as the tool they need me for? – not for themselves, but for out there!

(Pause.)

So, you who watch, you who read, and probably you who write, you need to take over. To do what is needed. To change what is at stake. To frame what needs decisions. Open to what needs help. To free what needs to be released. To practice what needs to be changed. I'm available at all times. I'm just the hopeless CASE. I need your hope to survive!

END

INSIDEOUT

PARTICIPANTS/ ALUMNI

Abhilash Ningappa
Adriana La Selva
Adriano W. Jensen
Adrijana Gvozdenović
Adva Zakai
Aela Royer
Agnes Schneidewind
Agnese Cornelio
Alejandro Petrasso
Aleksandra Borys
Aleksandra Janeva Imfeld
Alessandra Coppola
Amelie van Elmbt
Amy Pickles
Ana Casimiro
Anna Lugmeier
Asli Hatipoglu
Ana Paula Camargo
Andrea Zavala Folache
Anna Sörenson
Anouk Llaurens
Antye Guenther
Ariane Loze
Arianna Marcolini
Aubrey Birch
Audrey Cottin
Breg Horemans
Brendan Heshka
Bruno Stappaerts
Camila Aschner Restrepo
Carlotta Scioldo
Carolina Goradeszky
Carolina Mendonça
Caroline Daish
caterina daniela mora jara
Catherine Lé
Cecilia Molano
Charlotte Brouckaert
Chloe Chignell
Chloë Janssens
Chris Dupuis
Christian Hansen
Christina Stadlbauer
Christophe Engels
Constanze Schellow
Damla Ekin
Daniel Kok
Danny Neyman
Davide Tidoni
Dianne Weller
Diego Echegoyen
Doris Stelzer
Einat Tuchman
Ekaterina Kaplunova
Eleanor Ivory Weber
Elen Braga
Elise Goldstein
Elizabeth Ward
Esta Matković
Esteban Donoso
Eszter Nemethi
Eunkyung Jeong
Fanny Zaman
Federico Protto
Fien Wauters
Flávio Rodrigo
Fleur Ordoukhani
Frank Pay
Federico Vladimir Strate Pezdirc
Gable Roelofsen
Gabriela Karolczak
Gary Farrelly
Gerald Kurdian
Goda Palekaitė
Gosie Vervloessem
Geert Vaes
Hanne Jacobs
Hans Van Wambeke
Heike Langsdorf
Hektor Mamet
Helena Dietrich
Hoda Siahtiri
Inga Gerner Nielsen
Iris Bouche
Isabel Burr Raty
Iuliana Varodi
Ive Leemans
Jaime Conde-Salazar Pérez
Jaime Llopis
Jeremiah Runnels
Jimena Pérez Salerno
João Fiadeiro
Josef Wouters
Juan Dominguez
Juan Duque
Julia Clever
Julie Pfleiderer
Karl Philips
Karolien De Schepper
Kasia Tórz
Katinka van Gorkum
Katrin Lohmann
Katrine Turner
Shervin Kianersi Haghighi
Kim Lien Desault
Klaas Devos
Kleoni Manousakis
Kurt Van Overbeke
Laura Pante
Leo Kay
Leonie Kuipers
Lieselot Jansen
Lili M. Rampre
Lisa Charlotte Baudouin
Lore Rabaut
Luanda Casella
Lucia Rainer
Lucia Palladino

Lucie Eidenbenz
Luisa Fillitz
Luiza Crosman
Luk Sips
Maarten Van den Bussche
Magdalena Ptasznik
Maité Liébana Vena
Maja Hammarén
Mala Kline
Manon Avermaete
Marcelo Mardones
Marcos Simões
Margareth Kaserer
Maria Lucia Cruz Correia
Marilyne Grimmer
Marialena Marouda
Martin Sieweke
Martina Petrović
Mathilde Maillard
Maurice Meewisse
Mavi Veloso
Michel Yang
Michiel Reynaert
Muslin Brothers
Nada Gambier
Nassia Fourtouni
Nathaniel Moore
Nibia Pastrana Santiago
Oshin Albrecht
Philippe Severyns
Philippine Hoegen
Pia Louwerens
Piero Ramella
Quinsy Gario
Raquel Santana de Morais
Rareş Crăiuţ Augustin
Rebecca Louise Collins
Ricardo Santana
Rob Ritzen
Robin Amanda Creswell Faure
Rodolphe Coster
Esther Rodriguez-Barbero
Rui Calvo
Ruth S. Noyes
Samah Hijawi
Sana Ghobbeh
Sara Dandois
Sara Manente
Sara Santos
Sara Vilardo
Sarah Pletcher
Sébastien Hendrickx
Signe Frederiksen
Silvia Pereira / Omniadversus
Simon Asencio
Simon Loeffler
Sina Seifee
Sofia Caesar
Stef Meul
Stefan Jonathan Govaart
Stephen Bain
Sven Dehens
Sven Goyvaerts
Thiago Antunes
Timothy Segers
Tinna Ottesen
Túlio Rosa
Vanja Smiljanić
Varinia Canto Vila
Vera Sofia Mota
Veridiana Zurita
Verónica Cruz
Vicente Arlandis Recuerda
Vick Verachtert
Victoria Myronyuk
Vijai Maia Patchineelam
Xiri Tara Noir
Yaari Shalem
Zoumana Méïté

CONTRIBUTORS

Abu Ali * Toni Serra
Agnes Quackles
Akira Hino Sensei
Alberto Cossu
Alessandra Bergmaschi
Alex Arteaga
Alexander Baervoets
Alexander Schellow
Alexandre Lepetit
Alice Chauchat
Alma Soderberg
An Mertens
Ana Hoffner
Andre Lepecki
Anette Baldauf
Angelo Vermeulen
Anja Steglich
Anna Rispoli
Anne Juren
Ant Hampton
Antonia Baehr
Antonija Livingstone
Antonio Araújo
Aras Ozgun
Arco Renz
Barbara Van Lindt
Bart Van den Eynde
Bart Verschaffel
Bernard Stigler
Bleri Lleshi
Bojana Cvejić
Brandon LaBelle
Brian Massumi
Bruno De Wachter
Caroline Godart

Chantal Mouffe
Christian Rizzo
Christophe Meierhans
Claudia Bosse
Constant vzw
Daniel Blanga-Gubbay
Daniela Bershan
Dalila Honorato
David Bade
David Bergé
David Helbich
David Moss
Davis Freeman
Dieter Lesage
Dora Garcia
Dries Verhoeven
Edward George
Elke van Campenhout
Els Viaene
Emma Cocker
Epifania Amoo-Adare
Eric Thielemans
Erin Manning
Eva Berghmans
Eve Kalyva
Fabrizio Terranova
Femke Snelting
Florian Feigl
Fotini Lazaridou-Hatzigoga
Gabriëlle Schleijpen
Geert Opsomer
Gijs de Heij
Gonçalo Pena
Guillermo Gómez-Peña
Guy Gypens
Heather Kravas
Hendrik Willekens
Hicham Khalidi
Huib Van der Werf
International Errorist
Jack Hauser
Jacob Wren
Jan Maertens
Jan Masschelein
Jan Ritsema
Janez Janša
Jennifer Lacey
Jeremy Wade
Joanna Baillie
Johan Dehollander
Johan Grimonprez
Jovial Mbenga
Joël Verwimp
Julien Bruneau
Kate Rich
Katrien De Graeve
Kattrin Deufert
Klaus Janek
Kobe Matthys
Koen Tachelet
Koen Van Singhel
Kris Verdonck
Kristien Van den Brande
Krõõt Juurak
Lars Frers
Laurence Rassel
Laurent Liefooghe
Laurent van Lancker
Leo De Nijs
Lilia Mestre
Lisa Nelson
Livia Andrea Piazza
Luc Van den Dries
Ludi Loiseau
Luigi Coppola
Lynda Gaudreau
Magda Tyzlik-Carver
Marc Vanrunxt
Marcelo Rezende
Marcus Bergner
Marianne Van Kerckhove
Marie de Brugerolle
Mariella Greil
Martin Schick
Martino Morandi
Mathijs van de Sande
Medicine Man Oscar Parada
Meg Stuart
Mette Edvardsen
Michael Bauwens
Michael Kliën
Michiel Vandevelde
Miguel Clara Vasconcelos
Mika Elo
Mika Juusela
Milena Kipfmüller
Miriam Hempel
Moritz Frischkorn
Myriam van Imschoot
Nico Dockx
Nicolas Y. Galeazzi
Nicolas Malevé
Nikolaus Gansterer
Olga de Soto
Ong Keng Sen
O.S.P.
Patricia Reed
Paul Craenen
Paz Rojo
Peggy Pierrot
Peter Pal Pelbart
Peter Stamer
Petra Van Brabant
Pierre Joachim
Pierre Rubio
Pieter Vermeulen
Philipp Gehmacher
Pietro Fortuna
Philippe Riera

Robert Steijn
Rabih Mrouéh
Raphaële Jeune
Renée Copraij
Rogerio Liro
Rudi Laermans
Sabina Holzer
Sabine Cmelniski
Seda Guerses
Sol Archer
Stef Stessels
Stefan Heinrich
Stefanie Claes
Stéphane Boudin-Lestienne
Terenja Van Dijk
Timmy Delaet
Tine Van Aerschot
Tom Engels
Tom Plischke
Toto Kisaku
Various Artists
Vera Mantero
Victoria Pérez Royo
Vincent Dunoyer
Vincent Meessen
Vladimir Miller
Wesley Meuris
Wouter De Raeve
Yosi Wanunu

A.PASS TEAM

Lilia Mestre
Kristof Van Hoorde
Joke Liberge
Steven Jouwersma

A.PASS BOARD

Agnes Quackles
Frederik Le Roy
Guy Gypens
Hendrik De Smedt
Leonie Persyn

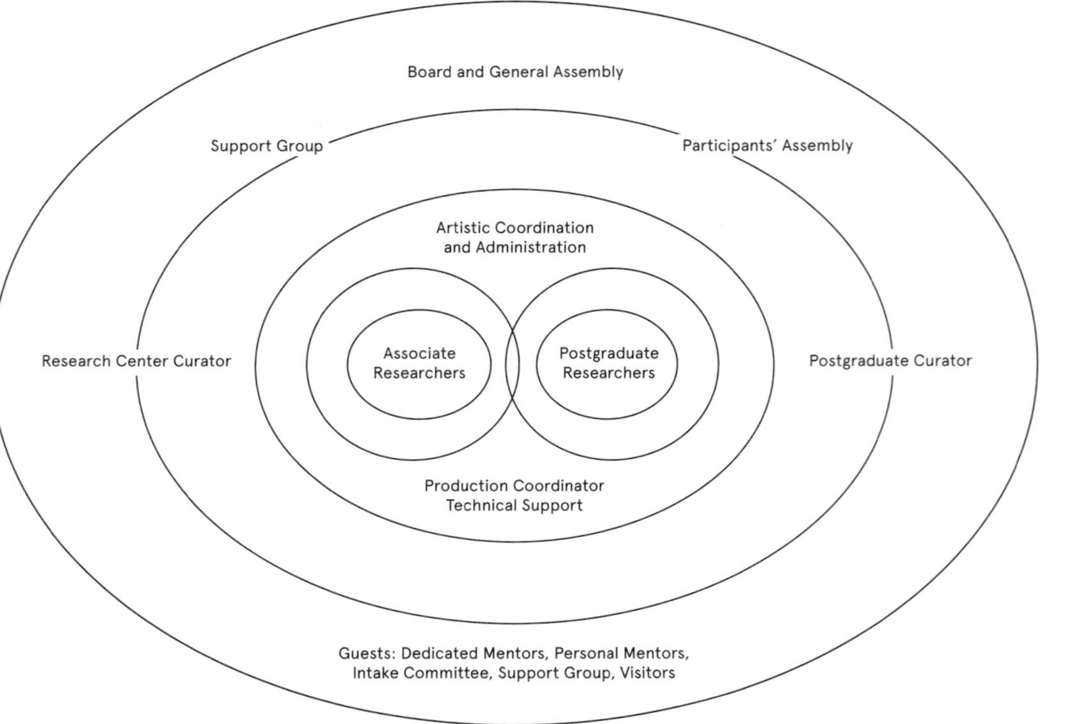
Board and General Assembly
Support Group
Participants' Assembly
Artistic Coordination
and Administration
Research Center Curator
Associate
Researchers
Postgraduate
Researchers
Postgraduate Curator
Production Coordinator
Technical Support
Guests: Dedicated Mentors, Personal Mentors,
Intake Committee, Support Group, Visitors

ARTISTIC RESEARCH
a.pass activates the practice of artistic research by accumulating its processes and critique. Embracing the fact that artistic research is becoming a category of production in the cultural field, a.pass does not claim to delineate its borders but affirms this apparent lack of definition as an opportunity for its development. Artistic research in a.pass is not oriented towards the production of a single solution or an artwork, but towards generating a setting for engagement with a particular topic or challenge. Artistic research processes aim at adding complexity to a question, rather than simplifying, bringing conflicting viewpoints, theories and ontologies in proximity to one another. The results are often transitory rather than conclusive.

ASSOCIATE RESEARCHERS
are seen as partners of a.pass with non-academic and academic research affiliations and support structures. They come together in a facilitated peer-to-peer group for the duration of a one-year cycle and contribute their research methodologies to the collective a.pass environment. The activities of the Associate Researchers are organised around performative publishing, engagement with external research situations and peer reviewing/collective mentoring. Research is developed, shared and performed in public lectures, workshops, conferences, publications, performances and other experimental set-ups.

BLOCK (POSTGRADUATE PROGRAMME)
The one-year programme is organised in three 'blocks' of four months, each of them divided in three months of curated curriculum and one month focused on self-organised work. When participants want to interrupt their studies for professional activities or to intensify their personal studies, it is possible to skip one block and to extend the duration of the programme to a maximum of 17 months. A block is structured by three mandatory collective moments of research presentations: Opening Week, Halfway Days and End Week (mostly in PAF – Performing Arts Forum). Each block, three to four participants enroll in the postgraduate programme and three to four participants complete the programme. Quarterly, this creates a new group of researchers in three developmental phases.

BOARD
The board is constituted of professionals working at the crossroads of art and education. The individual members have an advisory function depending on their respective expertise and institutional affiliation. They meet twice a year to evaluate and be updated on the position of a.pass within the broader context of art education. In case of conflict or the need for clarity, the board is the ruling instance in matters of policy and personnel.

BUDGETS
There are several budgets in a.pass dedicated to collaborative management of resources and are organised by different groups. They include: postgraduate curatorial block budget, participants' personal budget, materials budget, Participants' Assembly budget, End Presentation budget, Research Center budget and the Kinship budget which supports propositions from alumni, collaborators or third parties.

CURATOR
An a.pass curator (or team of curators) is responsible for the proposition and realisation of a block within the postgraduate programme, or in the case of the Research Center, a one-year long working period. Within this time frame, the curator develops a platform for practical and theoretical exchange between the a.pass participants and the other contributors to the programme (mentors, workshop facilitators, a.pass alumni). They work in close collaboration with the artistic coordinator.

CURATORIAL ASSEMBLAGE
The curatorial practice of a.pass consists of creating an environment for both focus and inclusion. The sources for curatorial arrangement are the concerns and practices of the participants manifested by the Participants' Assembly, the proposals of the Support Group, the research proposals of the Associate Researchers and from external professionals or institutions.

END PRESENTATION
The End Presentation can be organised individually or in collaboration, and aims explicitly towards the communication of the research done in a.pass towards a wider audience of spectators, witnesses and research participants. After their End Presentation, the a.pass researchers

receive a certificate of 60 credits and a written reflection of the work developed by the visitors.

GENERAL ASSEMBLY
The General Assembly consists of several committed alumni, mentors and curators who know the programme from the inside out, and through the years continue to follow the programme closely. They are invited in person to the activities (workshops, conferences, book launches, End Presentations of participants) and are the first addressee for feedback from a semi-outside position. There are annual meetings with members of the General Assembly including the board members. They approve the annual working of the institution and they evaluate the work of a.pass, they can give advice, approve the accounts and can fire or hire someone.

GUESTS
a.pass has a consistent pool of alumni, affiliated researchers and artists who are employed on a temporary basis as curators, dedicated and personal mentors, visitors to End Presentations, and as members of the Intake Committee for the selection of new participants.

INTAKE COMMITTEE
Intakes occur three times a year, every four months. The selection process is done by a group of four people: the artistic coordinator, the Research Center curator, one external curator or mentor and an ex-participant. To maintain the diversity and inclusive attitude of the intakes, the two external members of the jury are always different.

MENTOR
a.pass mentors engage in dialogue, feedback, contextualisation, critique and thinking together with the researchers. The mentors are invited professionals from different artistic, research and theoretical approaches to follow-up the postgraduate participants. They are part of a steady group of professionals that support and evaluate the participants and the programme. They are selected by the block curator or the participants in conversation with the artistic coordination. There are three dedicated mentors per block of four months. They are present in the mandatory moments and give individual mentoring sessions to the participants. Personal mentors: each participant obtains a virtual budget to spend on 'personal mentoring' to inform their research with knowledge that a.pass doesn't provide itself. Coordination mentoring is a follow-up of the participant research and trajectory in a.pass. These sessions take place every block with the artistic coordinator.

PARTICIPANTS/RESEARCHERS
Researchers following the a.pass programme develop a practice-based research, take an investigative look at their artistic trajectories and engage in a particular discursive approach. Researchers are engaging in a largely self-organised and collaborative environment where they take up an active role in the development of the a.pass research environment and act as responsive agents in (re)thinking artistic research methodologies, collective feedback strategies and practical organisation.

PARTICIPANTS' ASSEMBLY
A self-organised group that represents the interests of the a.pass participants and can act on behalf of them. a.pass encourages the participants to join the assembly or to take note of its activities. The PA has a budget per block to organise collective curatorial proposals to the programme.

PEDAGOGY RESEARCH
a.pass is building its curriculum by bringing together practitioners in the arts within a curated framework of workshops, ateliers, collective spatial practices and scores. This collective exploration is the space where experimental research formats are proposed and developed. The process of learning, development and critique engages all parts of the institute. a.pass sees itself as an ongoing research into the formation and politics of educational institutions. By collecting innovative methodologies of research, facilitating educational experimentation and by maintaining an institutional openness, a.pass affirms and continues to be an experimental institution, a place of engaged research of what education in the arts can be today.

PERFORMATIVE PUBLISHING
a.pass continuously develops and supports different and specific modes of presentation which are emerging from the research practiced at the institution. A large part of the programme is based on modes of making public research within the programme and towards the

larger public. These publishing moments are organised systematically within the programme and reach a larger audience with the End Presentations, Research Center publications, seminars, website publications and the archive. The aim of this work is to allow for performative publishing to present research as a work in the making and to develop modes of presentation that shift from the product paradigm towards a modality of witnessing a process in its unfinished and searching vulnerability.

RESEARCH CENTER
The Research Center at a.pass is a platform for advanced research practices in the arts. It invites five to six Associate Researchers per one-year cycle to follow their artistic research practice in an environment of mutual criticality and institutional support. The Research Center welcomes radical and inventive research methodologies in order to contribute them to the larger a.pass research environment. The Research Center welcomes researchers with both non-academic and academic research affiliations and support structures. The Research Center programme is facilitated by the Research Center curator.

SUPPORT GROUP
The Support Group functions as an autonomous advisory module and is implicated in the theoretical and meta discourse produced at a.pass in relation to the fields of artistic research and education. The major assignment for the Support Group is to generate content, evaluate a.pass activities in relation to the fields of art and academia outside a.pass, initiate projects and collaborations. Metaphorically, the group functions as a 'window to the outside'. This group gathers twice a year for two days in a sort of 'internal seminar approach'.

TEAM
a.pass has a fixed team of employees: the artistic coordinator, the administrator, the technical and scenography support and production coordinator. The artistic coordinator and administrator are accountable for the development and continuation of the institution on the level of content and business management. They together decide on the general management of the institution. The artistic coordinator is responsible for accompanying and supporting the research developed at a.pass and reviewing the contributions of the a.pass community. They are accountable for the pedagogical and artistic development of the organisation. The administrator is responsible for the business management of the Posthogeschool: implementation of the subventions, finances and budget follow-up, administration of the students, staff and co-workers, insurances, rent and legal matters. The production coordinator is responsible for the co-organisation and execution of the activities produced at a.pass, their budgets, the coordination of logistics and the production and distribution of the a.pass publications. The person doing technical and scenography support is responsible for the scenography components of the a.pass public research presentations and of the work spaces. They manage the technical material at a.pass and their good condition, availability and usage, as well as a follow-up on the technical budget.

VISITOR
For the End Presentations, a.pass invites three visitors who closely read the portfolios, attend the presentations, have a final feedback conversation with the researchers and contribute a written reflection on the work developed. Visitors are professional artists, curators or academics with an invested interest in artistic research. a.pass explicitly chooses a feedback format rather than an evaluation procedure. After concluding the postgraduate programme, the participant will receive the title of Laureate of the Higher Institute for Fine Arts Posthogeschool voor Podiumkunsten (the programme equals 60 credits).

ADRIJANA GVOZDENOVIĆ (1986) is an artist, a.pass alumna (2019) and Associate Researcher (2020). She co-curated the a.pass block 'Not in the Mood' (2021). With a background in visual arts, she is 'Archiving Artistic Anxieties' and she is interested in 'Exhibiting Otherwise'. Recently she did a research project 'Anthropomorphic Trouble' (with Goda Palekaite) at Art Catalyst, Sheffield and Whitechapel Gallery, London (2021), performed '7 anxieties and the world' for 'The art of lecture', Glasmoog Gallery, Cologne and presented her work in the exhibition *This situation has developed over a long time*, ŠKUC gallery, Ljubljana (2021). gadi.me

---

AMY PICKLES (1990) is an artist and loosely formed educator. She is a current participant a.pass, finishing in 2022. Her work experiments with ways to hold onto, and consider, the pervasive colonial infrastructures we are a part of. She teaches at the Willem de Kooning Academy, Rotterdam NL, in Autonomous Practices, and is a member of Varia, a collective initiative on everyday technology. Pickles lives and works in Rotterdam and Brussels.

ANA HOFFNER ex-Prvulovic* (1980 *On the crossroads of those who were born in Paraćin, Yugoslavia, who were moved in 1989, and received capitalist citizenship in Austria with a new name in 2002), is an artist, researcher and writer. She was a mentor workshop facilitator at a.pass in 2012-15. She* works explicitly against the current domination of corporate aesthetics, images of disgust and horror and the right-winged establishment by insisting on analysis, contextualisation and reflection. In 2020, she became Professor for Artistic Research at the University Mozarteum Salzburg. Hoffner ex-Prvulovic* lives and works in Salzburg. anahoffner.com

ANOUK LLAURENS (1969) is a dancer, teacher, researcher and shiatsu practitioner. She is a former a.pass participant (2016) and graduated from CNDC d'Angers (1992). She teaches at the Royal Conservatory of Antwerp, ImPulsTanz Vienna, Warsaw CI FLOW, Freiburg Contact Festival, Independent Dance London, and other art programmes in Europe. Through her research on poetic documentation, Llaurens investigates the notion of 'experience as document'. She develops 'live documents' in the form of performances and participatory practices: 'The wave' (2019); The breathing archive' (2017); 'Live documents' (2015). Recent publications include 'Mind the dance' online publication (2018). She collaborates with Belgian artist Julien Bruneau. She lives in Brussels. anoukllaurens.be

---

CATERINA DANIELA MORA JARA (1988) is an artist-translatress-tango dancer practitioner-life model, married-for-papers, a.pass alumna (2018-2019). She is house artist in Workspace Brussels 2021-2022 and PhD candidate at Uniarts (SKH), Department of Dance. She works with intimacy as procedure and explores translation as transgression. She is the creator of the ongoing series of bastard-cheap lecture-performances and a member of team editor: 2nd Handbooks of Dance. She navigates a little boat, doesn't have Instagram and has never been to IKEA. She lives and works in Brussels and Stockholm. caterinamora.jimdofree.com

---

CHLOE CHIGNELL (1993) is an artist based in Brussels working across text, choreography and publishing. She attended a.pass (2020) and the research cycle at P.A.R.T.S (2018). Chignell takes the body as the central problem, question and location of her research. She invests in writing as a body building practice, examining the ways in which language makes us up. She co-runs rile*, a bookshop and project space for publication and performance with Sven Dehens. chloechignell.com

CHLOË JANSSENS (1991) is an artist with a background in graphic design, a current a.pass participant since January 2021 and studied Visual Arts, Graphic Design at LUCA School of Arts, Ghent. Her work orbits around topics such as soil, climate emergency, community organising and fiction. She was recently in 'Down, Dwars, Dela', See U, Etterbeek (2021) and published *Handboek voor de circulaire economie* (2020), co-created with Isabelle Vanhoutte for Henri Lejeune, ISBN 9789464072297. Janssens lives, works and hurries between Geel, Brussels and Paris.

AUBREY BIRCH (1988), a.pass alumna (2019), is an artist and academic whose work revolves around the place where science and mysticism meet, using language and performance to travel across scales and planes of experience, from the very large to the very small, the abstract to the intimate and the deep past to the instant. Birch lives and works between Europe and the Australian outback. ophioglossum.site

---

ELKE VAN CAMPENHOUT (1971) is a monk, performer, writer and body work researcher. In 2007, she began the post-master programme in artistic research, a.pt (advanced performance training), which would later become a.pass. From 2007-2017 she worked as head of the a.pass programme, as a mentor, organising and leading workshops, and co-creating the vision of the house. Since then she has been an occasional guest mentor and curator. Her current work revolves around performative shadow work, rituals and the development of the experimental spiritual-artistic site The Monastery Live. themonastery.live

---

FEMKE SNELTING (1964) develops projects at the intersection of design, feminisms, and Free Software. She is a member of a.pass and has collaborated with the programme and Research Center in many shapes and forms. With Seda Guerses, Miriyam Aouragh and Helen Pritchard, she runs The Institute for Technology in the Public Interest. She co-edited *Volumetric Regimes: Material cultures of quantified presence* (with Jara Rocha, forthcoming). Additionally, Snelting supports artistic research at PhdArts, Leiden, and MERIAN, Maastricht. She occasionally teaches at XPUB in Rotterdam. snelting.domainepublic.net

---

GUY GYPENS (1962) is currently Head of Performing Arts at KANAL-Centre Pompidou in Brussels. He has been a member of the a.pass board of directors since 2013. After obtaining a master's degree in economic science, he became the administrator of the Beursschouwburg in Brussels from 1987 to 1991. In 1991 until 2007, he was the general manager of Anne Teresa De Keersmaeker and her dance company, Rosas. Concurrently, he was manager of both the theatre company tg STAN and contemporary music ensemble Ictus. From 1996 to 2000, he directed the Springdance Festival in Utrecht. In 2007 until 2019, he was the general and artistic director of the Kaaitheater Arts Centre in Brussels. Gypens lives and works in Brussels.

ISABEL BURR RATY (1979) is a filmmaker, artist and Sexual Kung Fu coach. Her relationship with a.pass spans from completing the post-master and Research Center to mentoring and co-curating. In 2018, Amsterdam Arts Fund partnered her to Waag and Mediamatic. She is a member of the EU project Staying in Touch, curatorial practices of the Future, and lectures in New Media Art History at ERG (BE). Her hybrid performance-installations, which invite the public to embody Sci-Fi such as 'Beauty Kit', have been shown internationally. With the support of Flanders State of the Arts, she is currently developing 'The Power Plant' project. isabel-burr-raty.com

JOKE LIBERGE (1972) is a former film-maker who made several (award winning) short films. After studying in Amsterdam (UvA and NFTVA) she moved to Brussels in 2001 to connect with her French roots. Other professional experiences include press attaché (International film festival Rotterdam) and adviser for the Ministry of Culture in the Netherlands. While continuing artistic and other collaborations, her main professional commitment has been with a.pass since 2013. As the production coordinator she translates the artistic goals at a practical level and supports their realisation. Liberge lives and works in Brussels.

KATE RICH (1968) is an artist, trader, feral economist and a.pass mentor (2016-2019). She is currently establishing the 'Feral MBA', a radically different training course in business for artists and others. Current business interests include administrative roles at Bristol's Cube Microplex; convening the 'Institute of Experiments with Business' (Ibex) with transnational network FoAM; 'Cube-Cola', an open source drink manufacturing partnership with worldwide distribution; and 'Feral Trade', a sole trader grocery business (since 2003). Rich lives and works in Bristol UK and temporarily in Tasmania, Australia. feraltrade.org/krcv

---

KRISTIEN VAN DEN BRANDE (1981) is a hybrid maker, shapeshifting between periods of writing, editing, research, performing, dramaturgy, institutional work, activism and domestic work – all of which she enjoys equally. She has been involved with a.pass as a curator, mentor and assistant coordinator since 2008. Her research trajectory spans from role-play to experimental pedagogy, from urbanism and sex-positivity to expanded writing. Her work is indebted to intense collaborations with artists (Mette Edvardsen, Lilia Mestre, Myriam Van Imschoot, Sarah Vanhee, Wim Cuyvers) and research institutions such as SARMA, Jan Van Eyck Academy, and a.pass. Van den Brande lives and works in Brussels.

KRÕÕT JUURAK (1981) is an artist, performer and stand-up comedian and a mentor at a.pass in 2019-2020. Juurak studied dance and choreography at ArteZ Arnhem and Fine Arts at the Sandberg Institute, Amsterdam. Their work addresses both human and non-human audiences and is whimsical-marxist by nature. Recent exhibitions and performances include the *Baltic Triennial 14: The Endless Frontier*, Vilnius (2021); 'You're So Busy' at Shedhalle, Zürich, (2021, 2022); 'Thinking Like an Octopus' at Wilhelm-Hack-Museum, Ludwigshafen, 2021; 'Art for Animals: A Perspective Change' Opelvillen Stiftung, Rüsselsheim (2020, 2021); 'Cohabitation' Silent Green, Berlin, 2021 i.e. Juurak lives and works in Vienna and Tallinn.

LAURA PANTE (1983) is a dancer and researcher. She attended the postgraduate programme at a.pass in 2018-2019. Since 2020, she is a PhD researcher at IUAVat University of Architecture in Venice with a thesis titled, '2DDance: a *quasi* concept'. She collaborates, both as a dancer and as a researcher, with artists and choreographers to analyse the development of the relation between body and movement techniques in their pedagogical practices. She is touring with the project titled 'Laura Pante' by Jerome Bel. She studied with Romeo Castellucci, Cristina Rizzo, Cindy Van Acker, Yasmine Huggonet. Pante lives and works in Venice.

LEO KAY (1972), a.pass alumnus, is a performance maker, writer and facilitator, combining live art and social art practice. Work includes: 'It's Like He's Knocking', UK/international tours, including Battersea Arts Centre, London, 2010-14; 'Only Wolves and Lions', UK/international tours, including Southbank Centre, London, Nafpaktos Performance Festival, Greece (2012-15); 'Change My Mind' – performance research project, UK residencies including Barbican Centre, London (2013-15); 'The Spinning Wheel', The Roundhouse, London (2015) & BRIC House, New York (2016); 'The Bakery of Slow Ideas', UK/international tours (2019-present), including Tanzkongress 19, Dresden & Performatik, Brussels (2019). Kay lives and works in London and Bari. thisisunfinished.com

LILIA MESTRE (1968) is a performing artist, dramaturge and researcher working mainly in collaborative formats. She has been involved in a.pass since 2008 as associate programme curator and core member (2014-17) and since 2017 as artistic coordinator. Mestre works with scores: inter-subjective set-ups and other chance-induced processes as emancipatory artistic and pedagogical tools, which have been documented in various publications. She is interested in forms of organisation created by and for artistic practice as alternative study processes for social political reflection. She was co-founder and latest coordinator of Art Laboratory Bains Connective in Brussels (1997-2017). Mestre lives and works in Brussels.

LIVIA ANDREA PIAZZA (1986) works as a researcher and practitioner in performing arts. She is part of the a.pass' Support Group. Since 2019, she is a research and teaching fellow for artistic practice at the Institute for Applied Theatre Studies in Giessen. Her current academic research focuses on the political economy of performance. She works as an independent dramaturge and as a curator for theory formats within festivals. Recently she co-initiated *Spot on Economies* at PACT Zollverein (2021) and published *A Live Gathering* (co-edited with Ana Vujanović) (2019). Piazza lives and works in Brussels and Giessen.

LOES JACOBS (1984) is a cultural worker and connected to a.pass through the Support Group since 2020. She studied art history at VUB and currently works as the artistic coordinator of nadine. Her work involves listening, bringing people together and transferring knowledge in the field of contemporary art. (Co-)curatorial projects include 'Wandering Arts Biennial', Brussels, 2014-2020, 'Kunst & Zwalm 2019', public space in East Flanders, 2019; 'Plain/Purl', Design Museum, Ghent, 2016. She co-edited the 2nd (2019), 3rd (2021), 4th (2022) WABook, and Dannie.n, published by nadine. Jacobs lives and works in Brussels. nadine.be

MATHILDE VILLENEUVE (1981) is the artistic director of Buda Arts Centre in Kortrijk, workplace for artists, festivals and a 'Learning Together' programme. From 2013 to 2018 she co-directed Les Laboratoires d'Aubervilliers, a place of research and experimentation in art, open to all artistic fields, linking art to social and political concerns. From 2006 to 2012, she coordinated the outdoor projects of the Arts school in France (ENSAPC). She has also worked as an independent curator and art critic. She has co-edited 2 books: *Re-publications* (Archive Books, Berlin, 2012) and *Ateliers des Arques* (Editions B42, Paris, 2008). She directs a new literary collection at the Publishing house B42.

MICHÈLE MEESEN (1976) was the administrator of a.pass from 2011 to 2021. Meesen studied law and cultural sciences at Maastricht University. After 10 years of mainly addressing legal skills, she decided 'to give the floor' to her other interests: art and teaching. Meesen lives in Hasselt.

MIRIAM HEMPEL (1979) is a designer engaged within the realms of the socio-political and the cultural field. She has been affiliated with a.pass as an institution and with numerous participants since 2011. Miriam sees design as an exploratory, collective, and collaborative process, and works in close co-conceptualisation with her clients, stimulating and facilitating the development of bespoke visual communication strategies. Recent collaborations include: *What is Work: Episode 1-3*, Kunsthal Gent (2021/22) with P. Hoegen and J.Reist; *Maastricht Tracks* (2021) a self-performative publication with D. Helbich and a new website for arts management agency *Hiros* (2021). daretoknow.co.uk

MUSLIN BROTHERS – TAMAR LEVIT & YAEN LEVI. Established in 2011 in Tel Aviv and currently located in Brussels, the work of a.pass alumni Muslin Brothers (fashion practitioners Tamar Levit and Yaen Levi) overlaps fashion, art and research to speculate on the way personal and social systems are shaped through clothing. The duo will participate in the Jan Van Eyck Academie (2023) and hold a B.A. in fashion design from Shenkar, college of design and art, Israel (2010). Their work has been shown at KANAL – Centre Pompidou, Brussels, Stockholm Art University, London Fashion Week, Tisch Gallery, New York, Tel Aviv Museum of Art and Jerusalem Design Week. They live and work in Brussels.

NICOLAS Y. GALEAZZI (1972) is an artist, curator and coach and has been connected to a.pass since 2009 as a mentor, coordinator (2013-16), curator of blocks and workshops and a member of the core team (2017-20). Trained as an educator and theatre director (1992-99), he has worked in performance art and art education. In the MA CAPAD at Dartington College of Art (2007-09), he focussed on artistic research and its side effects. Since then, his interests have revolved around relating art, economics, and ecology by setting up commons structure for the arts, engaging in Fair Practice (SOTA), and climatic and emotional collapses. Galeazzi lives and works in Brussels.

PEGGY PIERROT (1973) is an intellectual worker, teacher, radio host and writer with a background in sociology. She has been an a.pass mentor, workshop facilitator and curator since 2016. She teaches as a member of the logistic and administrative staff at Erg, Brussels, after having rethought and practiced an experimental training programme for adults in Le Magasin des Horizons (Grenoble) les Ateliers des horizons for two years. Pierrot lives and works in Brussels.

PHILIPPINE HOEGEN (1970) is a visual artist, a.pass alumna (2014/15), mentor (2016-20), member of the Support Group and General Assembly of a.pass. She is a Researcher at the Professorship Performative Creative Processes, HKU, Utrecht, and Caradt, Avans University, Breda, with the project 'Performing Working'. In her performative practice, she explores the ways in which we create versions of ourselves, the apparatuses and processes we use and what that means for our understanding of 'self'. Recent performance projects include: 'What is Work: Episode 1-3', Kunsthal Gent, 2021. Recent publications include 'ANOTHER VERSION: Thinking Through Performing' (2020). Hoegen is part of State of the Arts, and lives and works in Brussels. philippinehoegen.com

---

PIA LOUWERENS (1990) is an artistic researcher, artist and writer. She completed the postgraduate programme at a.pass and was part of the fellowship programme. From 2019-2021, she was the Junior Embedded Artistic Researcher in the NWO-funded research project 'Making Matters'. In 2021, she self-published her book *I'm Not Sad, The World Is Sad*, an autotheoretical, semi-fictional account of the increasingly paranoid relationship between an artistic researcher and the art institution where she is 'embedded'. Alongside her artistic practice, Louwerens has written texts for a.o. De Witte Raaf, Metropolis M, Tubelight and Het Parool. Louwerens lives and works in Brussels.

PIERRE RUBIO (1962) works as an artist, interdependent researcher, and dramaturge. He was involved at a.pass as co-curator (2014-2020) and mentor (2009-2013). He studied at Aix-Marseille University and within the Contemporary Dance National Centre (France) and has developed numerous projects in dance, choreography and performance (1985-2011). Today, encompassing issues of matter's agencies and memory's arrangements, his work questions modes of individuation and transindividuation to explore contemporary productions of human and post-human subjectivity. Rubio lives and works in Brussels. instagram.com/_pierre_rubio_formula_green

RUI CALVO (1982) is a Brazilian filmmaker who works as a screenwriter, director and editor. He attended a.pass (2021) and graduated from the University of São Paulo with a degree in Audiovisual Arts. Calvo considered a.pass a way to distance himself from the field of cinema so as to think about audiovisual narrative in different ways. Calvo addressed how to film bodies and not imprison them in rational discourse by giving instructions to performers (that resist character building) to play with in front of the camera, and situate them in film settings that do not evoke a fictional background. His short films include, 'Whole Man' and 'Quito', which were screened at festivals in countries such as Canada, UK, South Africa and Argentina. 'The Death of Helena', his first feature film as a director and screenwriter, was the recipient of a grant for film project development in Brazil. Calvo lives and works in São Paulo.

SAMAH HIJAWI (1976) is an artist and researcher. She attended a.pass in 2014. Since 2020, she has worked on the project *Kitchen. Table.* which looks at the movement of food practices over time and across geographies, and the body as a site of food memory. Her earlier work focused on the political gesture in artistic works that allude to the histories of Palestine. The question of where the political is embedded in artistic work continues *Aesthetics of the Political* (2020-ongoing), a project that involves creating artist to artist encounters to explore how political ideas are translated to artistic form. Hijawi lives and works in Brussels.

SARA MANENTE (1978) is an artist and researcher, former a.pass participant (2008), mentor, Support Group member, Associate Researcher (2019), and curator (2021). Trained in classical and contemporary dance, she holds a master's degree in Communication Sciences from the University of Bologna (2003). In her work, dance has been triggered by literary devices, paranormal practices and living cultures, resulting in choreographies, moving images, situations, sculptures and publications. Recently, she was artist-in-residence at Wiels for the project MOLD and editor of ROT magazine, with the research grant *Wicked Technology/Wild fermentation* (2019). Her work is supported by the Flemish government and has been presented internationally. Manente lives and works in Brussels.

SARAH CALE (1977) is a visual artist and has worked as a proofreader for a.pass and other institutions since 2017. Her work with painting and textiles occupies a performative position where handcrafted labour and its materiality produce the work's meaning, intentionally undermining historical vocabularies. Her work is currently funded by the Canada Council (2018-2022). Recent work has been shown at n0dine, Brussels (2021); CRG, Toronto (2021, 2020); Sointula Art Shed, Sointula (2021); McIntosh Gallery, London (2019); Vancounver Art Gallery, Vancouver (2017). She has worked as a visual art instructor since 2004, most recently in the master's programme at La Cambre, Brussels (2017-2021). She lives and works in Brussels. sarahcale.com

---

SINA SEIFEE (1982) is an artist. He attended a.pass (2016) and later as an Associate Researcher (2019). In addition to other collaborations with a.pass, he has worked with the institution as a mentor, curator and currently as digital support. Seifee's artistic practice looks at how epistemologies and knowledges get shaped, with emphasis on the heritage of zoology in West Asia. He has presented internationally in BOZAR, Brussels (2021); Wiels, Brussels (2020); SAVVY Contemporary, Berlin (2016); Sharjah Art Foundation, UAE (2018); Haus der Kulturen der Welt, Berlin (2017); Temporary Gallery, Köln (2019); and Akademie der Künste der Welt, Köln, (2015). Seifee lives and works in Brussels since 2017. sinaseifee.com

STEVEN JOUWERSMA (1982) is an artist. He works for a.pass as technical and scenographic support since 2013. He supports all the practical needs within a.pass with a focus on the execution of artistic research through materials, scenography and media. As an artist he makes public saunas and paintings of magic realism. Jouwersma lives and works in Brussels.
stevenjouwersma.com

TÚLIO ROSA (1989) is an artist and independent researcher and attended a.pass (2020-22). He holds a master's degree in Performing Arts and Visual Culture from the University of Castilla-La Mancha/Reina Sofia Museum (Madrid, 2016), and bachelor's degree in Contemporary Dance from Angel Vianna Dance School (Rio de Janeiro, 2011). His work focuses on the relationship between the body and the field of images, reflecting on the mechanisms and ethics of representation as well as the status of the image in relation to our political imagination. His current research, 'Arquivo Atlântico' [Atlantic Archive], focuses the memory and legacies of colonialism in the different territories bordered by the Atlantic Ocean.

VANJA SMILJANIĆ (1986) is a visual artist and a.pass alumna (2015). She holds an MFA from Kunsthochschule für Medien Cologne (2019), Dutch Art Institute (2012) and a degree in Fine Arts from the Faculdade de Belas Artes de Lisboa (2009). Connecting otherwise unparalleled reality systems, Smiljanić's work attests the foundation of ideologies as alienated regimes, recurring to her own body as a vessel for narration, often shifting between the position of oracle and storyteller. Recent projects include 'Young Artist Biennale/School of Waters' San Marino (2021); 'Cybernetics of the Poor' Kunsthalle Wien (2020); 'Right Wing Complex' HMKV Dortmund (2019).

VERIDIANA ZURITA (1982) is an artist, researcher, performer, filmmaker and essayist. She is an a.pass alumna (2012), mentor (2013-2015) and Associate Researcher (2013-2015). She is currently doing a master's in Social Sciences at UFABC-SP/BR (2022-2024), holds a 'diploma superior' in 'Technology, Subjectivity and Politics' at Clacso (2021), a master's degree in fine arts from DAI - NL (2010), and studied 'Communication of Body Arts' at the PUC-SP/BR (2005). Zurita produces the YouTube channel SAIFETICHE, writes for Outras Palavras (BR) and co-organises the sector Technologies and Anti-Surveillance/Socialism and Liberty Party, PSOL (BR). Her work focuses on the construction of social roles and creates situations where such constructions can be questioned, revisited and re-imagined. She lives and works in São Paulo.
veridianazurita.wordpress.com

VLADIMIR MILLER (1978) is an artist, researcher, dramaturge and scenographer. He has been working with a.pass since 2009 in various functions, most recently as the curator of the Research Center Cycle 3. In his research practice, Miller uses collective building processes to shift the relationships between practice, space and authorship within institutional environments towards commoning and self-organisation. Miller is currently completing his doctoral thesis at the Academy of Fine Arts, Vienna (PhD in Practice), where he was part of the Spaces of Commoning research group and co-edited the resulting publication.

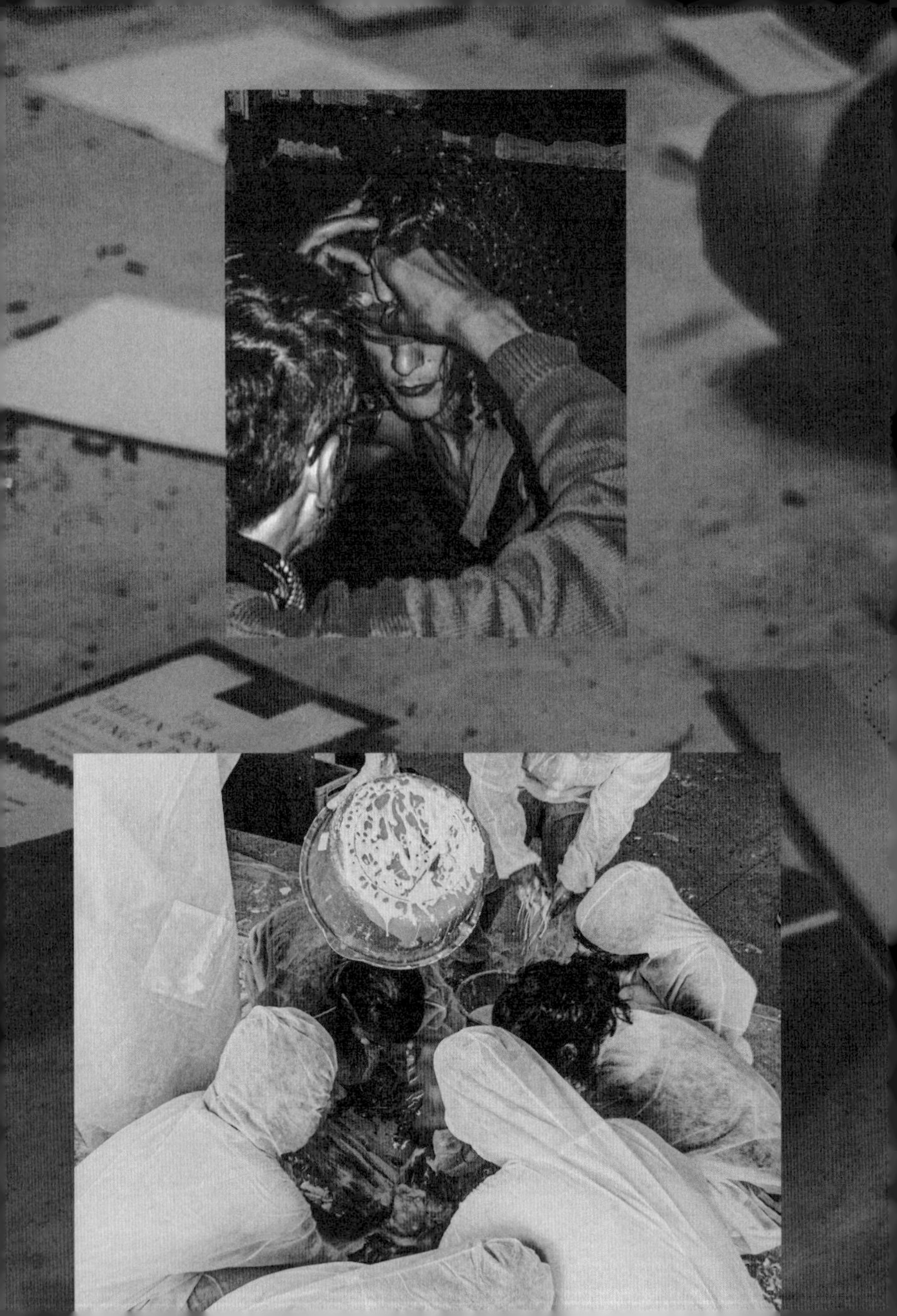

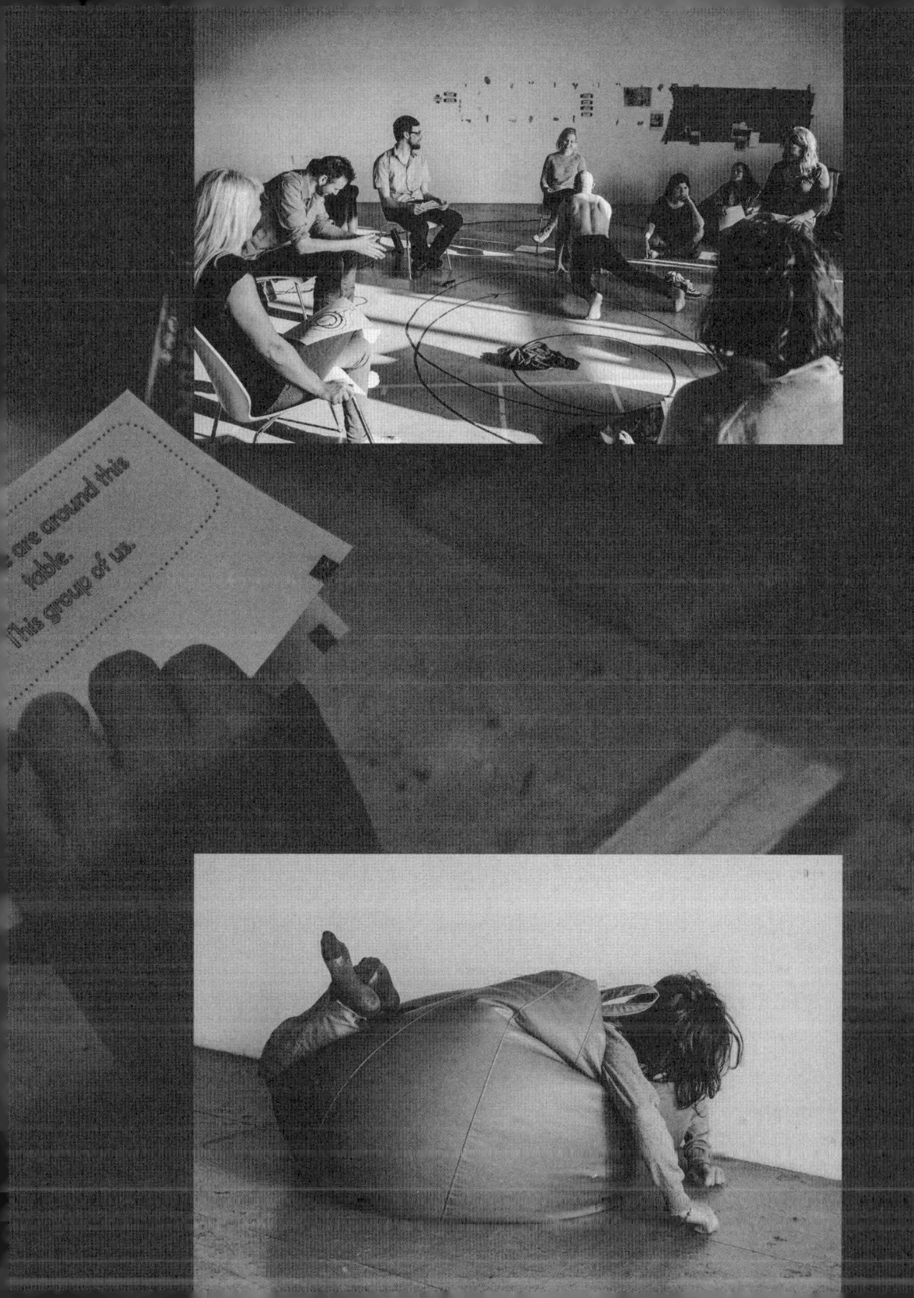
are around this
table.
This group of us.

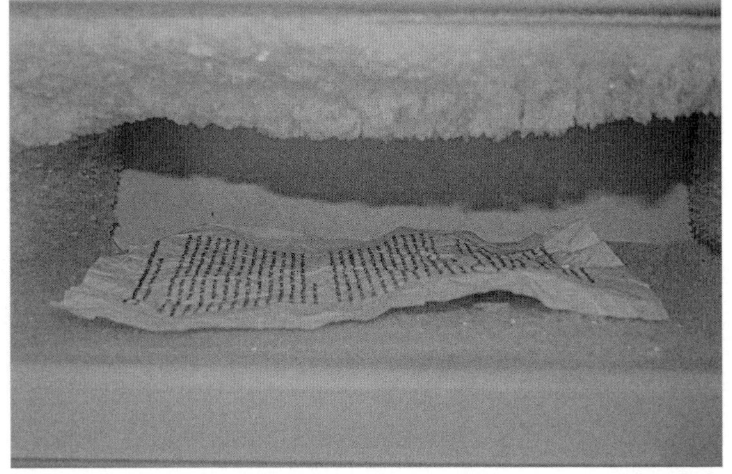

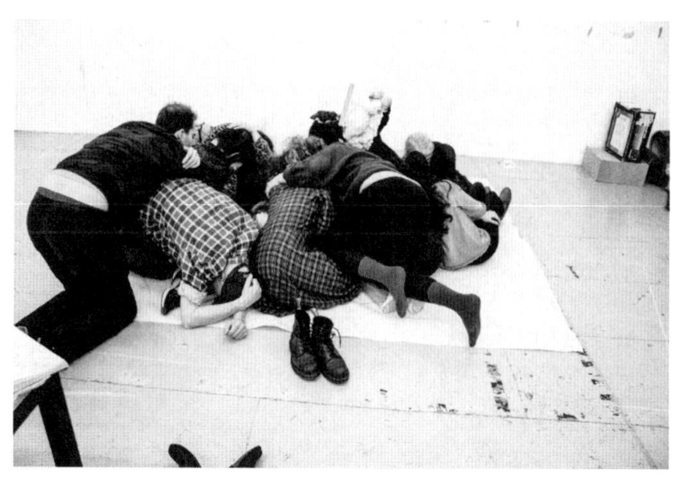

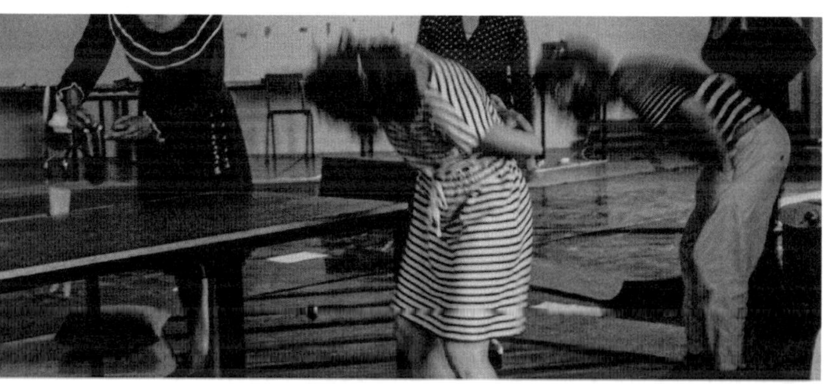

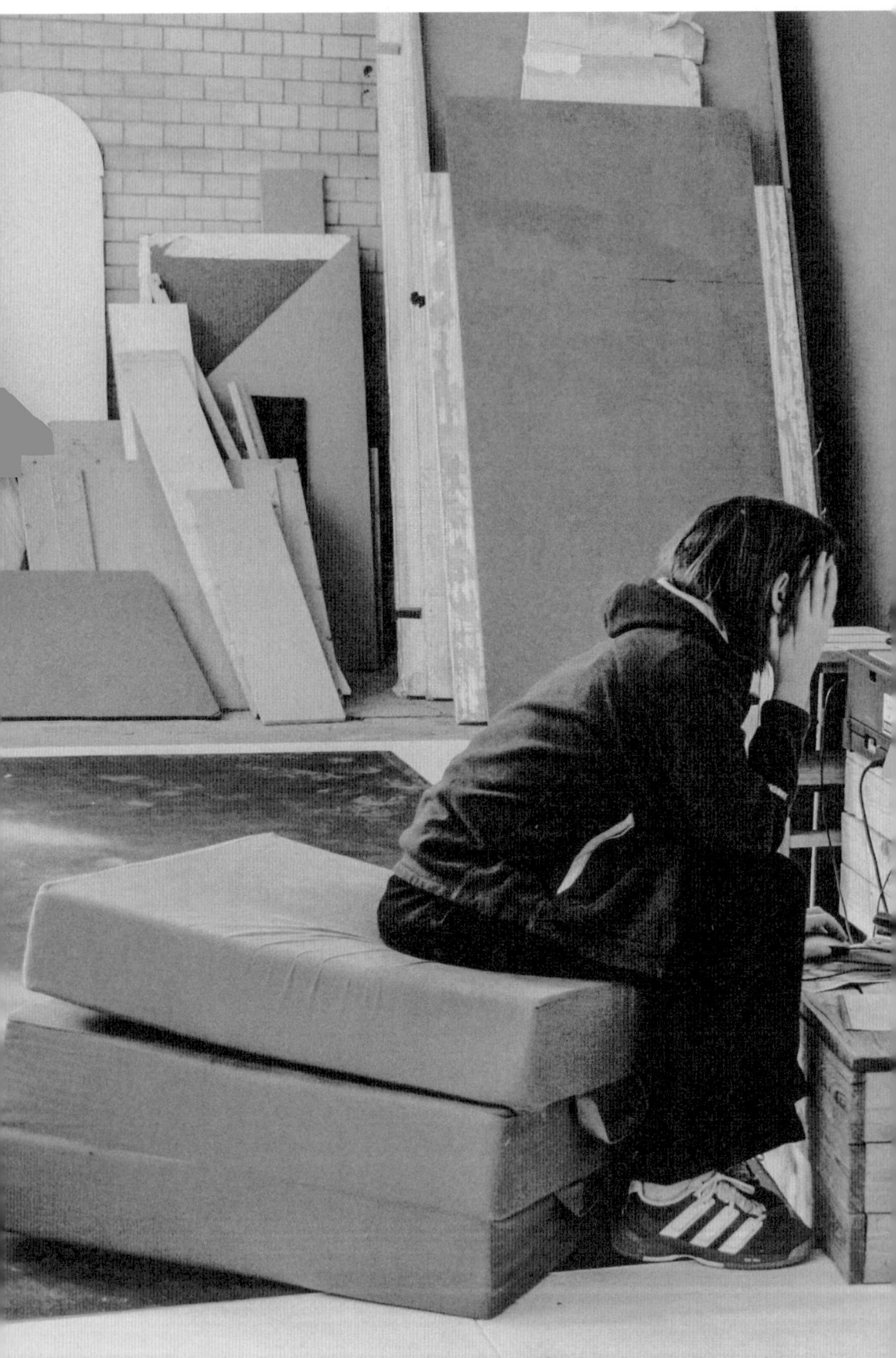

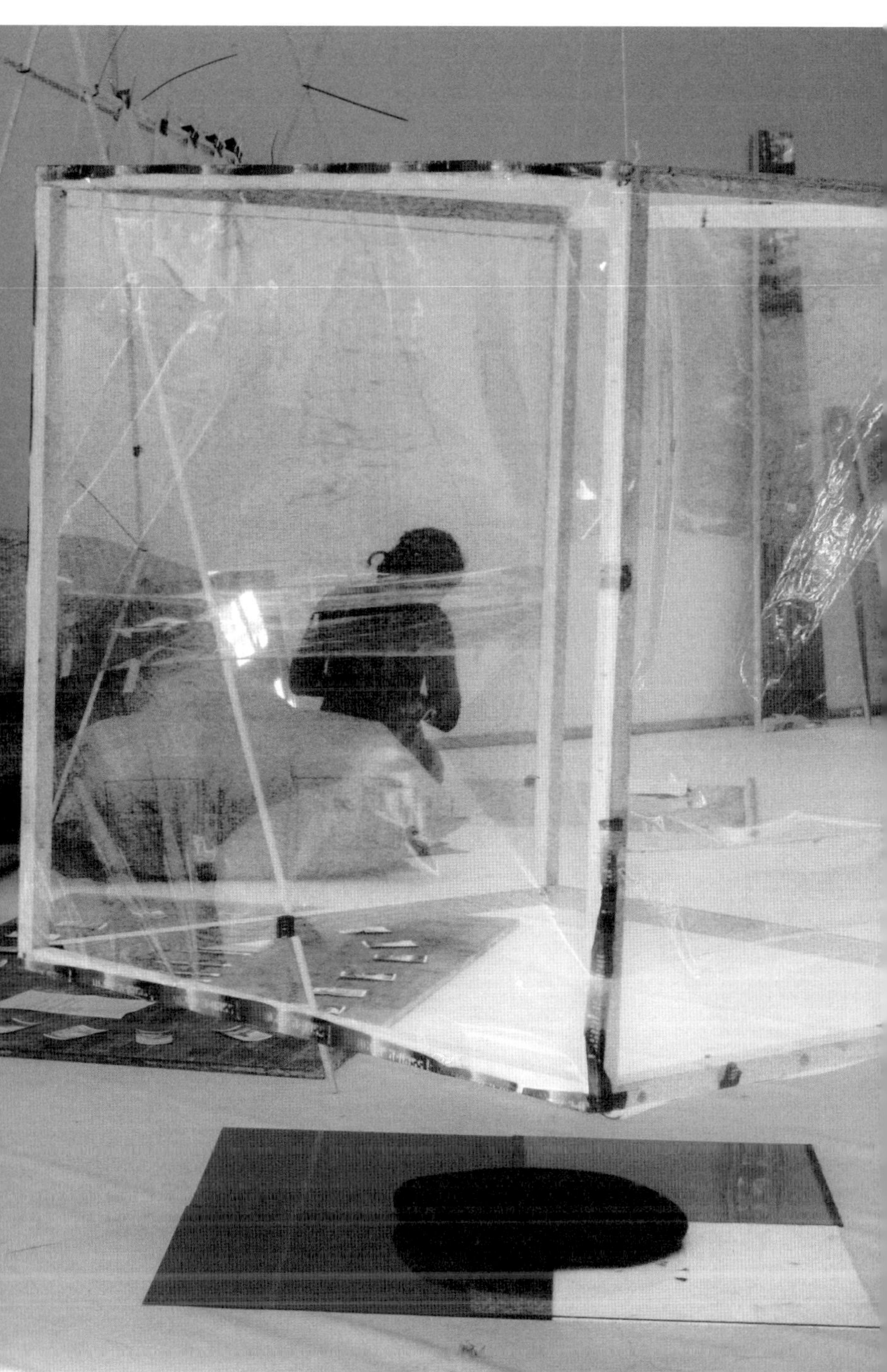

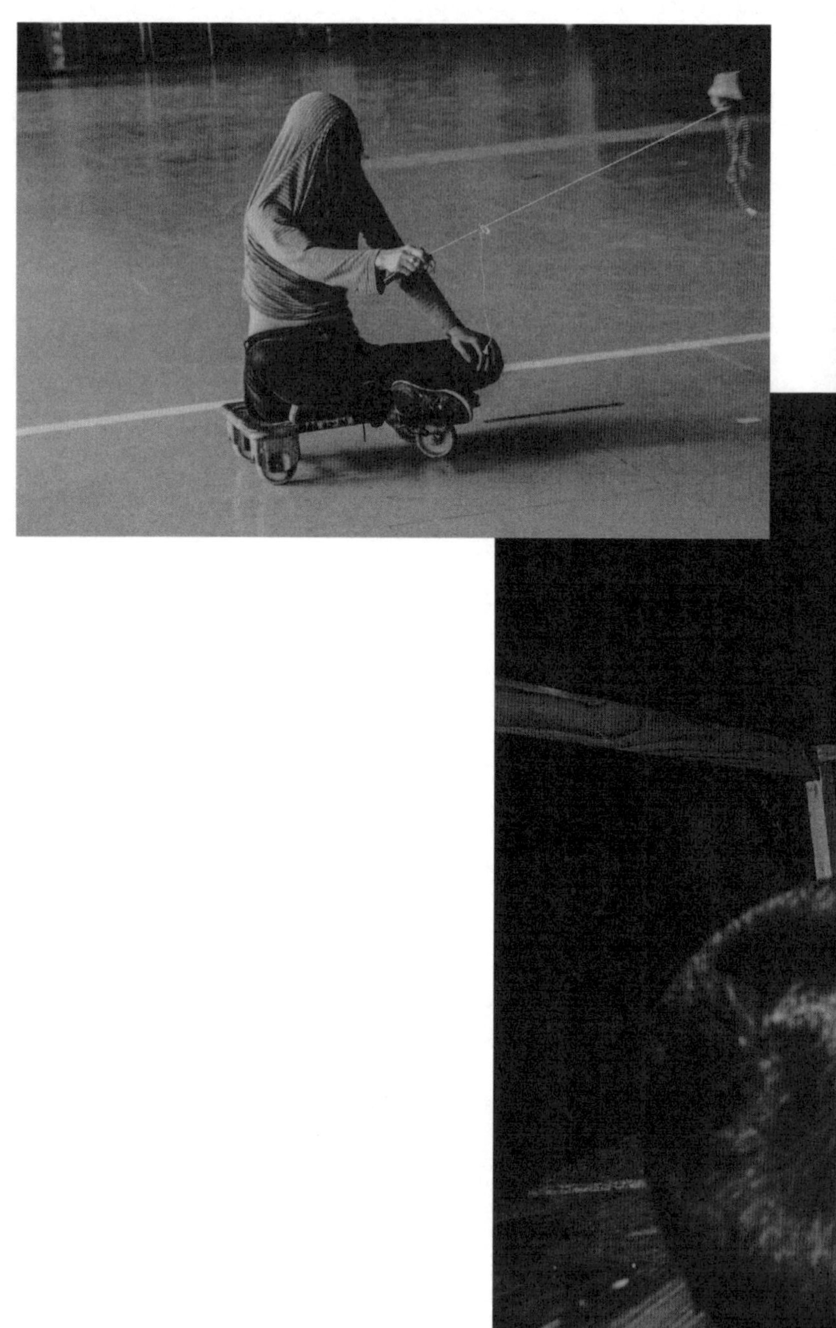

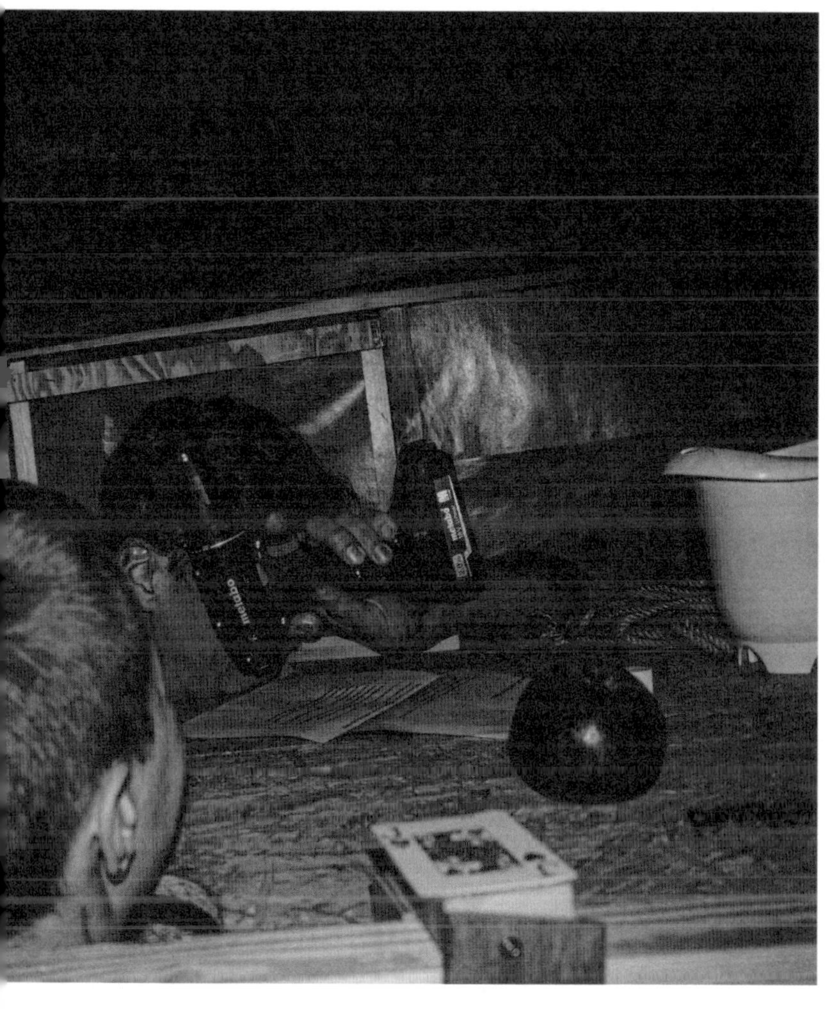

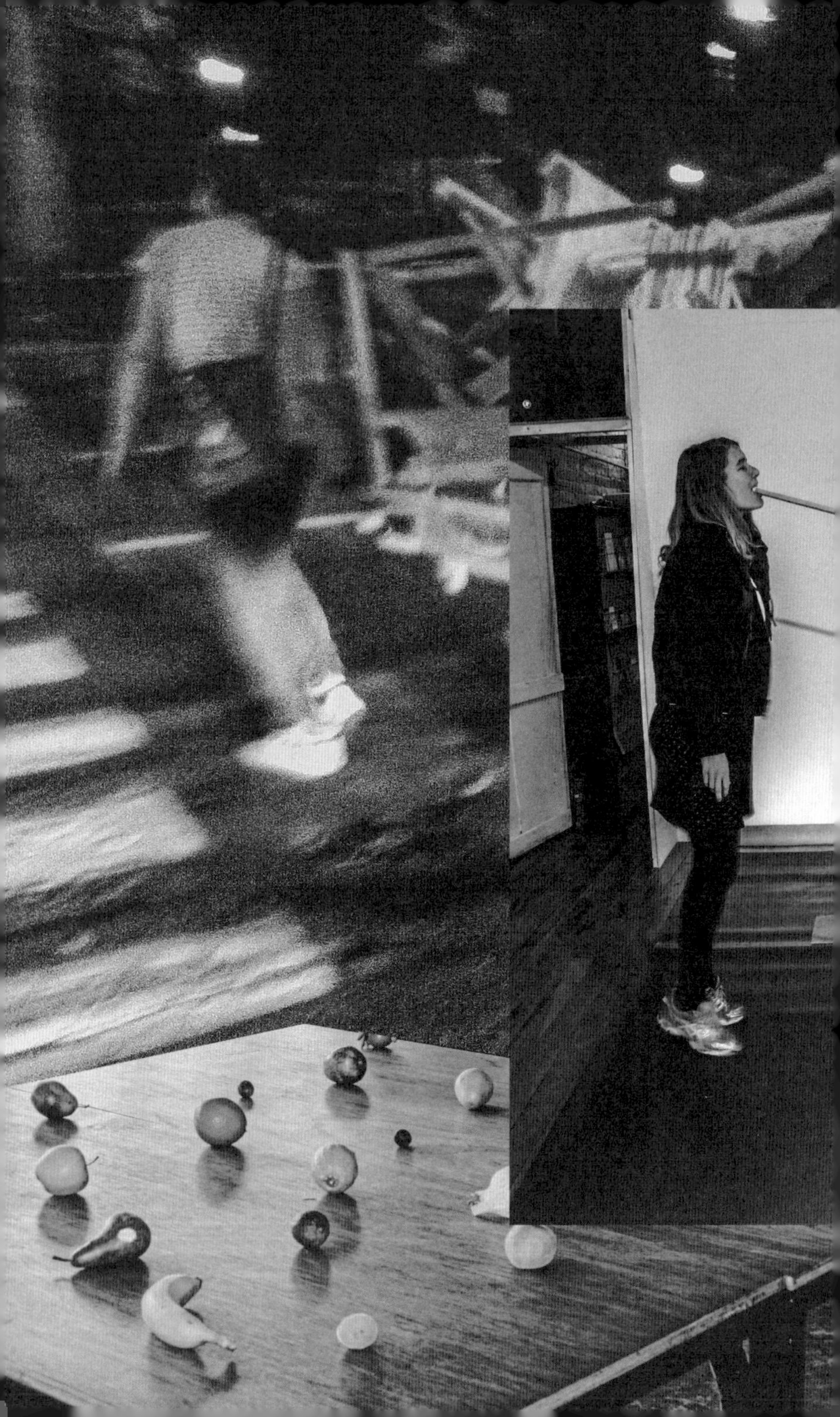

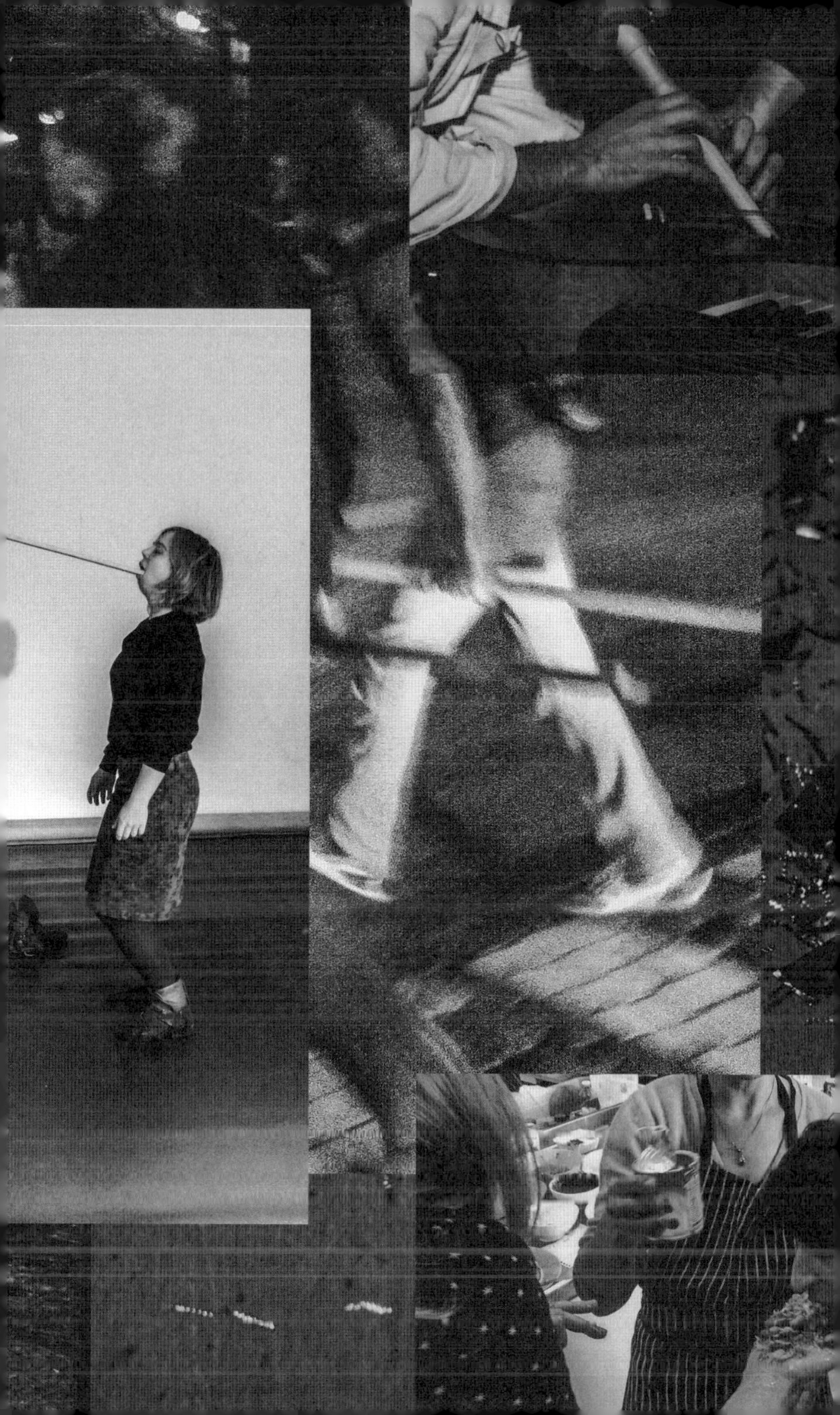

Onomatopee 181

In these circumstances: On collaboration, performativity, self-organisation and transdisciplinarity in research-based practices

ISBN: 978-94-93148-85-7

Editor: Philippine Hoegen

Editorial support: Lilia Mestre

Contributing authors: Adrijana Gvozdenović, Amy Pickles, Ana Hoffner, Anouk Llaurens, Aubrey Birch, caterina daniela mora jara, Chloë Janssens, Elke Van Campenhout, Femke Snelting, Guy Gypens, Isabel Burr Raty, Kate Rich, Kristien Van den Brande, Krõõt Juurak, Laura Pante, Leo Kay, Lilia Mestre, Livia Andrea Piazza, Loes Jacobs, Mathilde Villeneuve, Muslin Brothers - Tamar Levit & Yaen Levi, Nicolas Y. Galeazzi, Peggy Pierrot, Philippine Hoegen, Pia Louwerens, Pierre Rubio, Rui Calvo, Samah Hijawi, Sara Manente, Sina Seifee, Steven Jouwersma, Túlio Rosa, Vanja Smiljanić, Veridiana Zurita, Vladimir Miller

Text editors: Chloe Chignell, Sarah Cale, Kristien Van den Brande

Proofreader: Sarah Cale

Production coordination: Joke Liberge

Administration: Michèle Meesen, Kristof Van Hoorde

Graphic design: Miriam Hempel, www.daretoknow.uk

Fonts: *SangBleu Kingdom*, Swiss Typefaces, *Standard*, Bryce Wilner

Paper: Munken Lynx Rough

Printer: Snel, BE

Images from the a.pass archive, and on their respective pages by: Leo Kay, Femke Snelting, Vanja Smiljanić, Kate Rich, Rui Calvo, Muslin Brothers, Anouk Llaurens, Vladimir Miller, Samah Hijawi, Sina Seifee, Steven Jouwersma

Produced by a.pass Posthogeschool voor Podiumkunsten vzw.

a·pass | advanced performance and scenography studies

www.apass.be

First edition, Brussels, 2022

Onomatopee Projects

www.onomatopee.net

Made with the support of the Flemish Ministry of Education:

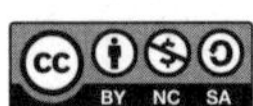